The German Economy in the
Twentieth Century

Contempory Economic History of Europe Series
Edited by Derek Aldcroft

The Economy of Yugoslavia
Fred Singleton and Bernard Carter

The Economic Development of the USSR
Roger Munting

The Norwegian Economy
Fritz Hodne

The Spanish Economy
J.R. Harrison

The Polish Economy in the Twentieth Century
Zgibniew Landau and Jerzy Tomaszewski

The Hungarian Economy in the Twentieth Century
Ivan T. Berend and György Ránki

The Bulgarian Economy in the Twentieth Century
John R. Lampe

The Danish Economy in the Twentieth Century
Hans Christian Johansen

The Greek Economy in the Twentieth Century
A.F. Freris

The Romanian Economy in the Twentieth Century
David Turnock

The Czechoslovak Economy 1918–1980
Alice Teichova

*The Economic Development of Ireland in
the Twentieth Century*
Kieran A. Kennedy, Thomas Giblin and Deirdre McHugh

The German Economy in the Twentieth Century

Hans-Joachim Braun

R

Routledge
London and New York

First published 1990
by Routledge
11 New Fetter Lane, London EC4P 4EE

Simultaneously published in the USA and Canada
by Routledge
a division of Routledge, Chapman and Hall, Inc.
29 West 35th Street, New York, NY 10001

© 1990 H.J. Braun

Printed and bound in Great Britain by Mackays of Chatham PLC, Kent

British Library Cataloguing in Publication Data

Braun, H.J.
   The German economy in the twentieth century:
   the German Reich and the Federal Republic.
   – (Routledge contemporary economic history
   of Europe)
   1. Germany. Economic condition, history
   I. Title
   330.943
   ISBN 0-415-02101-4

Library of Congress Cataloging in Publication Data

Braun, Hans-Joachim.
   The German economy in the twentieth century / Hans-Joachim Braun.
      p.   cm. – (Contemporary economic history of Europe series)
   Bibliography: p.
   Includes index.
   ISBN 0-415-02101-4
   1. Germany – Economic conditions – 20th century. 2. Germany
(West) – Economic conditions. I. Title. II. Series.
   HC286.B74   1990
   330.943'08–dc20   89-10480
                                                          CIP

For Salina

CONTENTS

Figures   viii

Tables   x

Introduction   1

Editor's Introduction   7

Part I: 1870-1948

1. The Economy of the Kaiserreich, 1871-1914   19
2. The First World War   25
3. Reparations and Inflation   33
4. Relative Stabilisation   44
5. The Great Depression   64
6. The National Socialist Economy   78
7. The Second World War   109
8. The Post-War Economy, 1945-1948   144

Part II: The Federal Republic of Germany 1949-1985

9. Economic Growth and Fluctuations   165
10. Economic Doctrine and Policy   176
11. Public Finance   195
12. Capital and Labour   208
13. Structural Change   223
14. Foreign Trade   237

Select Bibliography   255

Index   264

FIGURES

3.1   The development of inflation 1919-1923   38

4.1   Growth of German industrial
        production 1914-1931   48

4.2   German producer goods and consumer
        goods production per capita 1920-1935   49

7.1   National income and government ex-
        penditure of the "Greater German Reich"
        1940-1944   112

7.2   Germany's foreign trade, September 1939
        to September 1941 (in RM million)   120

7.3   Supply of the German population with
        victuals (calories per day per person)
        from 1938 to 1946   127

7.4   Index of total armament production
        1942-1945   137

8.1   Indices of industrial production in the
        Bizone and the French zone of occupation
        1946-1949   147

9.1   Gross national product 1950-1985   167

9.2   Real growth rates of GNP 1951-1985   170

10.1   Central bank monetary targets and
        growth 1975-1986   189

11.1   Government receipts and expenditure
        1950-1985   195

11.2   Public debt 1950-1985   201

12.1   Investment in manufacturing 1956-1978   209

12.2   Unemployment 1950-1985   212

12.3   Annual growth rates of net wages
        per capita 1950-1985   215

12.4   Annual growth rates of labour pro-
        ductivity in the manufacturing sector
        1952-1985   216

12.5   Wage share 1950-1985   218

13.1   Share of sectors in gross value
        added (left); share of gainfully
        employed persons in sectors (right)
        1950-1985   224

13.2   R&D expenditures 1950-1985   232

14.1   Export and import shares 1950-1985   238

14.2   Components of the current account
        balance 1950-1985   240

14.3   DM/US dollar exchange rates 1953-1985,
        annual averages   241

14.4   Average export and import prices, terms
        of trade, 1952-1985   242

14.5   Federal German foreign direct investment
        1956-1985 and foreign direct investment
        in the FRG 1962-1985   245

TABLES

2.1   Changes in industrial employment during
      the First World War. Increase or decrease
      of employees (in %) in 1918 compared
      to 1913 in firms with more than 10
      employees   28

4.1   Growth of output per hour (in constant
      prices) in selected industrial branches
      1926-1930 in per cent   51

4.2   German industry and artisan production
      1925-1932: hourly wages and productivity   53

4.3   Agricultural yields in Germany 1913,
      1920, 1924 and 1928   55

4.4   Indices of German export volumes,
      1924/5-1928/9   57

4.5   Terms of trade 1924-1935   59

6.1   Public expenditure in Germany by category
      1928-1938   84

6.2   The production of selected goods under
      the Four Year Plan   88

6.3   Statistics on German finance 1932/3-
      1938/9   90

6.4   Economic recovery in Germany 1932-1938   92

6.5   Wages and wage shares 1933-1939   95

6.6   Degree of self-sufficiency in the
      agricultural sector 1927/8-1938/9   100

6.7   Germany's foreign trade 1930-1939.
      Foreign trade, gold and foreign-
      exchange movements   103

7.1   Development of the public debt 1939-
      1945   115

7.2   Mobilisation of labour 1939-1944   122

7.3   Fighter production in 1944   132

8.1   Gross fixed industrial assets in the
      territory which is now the Federal
      Republic of Germany 1939-1948   145

8.2   Age structure of fixed assets in
      industry   147

8.3   West German balance of payments 1945-
      1952   157

11.1 Federal government revenue 1950-1985   197

11.2 Expenditure of the Federal government,
      the regional and the local authorities
      by functions, 1950-1985   199

11.3 New public debt and interest rates 1974-
      1985   202

13.1 Employment and labour productivity in
      the primary sector 1950-1985   227

13.2 Share of selected industrial branches
      in gross value added of total industry
      1960-1980   229

INTRODUCTION

When dealing with a comparatively long time span of economic development - in this case almost one hundred years - the problem arises whether it would be preferable to concentrate on long-term trends in fields like economic growth and fluctuations, public finance and foreign trade or divide them into smaller periods of time and then investigate the particular features of those periods in more detail. While the first option would have had much to commend it I have mainly relied on the second alternative, although in the second half of the book I have stressed trends which were in the forefront of Federal German economic development in the second half of the twentieth century and which originated in the first half or even in the nineteenth century. In dealing with the first half of the twentieth century I have relied on divisions familiar from political history.

The main reason for this procedure is the specific course of German history in the twentieth century. While some businessmen and politicians in the Federal Republic find pleasure in pointing out that the FRG has, in recent years, been *Weltmeister* (world champion) in exports, and, during the last decades, in low inflation rates, this title certainly belongs to Germany if one considers her twentieth century political development with its unique and partly tragic sequence of imperial monarchy, (Weimar) democracy, (National Socialist) dictatorship and Western parliamentarian democracy in the West and Socialist *Volksdemokratie* in the East. These radical changes had, of course, a marked influence on the economic framework and on economic growth, although the latter is more difficult to pinpoint. Moreover, two world wars, especially the second, have changed the German political boundaries to such an extent that economic life has also been deeply influenced. The Federal German state of 1949 extended to only a little more than half of the area of "Greater Germany" in 1937. It is therefore obvious that the attempt to delineate long-term trends of economic development creates great problems.

After having treated Germany as a whole until the end of the Second World War, only the western zones of occupation and the Federal Republic of Germany will be dealt with thereafter. This does not imply a new subtle - or crude - *neo*-imperialist strategy, in which the author lets the FRG speak for the two German states. The rather undramatic reason is that there will be a separate volume on the GDR in the series on the contemporary economic history of Europe written by Mr. W. Forsyth from Aberdeen. Also, to avoid misunderstanding, it should, as to the subtitle of the present book, *The Federal Republic and the German Reich*, be made clear that the main focus of the book is not on the *relationship* between the *Reich* and the FRG (although some aspects of this problem will be treated), but on the *Reich* first and the Federal Republic second.

In stressing the caesura between the pre-1945 German *Reich* and the Federal Republic it should not, however, be overlooked that there are several trends in recent German economic history which stretch over the whole century and can be regarded as being inherent in the logic of economic development of western industrialised nations in the twentieth century. Apart from the particular geographic location and the relatively high dependence on world trade there are others, like the continuity of business cycles. These had already originated before the foundation of the German *Reich* and lasted approximately 9 to 10 years in the 1880s, but only 4 to 5 years after 1949. There has also been a continuity in demographic factors like the declining birth rate common to all western industrialised nations and other processes connected with industrialisation, like urbanisation, industrial concentration and structural change with a constantly declining share of the agricultural sector, the stagnating and then falling share of the secondary sector and the growing share of the tertiary (service) sector. These trends have become particularly marked in the economic development of the FRG while - although also present in the first half of this century - they were often interrupted, sometimes hastened, sometimes retarded, especially as a consequence of two world wars and the policies leading to them.

In this book it has only been possible to give a brief survey of the economic development of the *Reich* and the Federal Republic of Germany. The reader is referred to the host of literature on particular aspects quoted in the select bibliography and the footnotes. I have tried to describe and analyse the main features of macroeconomic development leaving microeconomic aspects aside. Owing to lack of space, many interesting issues, especially in the economic development of the FRG, have been omitted or are only briefly hinted at, like banking and insurance, internal trade, transport and communication or the development of savings. A field which, as a historian of technology as well as an economic historian, I would have much liked to expand on, is the contribution of technology to economic development, a topic which most economists, who still regard technology as a "residual factor", usually neglect. A mere description of technical innovations would not, however, have been of much use in a brief survey of German economic development, and the contribution of technology to economic growth in the twentieth century is still - apart from a few exceptions - widely unexplored and full of methodological pitfalls; indeed, it is questionable whether it will ever be possible to tackle this issue adequately. Also, social and demographic factors were treated only very briefly, mainly in the context of social and labour policy.

The large number of controversies and open research problems in German twentieth century economic history make it difficult to stay abreast with current research in the field. For the Weimar economy, for example, there are controversies on the origin of the Great Depression and the objectives of Chancellor Bruening's economic and financial policies; for the National Socialist economy the role of big business in the National Socialist rise to power, the primacy of politics or economics, economic and social problems as a motive for Hitler's decision to attack Poland and thus risk the outbreak of war and the issue of the *Blitzkrieg* economy are some of the research problems. As far as the post-1945 period is concerned the extent of economic growth before the Marshall Plan and the currency reform, the role of the concept of the social market economy in economic growth and the reasons for weak business investment after 1974, to mention only a few topics, await further research. Most of those problems I have tackled briefly. The fact that some of them, for example the issue whether wages in the Weimar Republic contributed significantly to the depression in Germany, have some - indirect - implications for the contemporary debate on economic policy, extends their significance beyond the boundaries of historical interest.

Although the stock exchange crash of 19 October 1987 has affected the Federal German economy and those of the other western industrial nations less negatively than had been feared at the time the Federal German economy today has to cope with several problems the historical dimension of which has been sketched in this book. Unemployment seems to be the most acute one, especially juvenile unemployment, which is also - and foremost - a social problem of the first order. The demographic development will probably contribute to alleviating this problem in the near future (which is little consolation for those without work today), but the smaller number of gainfully employed persons in the future will contribute less to social insurance, which causes politicians and the next generation of pensioners some concern. Huge debts of several FRG trading partners and the fear of worldwide protectionism are other risks the Federal German economy has to face.

Apart from this, recent environmental disasters have - once again - made completely clear that a different attitude has to be adopted towards our environment, a plea directed not only to Federal German industrialists and politicians, but also to those of other nations irrespective of their capitalist or socialist economic order. It is no longer tolerable that we keep on destroying our natural living conditions according to the slogan *après nous le déluge*. This is, of course, an issue which far transcends the economic sphere.

During the process of writing this book and after completion of the manuscript I have received much help and timely advice from many colleagues to whom I am profoundly grateful. I want to thank Professor Derek Aldcroft from Leicester, the editor of this series, for many useful comments, and both him and Mr. Peter Sowden of Routledge for their patience. I am also grateful to Professor Wolfram Fischer, Berlin, who made available to me before publication parts of the *Handbuch der europaeischen Wirtschafts- und Sozialgeschichte*, vol. 6, edited by him, Professor Karl Hardach, Duesseldorf, who himself had suffered the strain of writing a book on the German economy in the twentieth century some time ago, and the late Professor Klaus H. Hennings, Hannover, with whom I had fruitful discussions in the early stages of the book. Professor Manfred Knapp, Hamburg, made useful comments on the immediate post-Second World War period, Dr. Gernot Mueller and Dr. Ulrich Nocken, both from Duesseldorf, gave hints on the Federal Republic, viz. on Weimar. To Dr.

Richard J. Overy, London/Cambridge, I am grateful for his comments on the National Socialist economy.

I have to thank my assistants Torsten Bardohn, Gabriele Ferk, Dr. Hartmut Knittel and Anne-Katrin Stammer for several useful hints and corrections, bibliographical and statistical help and the preparation of the index. Mrs. Heidi Windeit has - as always - done a superb job in coming to grips with a partly illegible manuscript and still remained cheerful. My wife Kathleen and my three children deserve my particular thanks for their patience and understanding with an overworked scholar. I dedicate this book to Salina, my younger daughter.

EDITOR'S INTRODUCTION

By comparison with the nineteenth century, the twentieth has been very much more turbulent, both economically and politically. Two world wars and a great depression are sufficient to substantiate this claim without invoking the problems of more recent times. Yet despite these setbacks Europe's economic performance in the present century has been very much better than anything recorded in the historical past, thanks largely to the super-boom conditions following the post-Second World War reconstruction period. Thus in the period 1946-75, or 1950-73, the annual increase in total European GNP per capita was 4.8 and 4.5 per cent respectively, as against a compound rate of just under 1 per cent in the nineteenth century (1800-1913) and the same during the troubled years between 1913-50. As Bairoch points out, within a generation or so European per capita income rose slightly more than in the previous 150 years (1947-75 by 250 per cent, 1800-1948 by 225 per cent) and, on rough estimates for the half-century before 1800, by about as much as in the preceding two centuries.[1]

The dynamic growth and relative stability of the 1950s and 1960s may however belie the natural order of things as the events of the later 1970s and early 1980s demonstrate. Certainly it would seem unlikely that the European economy, or the world economy for that matter, will see a lasting return to the relatively stable conditions of the nineteenth century. No doubt the experience of the present century can easily lead to an exaggerated idea about the stability of the previous one. Nevertheless, one may justifiably claim that for much of the nineteenth century there was a degree of harmony in the economic development of the major powers and between the metropolitan economies and the periphery which has been noticeably absent since 1914. Indeed, one of the reasons for the apparent success of the gold standard post 1870, despite the aura of stability it allegedly shed, was the absence of serious external disturbances and imbalance in development among the major participating powers. As Triffin writes, "the residual harmonization of national monetary and credit policies depended far less on *ex post* corrective action, requiring an extreme flexibility, downward as well as upward, of national price and wage levels, than on an *ex ante* avoidance of substantial disparities in cost competitiveness and the monetary policies that would allow them to develop".[2]

Whatever the reasons for the absence of serious economic and political conflict, the fact remains that up to 1914 international development and political relations, though subject to strains of a minor nature from time to time, were never exposed to internal and external shocks of the magnitude experienced in the twentieth century. Not surprisingly therefore, the First World War rudely shattered the liberal tranquility of the later nineteenth and early twentieth centuries. At the time few people realised that it was going to be a lengthy war and, even more important, fewer still had any conception of the enormous impact it would have on economic and social relationships. Moreover, there was a general feeling, readily accepted in establishment circles, that following the period of hostilities it would be possible to resume where one had left off - in short, to recreate the conditions of the prewar era.

For obvious reasons this was clearly an impossible task, though for nearly a decade statesmen strove to get back to what they regarded as "normalcy", or the natural order of things. In itself this was one of the profound mistakes of the first postwar decade since it should have been clear, even at that time, that the war and postwar clearing-up operations had undermined Europe's former equipoise and sapped her strength to a point where the economic system had become very sensitive to external shocks. The map of Europe had been rewritten under the political settlements following the war and this further weakened the economic viability of the continent and left a dangerous political vacuum in its wake. Moreover, it was not only in the economic sphere that Europe's strength had been reduced; in political and social terms the European continent was seriously weakened and many countries in the early postwar years were in a state of social ferment and upheaval.[3]

Generally speaking, Europe's economic and political fragility was ignored in the 1920s, probably more out of ignorance than intent. In their efforts to resurrect the prewar system statesmen believed they were providing a viable solution to the problems of the day, and the fact that Europe shared in the prosperity of the later 1920s seemed to vindicate their judgement. But the postwar problems - war debts, external imbalances, currency issues, structural distortions and the like - defied solutions along traditional lines. The most notable of these was the attempt to restore a semblance of the gold standard in the belief that it had been responsible for the former stability. The upshot was a set of haphazard and inconsistent currency stabilisation policies which took no account of the changes in relative costs and prices among countries since 1914. Consequently, despite the apparent prosperity of the latter half of the decade, Europe remained in a state of unstable equilibrium, and therefore vulnerable to any external shocks. The collapse of US foreign lending from the middle of 1928 and the subsequent downturn of the American economy a year later exposed the weaknesses of the European economy. The structural supports were too weak to withstand violent shocks and so the edifice disintegrated.

That the years 1929-1932/33 experienced one of the worst depressions and financial crises in history is not altogether surprising given the convergence of many unfavourable forces at that point in time. Moreover, the fact that a cyclical downturn occurred against the backdrop of structural disequilibrium only served to exacerbate the problem, while the inherent weakness of certain financial institutions in Europe and the United States led to extreme instability. The intensity of the crisis varied a great deal but few countries, apart from the USSR, were unaffected. The action of governments tended to aggravate rather than ease the situation. Such policies included expenditure cuts, monetary contraction, the abandonment of the gold standard and protective measures designed to insulate domestic economies from external events. In effect these policies, while sometimes affording temporary relief to hardpressed countries, in the end led to income destruction rather than income creation. When recovery finally set in in the winter of 1932/33 it owed little to policy contributions, though subsequently some western governments did attempt more ambitious programmes of stimulation, while many of the poorer eastern European countries adopted autarchic policies in an effort to push forward industrialisation. Apart from some notable exceptions, Germany and Sweden in particular, recovery from the slump, especially in terms of employment generation, was slow and patchy and even at the peak of the upswing in 1937 many countries were still operating below their resource capacity. A combination of weak real growth forces and structural imbalances in development would no doubt have ensured a continuation of resource under-utilisation had not rearmament and the outbreak of war served to close the gap.

Thus, by the eve of the Second World War Europe as a whole was in a much weaker state economically than it had been in 1914, with her shares of world income and trade notably reduced. Worse still, she emerged from the second war in 1945 in a more prostrate condition than in 1918, with output levels well down on those of the pre-war period. In terms of the loss of life, physical destruction and decline in living standards Europe's position was much worse than after the First World War. On the other hand, recovery from wartime destruction was stronger and more secure than in the previous case. In part this can be attributed to the fact that in the reconstruction phase of the later 1940s some of the mistakes and blunders of the earlier experience were avoided. Inflation, for example, was contained more readily between 1939 and 1945 and the violent inflations of the early 1920s were not for the most part perpetuated after the Second World War. With the exception of Berlin, the map of Europe was divided much more cleanly and neatly than after 1918. Though it resulted in two ideological power blocs, the East and the West, it did nevertheless dispose of the power vacuum in Central/East Europe which had been a source of friction and contention in the interwar years. Moreover, the fact that each bloc was dominated or backed by a wealthy and rival super-power meant that support was forthcoming for the satellite countries. The vanquished powers were not, with the exception of East Germany, burdened by unreasonable exactions which had been the cause of so much bitterness and squabbling during the 1920s. Finally, governments no longer hankered after the "halcyon" pre-war days, not surprisingly given the rugged conditions of the 1930s. This time it was to be planning for the future which occupied their attention, and which found expression in the commitment to maintain full employment and all that entailed in terms of growth and stability, together with a conscious desire to build upon the earlier social welfare foundations. In wider perspective, the new initiatives found positive expression in terms of a readiness to cooperate internationally, particularly in trade and monetary matters. The liberal American aid programme for the West in the later 1940s was a concrete manifestation of this new approach.

Thus despite the enormity of the reconstruction task facing Europe at the end of the war, the recovery effort, after some initial difficulties, was both strong and sustained, and by the early 1950s Europe had reached a point where she could look to the future with some confidence. During the next two decades or so virtually every European country, in keeping with the buoyant conditions in the world economy as a whole, expanded very much more rapidly than in the past. This was the super-growth phase during which Europe regained a large part of the relative losses incurred between 1914 and 1945. The Eastern bloc countries forged ahead the most rapidly under their planned regimes, while the western democracies achieved their success under mixed enterprise systems with varying degrees of market freedom. In both cases the state played a far more important role than hitherto, and neither system could be said to be without its problems. The planning mechanism in eastern Europe never functioned as smoothly as originally anticipated by its proponents, and in due course most of the socialist countries were forced to make modifications to their systems of control. Similarly, the semi-market systems of the West did not always produce the right results so that governments were obliged to intervene to an increasing extent. One of the major problems encountered by the demand-managed economies of the West was that of trying to achieve a series of basically incompatible objectives simultaneously - namely full employment, price stability, growth and stability and external equilibrium. Given the limited policy weapons available to governments this proved an impossible task to accomplish in most cases, though West Germany managed to achieve the seemingly impossible for much of the period.

Although these incompatible objectives proved elusive *in toto*, there was, throughout most of the period to the early 1970s, little cause for serious alarm. It is true that there were minor lapses from full employment; fluctuations still occurred but they were very moderate and took the form of growth cycles; some countries experienced periodic balance of payments problems; while prices generally rose continuously though at fairly modest annual rates. But such lapses could readily be accommodated, even with the limited policy choices, within an economic system that was growing rapidly. And there was some consolation from the fact that the planned socialist economies were not immune from some of these problems, especially later on in the period. By the later 1960s, despite some warning signs that conditions might be deteriorating, it seemed that Europe had entered a phase of perpetual prosperity not dissimilar to the one the Americans had conceived in the 1920s. Unfortunately, as in the earlier case, this illusion was to be rudely shattered in the first half of the 1970s. The super-growth phase of the postwar period culminated in the somewhat feverish and speculative boom of 1972-73. By the following year the growth trend had been reversed, the old business cycle had reappeared and most countries were experiencing inflation at higher rates than at any time in the past half-century. From that time onwards, according to Samuel Brittan, "everything seems to have gone sour and we have had slower growth, rising unemployment, faster inflation, creeping trade restrictions and all the symptoms of stagflation".[4] In fact, compared with the relatively placid and successful decades of the 1950s and 1960s, the later 1970s and early 1980s have been extremely turbulent, reminiscent in some respects of the interwar years.

It should of course be stressed that by comparison with the interwar years or even with the nineteenth century, economic growth has been quite respectable since the sharp boom and contraction in the first half of the 1970s. It only appears poor in relation to the rapid growth between 1950 and 1973 and the question arises as to whether this period should be regarded as somewhat abnormal with the shift to a lower growth profile in the 1970s being the inevitable consequence of long-term forces involving some reversal of the special growth promoting factors of the previous decades. In effect this would imply some weakening of real growth forces in the 1970s which was aggravated by specific factors, for example energy crises and policy variables.

The most disturbing feature of this later period was not simply that growth slowed down but that it became more erratic, with longer recessionary periods involving absolute contractions in output, and that it was accompanied by mounting unemployment and high inflation. Traditional Keynesian demand management policies were unable to cope with these problems and, in an effort to deal with them, particularly inflation, governments resorted to ultra-defensive policies and monetary control. These were not very successful either since the need for social and political compromise in policy-making meant that they were not applied rigorously enough to eradicate inflation, yet at the same time their influence was sufficiently strong to dampen the rate of growth thereby exacerbating unemployment. In other words, economic management is faced with an awkward policy dilemma in the prevailing situation of high unemployment and rapid inflation. Policy action to deal with either one tends to make the other worse, while the constraint of the political concensus produces an uneasy compromise in an effort to "minimise macroeconomic misery".[5] Rostow has neatly summarised the constraints involved in this context: "Taxes, public expenditure, interest rates, and the supply of money are not determined antiseptically by men free to move economies along a Phillips curve to an optimum trade-off between the rate of unemployment and the rate of inflation. Fiscal and monetary policy are, inevitably, living parts of the democratic political process."[6]

Whether the current problems of contemporary western capitalism or the difficulties associated with the planning mechanisms of the socialist countries of eastern Europe are amenable to solutions remains to be seen. It is not, for the most part, the purpose of the volumes in this series to speculate about the future. The series is designed to provide clear and balanced surveys of the economic development and problems of individual European countries from the end of the First World War through to the present, against the background of the general economic and political trends of the time. Though most European countries have shared a common experience for much of the period, it is nonetheless true that there has been considerable variation among countries in the rate of development and the manner in which they have sought to regulate and control their economies. The problems encountered have also varied widely, in part reflecting disparities in levels of development. While most European countries had, by the end of the First World War, achieved some industrialisation and made the initial breakthrough into modern economic growth, nevertheless there existed a wide gulf between the richer and poorer nations. At the beginning of the period the most advanced region was north-west Europe including Scandinavia and as one moved east and south so the level of per capita income relative to the European average declined. In some cases, notably Bulgaria, Yugoslavia and Portugal, income levels were barely half the European average. The gap has narrowed over time but the general pattern remains basically the same. Between 1913 and 1973 most of the poorer countries in the east and south (apart from Spain) raised their real per capita income levels relative to the European average, with most of the improvement taking place after 1950. Even so, by 1973 most of them, with the exception of Czechoslovakia, still fell below the European average, ranging from 9-15 per cent in the case of the USSR, Hungary, Greece, Bulgaria and Poland, to as much as 35-45 per cent for Spain, Portugal, Romania and Yugoslavia. Italy and Ireland also recorded per capita income levels some way below the European average.[7]

Germany's twentieth century history has been even more momentous than that of the previous century: defeats in two major wars, a spectacular inflation in the early 1920s and one of the worst depressions, all within the space of less than half a century. And yet the country rebounded after the postwar reconstruction in the late 1940s to become one of the most prosperous industrial nations of the West. It has been the envy of many other advanced nations, particularly Britain, for the ability to achieve what seemed to many the incompatible, namely high growth, a healthy balance of payments, low price inflation and full employment. At least this was the case until more recent years when Germany too has suffered from some of the tribulations following on from the two oil shocks of the 1970s.

Germany's resilience in the face of great disasters has been the subject of numerous studies which stress, with varying degrees of emphasis, the factors making for success. As Professor Braun's new study of the German economy shows, there is no one factor above all which can explain the phenomenon.

One can point to the way in which Germany adapted the structure of her economy to meet the changing pattern of world demand and the emphasis placed on cost containment and competitiveness within the framework of a national economic policy which gave priority to financial stability. One should also bear in mind that Germany has always placed great emphasis on the importance of *Technik*, the art of doing things, and her considerable investment in education has reflected this approach. Moreover, it should also be noted that the disasters which befell Germany in the first part of the century had a less severe impact on her capital and human resource base than often imagined. In view of this the potential for recovery from such calamities was stronger than might otherwise have been the case.

In recent years the German economy has shown signs of faltering in line with many other countries. It too has suffered some of the impediments of structural maladjustment. The crucial question for the future is whether it will be able to regain its former momentum by adapting to the new structure of activity and competitiveness now emerging within the world economy.

Notes

1. P. Bairoch, "Europe's Gross National Product: 1800-1975", *The Journal of European Economic History*, 5 (Fall 1976), pp.298-99.

2. R. Triffin, *Our International Monetary System: Yesterday, Today and Tomorrow* (1968, New York), p.14; see also D.H. Aldcroft, *From Versailles to Wall Street, 1919-1929* (1977), pp.162-64. Some of the costs of the gold standard system may however have been borne by the countries of the periphery, for example Latin America.

3. See P.N. Stearns, *European Society in Upheaval* (1967).

4. *Financial Times*, 14 February 1980.

5. J.O.N. Perkins, *The Macroeconomic Mix to Stop Stagflation* (1980).

6. W.W. Rostow, *Getting From Here to There* (1979).

7. See Bairoch, "Europe's Gross National Product", pp.297, 307.

PART I: 1871 - 1948

Chapter One

THE ECONOMY OF THE *KAISERREICH*, 1871-1914

Looking at Germany's economic development in the period 1871-1914 the figures are indeed spectacular: Germany's industrial production rose sixfold, whereas France could only treble and England could only double their industrial production. Between 1870-1913 German steel production grew more than tenfold.[1] By 1870 the phase of early industrialisation had come to an end and, during the period 1870-1913, the transformation from an "agrarian state" to an "industrial state" took place. The secondary sector, with industry, small trade and mining, overtook the primary sector. In 1871, 49 per cent of the German population had still been employed in agriculture; this figure declined to 35.2 per cent in 1907. In the same period the figure of those employed in industry rose from 31 to 40 per cent.

The transformation from an agrarian society to an industrial society did not happen without friction and was not completed at the outbreak of the First World War. There were still remnants of the old feudal society: most of the leading positions in diplomacy, state bureaucracy and the armed forces were reserved for members of the traditional ruling elite.

The German population grew from 41 million in 1871 to 49.7 million in 1891 and 65.3 million in 1911. Until the 1880s population growth had mainly been due to an increasing birth rate. From then onwards, birth rates declined, but mortality declined even further, mainly because of better medical provisions. Migration also played an important role. Until the beginning of the 1890s Germany had insufficient job opportunities for the rising population. This problem of insufficient jobs in industry was at the centre of the "social question".[2] Emigration, especially to North America, exceeded immigration.[3] With improving job opportunities in Germany the picture changed, however. There was increasing immigration into Germany by people of various nationalities. Of particular importance were the "Ruhr Poles" who found employment in the Ruhr industrial region.[4]

German agricultural production and productivity improved substantially in the late nineteenth and early twentieth century. Agricultural machinery in use rose about fourfold between 1880 and 1914 and the extensive use of fertilizers made higher agricultural yields possible.[5] In spite of this, German agriculture was in grave difficulties. After 1870 there was a rapid decline in grain prices on the European market mainly due to cheap American imports. The political turn to protectionism in 1878/9 tried to ease agricultural problems. As a result German farmers, especially the large estate owners in the East, were partly shielded from the world market with the consequence that the process of de-agrarianisation in Germany was slowed down.

Although German heavy industry, together with agriculture, successfully demanded a protectionist German foreign trade policy, German industry as a whole rapidly increased its share of the world market. This is particularly true of the "new industries", mainly the chemical, electrical, optical and high-precision engineering industries as opposed to the traditional consumer-goods industries, especially textiles. These "new", science-based industries depended to a large extent on the rapid expansion of applied science and technology in German universities and especially in Institutes of Technology (*Technische Hochschulen*). A high standard of technical education[6] and the foundation of governmental research and development institutes were, however, only one prerequisite for the rapid expansion of the new industries. Other factors were industrial concentration, in which the major German banks played an important role, and a state policy of assisting industrial growth. Germany had the advantage of a late start in industrialisation as compared to Britain. German entrepreneurs were in a position to avoid mistakes made by their colleagues of the "first industrial nation" and concentrated on the development of new industries while neglecting "old" ones such as the textile industry. The fact often deplored by contemporary observers that Germany had hardly any colonies implied the advantage that German entrepreneurs could not rely on colonies for imports and especially exports, and had to cope with the vagaries of and the keen competition on the world market.[7]

Concentration and cartelisation are not necessarily prerequisites for a superior industrial performance. They can make corporations inflexible and slow, and this often happened in the late nineteenth and early twentieth century. As a whole, however, German industrial concerns were - with exceptions - quite competitive on the world market. One of the reasons for concentration and cartelisation was the so-called "Great Depression" of the late nineteenth century[8] which caused corporations, especially in mining and iron and steel production, to regulate prices, production and sales. The banks played an active role in this process in their attempt to safeguard their loans and investment.[9]

Often the German economic system of the late nineteenth and early twentieth century is called "organised capitalism" as opposed to the "capitalism of free competition" which is supposed to have preceeded it.[10] The main features of "organised capitalism" are the concentration of capital, market regulation by formal, hierarchical and bureaucratic administrations, increasing pressure of organised interests to influence state political decision-making and systematic state intervention in the economy. According to the concept of "organised capitalism", there is an "organised interdependence of state and economy". Although this concept can be of some help as a heuristic device, it is misleading if it is applied to explain the economic, social and political reality in Germany in the late nineteenth and early twentieth century. There are some distinct ideological overtones implied in this concept and it is difficult to prove a transition from a "capitalism of free competition" to an "organised capitalism".[11]

Another label which is often attached to the period under consideration is that of the "Great Depression", which is supposed to comprise the years between 1873 and 1896. The cyclical upswing between 1869 and 1873, which was enhanced by the inflow of French reparations after the war of 1870/1, ended in the *Gruenderkrise* (foundation of the Empire crisis). From 1874 to 1879 net national income decreased by 15 per cent and Germany's decision to adopt the gold currency resulted in deflationary tendencies.[12] From 1876 to 1896 German wholesale prices fell by 2.2 per cent annually, while the cost of living showed an annual fall of 0.5 per cent. Considering the increases in productivity during the industrialisation period this development was quite normal.[13] There was indeed a sharp recession in the period 1874 to 1879, but after

1880 German industrial production increased, although with cyclical fluctuations. During the years 1880 to 1896 real growth was about three per cent, the same as in the following period 1896 to 1913. It is therefore highly problematic to apply the term "Great Depression" to the period 1873-96. From 1871 to 1913 nominal wages rose by about 1.6 to 1.9 per cent annually, the growth figures of real wages vary between 0.7 and 1.4 per cent.[14] Economic growth in Germany continued until the outbreak of the First World War, although there were recessions in 1900 and 1907.

In foreign trade Germany's share of the world market increased from 11 to 13 per cent between 1880 and 1913, while that of the other great powers stagnated or decreased. At the outbreak of the First World War Germany's export share amounted to 20.2 per cent. This impressive performance was often praised by contemporary German observers, but it also had a negative side to it: a marked dependence on the vagaries of the world market in a period of increasing world-wide protectionism. Germany's trade was to a large extent with industrial nations. Between 1890 and 1913 direct investment overseas played an increasing role. In the first years of the twentieth century Anglo-German trade rivalry became keener.[15] Around 1890 German industrial production had only amounted to two-thirds of the British, and her share of world trade was only half that of the British.

By 1913, however, Germany had overtaken Britain in industrial production and had almost drawn level with Britain in foreign trade. Britain was, however, still the leading trading nation in the world. Her capital exports surpassed those of Germany, the same goes for shipbuilding and the exports of textiles and textile machinery.[16]

There were also problems with France. In this country a "defensive nationalism" tried to check German economic expansion from 1911 onwards.[17] On the basis of her recently gained economic strength, Germany pursued a foreign policy which, although not deliberately aiming at war, nonetheless accepted the risk of a European war.[18] Internal socioeconomic conflicts also played a major role in this. The main conflict existed between the old and new socioeconomic elite in agriculture, commerce and industry - whose interests were, however, not uniform - on the one hand, and the industrial working class on the other. The latter was only "negatively integrated" into the state[19] with no freedom of association; a parliamentary system as in the Western democracies of the time was lacking. Financial policy, which overtly favoured the propertied classes by increasing indirect taxes, deepened the already existing antagonism.[20] Nationalism of the masses and the creation of the image of a beleaguered fortress - the German *Reich* - encircled by aggressive powers seemed to be a way of easing social tensions at home by directing them towards foreign enemies. The rhetoric of a "preventive war" led to the battlefields of 1914-18. Although an interpretation of German policy along these lines has much to commend it, it should be taken with more than a grain of salt.[21]

Notes

1. For this and the following see V.R. Berghahn, *Modern Germany. Society, economy and politics in the twentieth century* (Cambridge University Press, Cambridge, 1982), pp.1-9; Karl Erich Born, *Wirtschafts- und Sozialgeschichte des Deutschen Kaiserreichs (1867/71-1914)* (Steiner, Stuttgart, 1985); Gerd Hardach, *Deutschland in der Weltwirtschaft 1870-1970. Eine Einfuehrung in die Sozial- und Wirtschaftsgeschichte* (Campus, Frankfurt, New York, 1977), pp.32-9; Dietmar Petzina, *Die deutsche Wirtschaft in der Zwischenkriegszeit* (Steiner, Stuttgart, 1977), pp.5-73.

2. Werner Conze, "Vom «Poebel» zum «Proletariat». Sozialgeschichtliche Voraussetzungen fuer den Sozialismus in Deutschland", in Hans-Ulrich Wehler (ed.), *Moderne deutsche Sozialgeschichte* (Kiepenheuer and Witsch, Cologne, Berlin, 1966), pp.111-36.

3. Wolfgang Koellmann, "Bevoelkerungsgeschichte 1800-1970", in Hermann Aubin and Wolfgang Zorn (eds), *Handbuch der deutschen Wirtschafts- und Sozialgeschichte* (2 vols., Klett, Stuttgart, 1976), vol. 2, pp.30-3; Peter Marschalck, *Deutsche Ueberseewanderung im 19. Jahrhundert* (Klett, Stuttgart, 1973).

4. Christoph Klessmann, *Polnische Bergarbeiter im Ruhrgebiet 1870-1945* (Vandenhoeck and Ruprecht, Goettingen, 1978).

5. Harald Winkel, "Zur Anwendung des technischen Fortschritts in der Landwirtschaft im ausgehenden 19. Jahrhundert", *Zeitschrift fuer Agrargeschichte und Agrarsoziologie*, vol. 27 (1979), pp.19-31. Also Petzina, *Deutsche Wirtschaft*, p.43.

6. Karl-Heinz Manegold, *Universitaet, Technische Hochschule und Industrie. Ein Beitrag zur Emanzipation der Technik im 19. Jahrhundert* (Duncker and Humblot, Berlin, 1969).

7. Wilfried Feldenkirchen "Die wirtschaftliche Rivalitaet zwischen Deutschland und England im 19. Jahrhundert", *Zeitschrift fuer Unternehmensgeschichte*, vol. 25 (1980), p.84. See also Charles P. Kindleberger, "Germany's overtaking of England 1806-1914", Part 2, *Weltwirtschaftliches Archiv* vol. 111 (1975), pp.477-504; S.B. Saul, *Industrialisation and de-industrialisation? The interaction of the German and British economies before the First World War* (German Historical Institute London, The 1979 annual lecture).

8. Hans Rosenberg, *Grosse Depression und Bismarckzeit. Wirtschaftsablauf, Gesellschaft und Politik in Mitteleuropa* (de Gruyter, Berlin, 1967).

9. Fritz Blaich, *Kartell- und Monopolpolitik im kaiserlichen Deutschland. Das Problem der Marktmacht im deutschen Reichstag 1879-1914* (Droste, Dues-

seldorf, 1973).

10. Heinrich August Winkler (ed.), *Organisierter Kapitalismus* (Vandenhoeck and Ruprecht, Goettingen, 1974); Juergen Kocka, "Organisierter Kapitalismus im Kaiserreich", *Historische Zeitschrift*, vol. 230 (1980), pp.613-31.

11. Volker Hentschel, *Wirtschaft und Wirtschaftspolitik im wilhelminischen Deutschland. Organisierter Kapitalismus und Interventionsstaat?* (Klett-Cotta, Stuttgart, 1978), pp.9-21. See also Kenneth D. Barkin, "Organised Capitalism", *Journal of Modern History*, vol.47 (1975), pp.125-9.

12. Knut Borchardt, "Wirtschaftliches Wachstum und Wechsellagen 1800-1914", in Hermann Aubin and Wolfgang Zorn (eds), *Handbuch der deutschen Wirtschafts- und Sozialgeschichte* (2 vols., Klett, Stuttgart, 1976), vol. 2, p.266.

13. David S. Landes, *The unbound Prometheus. Technological change and industrial development in Western Europe from 1750 to the present* (Cambridge University Press, Cambridge, 1969), p.234.

14. Gerhard Bry, *Wages in Germany 1817-1945* (Princeton University Press, Princeton, 1960); A.V. Desai, *Real wages in Germany 1871-1913* (Clarendon Press, Oxford, 1968).

15. Paul M. Kennedy, *The rise of the Anglo-German antagonism 1860-1914* (Allen & Unwin, London, 1980), pp.41-58, 291-305.

16. See also Feldenkirchen, "Die wirtschaftliche Rivalitaet zwischen Deutschland und England im 19. Jahrhundert", pp.96-101 and Christoph Buchheim, *Deutsche Gewerbeexporte nach England in der zweiten Haelfte des 19. Jahrhunderts* (Scripta Mercaturae, Ostfildern, 1982).

17. Hermann Kellenbenz, *Deutsche Wirtschaftsgeschichte* (2 vols., Beck, Munich, 1981), vol. 2, p.341.

18. Hans-Ulrich Wehler, *Das deutsche Kaiserreich 1871-1918* (Vandenhoeck and Ruprecht, Goettingen, 1973), p.194. See also Fritz Fischer, *Germany's aims in the First World War* (Chatto and Windus, London, 1967).

19. Dieter Groh, *Negative Integration und revolutionaerer Attentismus. Die deutsche Sozialdemokratie am Vorabend des Ersten Weltkrieges* (Ullstein, Frankfurt, 1973).

20. Peter-Christian Witt, *Die Finanzpolitik des Deutschen Reiches von 1903 bis 1913. Eine Studie zur Innenpolitik des Wilhelminischen Deutschland* (Matthiesen, Luebeck and Hamburg, 1970).

21. See Gustav Schmidt, *Der europaeische Imperialismus* (Oldenbourg, Munich, 1985), pp.147-52 and the literature quoted there. See also Martin Kitchen, *The political economy of Germany* (Croom Helm, London, 1978), chapters 10 and 11.

Chapter Two

THE FIRST WORLD WAR

In August 1914, the German politicians reckoned with a short war. Most Germans thought that the war would be over by Christmas; the General Staff assumed a maximum duration of two years. All these predictions proved wrong. The war soon developed into a war of attrition for which no sufficient provision had been made.[1]

Germany's supply problems were partly caused by the British blockade imposed on 2 November 1914. As it also affected ships sailing under a neutral flag it was contrary to international law, a fact German politicians were quick to point out. Although the blockade impaired Germany's food and raw material supplies to a significant degree, there were several loopholes. Sweden kept on delivering substantial quantities of foodstuffs, iron ore and wood pulp, which became a substitute for cotton in the German powder and explosives industry. Norway, too, provided non-ferrous metals, Holland farm produce. During the war, imports fell to 40 per cent of the pre-war level. However, the main cause of Germany's economic decline was not so much the blockade, but excessive demands made on the economy.[2]

Shortly after the outbreak of the war, the *Kriegsrohstoffabteilung*, *KRA* (War Raw Materials Department) was established on 13 August 1914. It operated within the Prussian War Ministry and expanded rapidly, supervising about two dozen raw materials corporations by the end of the war.[3] Whereas the War Raw Materials Department controlled raw materials throughout Germany, fixed maximum prices, allocated raw materials and developed substitutes (*Ersatz*), the raw materials corporations, led by industrialists, were responsible for the acquisition, control and distribution of those materials, which were particularly important for the war effort.[4] In addition to this, a *Kriegsernaehrungsamt* (War Nutrition Office) was established in May 1916 to "regulate" the food supply system, in which "to regulate" meant in fact "to ration". The efforts of the War Nutrition Office were only partly successful, because a substantial amount of farm produce and meat was not sold on the regulated, but on the black market.

Owing to the British blockade and an insufficient raw material supply in Germany, *Ersatz*-materials of all kinds were developed. The synthetic fixation of nitrogen played the most important role. With the outbreak of the war, nitrogen imports from Chile ceased, which were necessary for the production of explosives and as a fertilizer in agriculture. With substantial financial assistance from the state the synthetic fixation of nitrogen was developed, which made a rapidly increasing output of powder and explosives possible. Other substitutes, which became particularly important after the First World War, were those for textiles, especially rayon and synthetic rubber for the tyres of army vehicles.[5] In foodstuffs, *Ersatz* was the word of the day, too. There was an *Ersatz* for practically everything: *Ersatz* wine, beer and sausage, coffee made from acorns and fat made from snails.[6]

In developing new products and providing goods for the war economy government and industry worked closely together to an extent which might justify the use of the term "symbiosis".[7] Contemporary observers spoke of "war socialism". This, however, reflects rather an ideology than historical facts. There was no transformation of the capitalist system, although the state and the military played a larger role in war production than they had done in the period before 1914.

This applies particularly to the last two years of the war, after a Supreme War Office (*Oberstes Kriegsamt*) had been established in November 1916. The huge expenditure of war material at Verdun and on the Somme made an even higher armament production effort necessary. The "Hindenburg Programme" of August 1916 laid down considerably increased production targets and was the starting point of a further militarisation of the German economy. The Supreme War Office, although nominally part of the Prussian War Ministry, was practically run by the Supreme Army Command. It had the powers of intervention in the production process and was put in charge of the War Raw Materials Department, the "War Substitutes and Labour Department" (*Kriegsersatz- und Ar-*

beitsdepartment) and the "Arms and Munitions Procurement Office" (*Waffen- und Munitionsbeschaffungsamt, WUMBA*) which had shortly before replaced the Prussian Ordnance Department. A "Standing Committee for the Integration of Factories" set up in December 1916 had the power to close down inefficient enterprises.

The most important part of the "Hindenburg Programme" was, however, the total mobilisation of labour. After various discussions in the second half of 1916, the "Patriotic Auxiliary Service Law" (*Gesetz ueber den Vaterlaendischen Hilfsdienst*) was promulgated on 5 December 1916. Males between the age of seventeen and sixty had to do compulsory service in areas relevant to the war economy. The law also restricted the mobility of labour, but the workers kept the right to move to a better paid job.

Government and industry realised that, in order to retain the *Burgfrieden*, the peace in industrial relations during the war, concessions had to be made to organised labour. Therefore, workers' committees were introduced in firms with at least 50 employees - the precursors of the workers' councils (*Betriebsraete*) and of the conciliation committees for bargaining. The workers' committees represented and voiced the employees' interests vis-à-vis the employers. They were recognised as equal partners in bargaining, a fact which has led historians to call their creation a "triumph of labour".[8] In view of the price labour had to pay, this is probably an exaggeration, but it is true that the First World War marked a decisive step in the development of organised labour rights in Germany.

In spite of the Hindenburg Programme and additional demands on labour, there was still a manpower gap in the German war economy. The war production drive and the difficulty of obtaining draft exemptions for skilled workers led to the importation of foreign labour mainly from Poland and Belgium. These labour imports soon degenerated into deportations, which had, however, to be stopped in February 1917 due to massive Dutch protests. The remaining labour gap was speedily filled by German female labour.[9]

Soon after the announcement of the Hindenburg Programme it became clear that its targets were unrealistic. From October 1916 onwards several factories had to discontinue their production owing to lack of coal. This was caused by inadequate coal output compounded by transport problems. During the year 1917 the Hindenburg Programme targets had to be gradually adapted to more realistic figures. By concentrating only on the most essential armament supplies, at least some of the Programme's targets could be reached by the beginning of 1918.[10]

Table 2.1:   *Changes in industrial employment during the First World War. Increase or decrease of employees (in %) in 1918 compared to 1913 in firms with more than 10 employees*

chemical industry	+ 170
engineering (electrical industry included)	+ 49
wood-working industry	+ 13
metalworking	+ 8
mining	- 5
leather	- 17
papermaking and processing	- 20
food and luxury food industries	- 24
printing	- 31
clothing	- 32
construction	- 57
war industries	+ 44
"peace industries"	- 40

Source: Wolfram Fischer, "Bergbau, Industrie und Handwerk 1914-1970" in Hermann Aubin and Wolfgang Zorn (eds), *Handbuch der deutschen Wirtschafts- und Sozialgeschichte* (2 vols., Klett, Stuttgart, 1976), vol. 2, p.800, Table 4b.

Already in the first phase of the war significant shifts took place in the German war economy. Private consumption was drastically curtailed and private investments fell except, of course, in the armament sector. Exports decreased, while imports increased continuously.[11] In industry, structural change was dramatic, as can be seen from the above table.

The chemical industry expanded rapidly and there was also an expansion in heavy industry and engineering, whereas the consumer goods industries declined.

Employment in industry fell by 8 per cent in firms with more than ten employees. Workers' productivity declined by about 20 per cent partly owing to a different composition of the labour force during the war: there was a larger share of unskilled and semi-skilled workers, juveniles and female workers. Workers' performance also decreased because of insufficient nutrition and falling real wages, which most probably contributed to lower productivity. The deterioration of the workers' morale in the last phase of the war and a growing resistance against its continuation also played a role.[12]

Although, taking industry as a whole, productivity decreased, there were also branches with substantial productivity gains. Examples are the engineering, electrical and chemical industries, where a rationalised system of production and standardisation was introduced. Changes in the organisation of production with flow production and the use of modern machine tools made it possible to employ semi-skilled workers, female workers and juveniles in increasing numbers. These changes were a basis for the rationalisation drive of the 1920s.[13]

Industrial production, especially armament production, was essential for the German war economy, but so was agriculture. Here the problems were particularly severe: agricultural production decreased, because many farmers were conscripted into the army and could no longer cultivate the land. Agricultural horses, seed, fertilizers and machinery were scarce. Although the synthetic fixation of nitrogen had been developed this was used almost exclusively for the production of explosives. The lack of crude phosphate imports, which were needed as fertilizers, proved to be disastrous for German agriculture.[14] In order to improve the food supply situation and to cut down stock farming the government issued a decree ordering about 9 million pigs to be slaughtered. Men and pigs had become competitors for scarce potato and grain supplies.

The insufficient supply of agricultural products caused a rapid increase in food prices. Already in August 1914 maximum prices for food were decreed in urban and rural districts and in October 1914 general price controls were introduced. These did not prove very effective, however, as black markets developed rapidly.[15] The tight supply situation worsened after the poor harvests of 1916 and 1917. Grain production, already well below its pre-war level, fell from 21.8 million to 14.9 million tons in these two years. The particularly hard winter of 1916/7 worsened the nutritional crisis which was compounded by a lack of heating materials and by transport difficulties. In this "turnip winter" of 1916/7 the starving urban population took refuge to consuming crops which so far had not been considered fit for human consumption.

After 1916, the scarcity and high price of food as well as long working hours and the intensification of the work process, especially in the armament industry, caused various strikes. In April 1917 workers in Berlin and Leipzig went on strike because of lower food rations. In later strikes, however, political demands became more and more important: the strikes in the Ruhr and Upper Silesia of June and July 1917 were also politically motivated with demands for an immediate peace treaty and a general and equal right to vote.

At the beginning of the war, the problem of war finance did not seem to exist at all: the conquered enemies would pay the bill and it would be a short war anyway. Until the bill could be handed over to the enemies, war loans and short term *Reich* treasury bills would provide the necessary funds for warfare. But the reparation dreams of the German government materialised only in one instance: in the peace treaty at Brest Litovsk on 3 March 1918 Russia had to pay the sum of 6 thousand million roubles. Even in the spring of 1918 the *Kaiser* rejoiced at the thought of imposing enormous reparation sums on the United States, Great Britain, France and Italy.

There were three different means of financing the war.[16] First: war loans amounting to the sum of almost RM 100 thousand million. The *Reich* offered five per cent war bonds which proved quite attractive in the first two years of the war, because nominal wages rose and the supply of goods declined so that there was sufficient liquidity.

Second: for her short-term debts the *Reich* issued interest-bearing treasury bills, which, at the end of the war, amounted to RM 51 thousand million. The German Central Bank, the *Reichs-*

bank, was given the right to rediscount in unlimited amounts against banknotes.

Third: additional taxes were raised from 1916 onwards, which, compared to the war bonds and treasury bills, played only a minor role. Among these taxes was a war profits tax, which was announced in December 1915 but introduced only in June 1916. In the meantime, war profiteers had ample opportunity to hide their profits. There were also a general turnover tax introduced in 1916 and a special tax on a number of luxury goods. Altogether, these taxes yielded RM 2.1 thousand million in 1916, 8 thousand million in 1917 and 7.4 thousand million in 1918. These figures show that the war expenditure of the German *Reich*, which amounted to about RM 150 thousand million, was almost completely financed by loans. The higher yields from the additional taxes just sufficed to service the public debt.

During the war, the money supply quintupled. The creation of additional money was of course a convenient means of raising the funds necessary to keep the war economy going. This caused inflationary tendencies which increased rapidly in the early 1920s. But the origins of the inflation were in the inflationary financing of the war.[17] Already in this period the effects of inflation made themselves felt: people with tangible assets generally remained unhurt by inflation and often made substantial profits, whereas those with only financial assets and the recipients of incomes, which did not keep up with price increases, found it hard to cope with the situation.

Notes

1. Lothar Burchardt, *Friedenswirtschaft und Kriegsvorsorge. Deutschlands wirtschaftliche Ruestungsbestrebungen vor 1914* (Boldt, Boppard, 1968). See especially Gerald D. Feldman, *Army, industry and labour in Germany 1914-1918* (Princeton University Press, Princeton, 1966); Gerd Hardach, *The First World War, 1914-1918* (Allen Lane, London, 1977); Juergen Kocka, *Facing Total War. German Society 1914-1918* (Harvard University Press, Cambridge, Mass., 1984); Friedrich Zunkel, *Industrie und Staatssozialismus. Der Kampf um die Wirtschaftsordnung in Deutschland 1914-1918* (Droste, Duesseldorf, 1974); Hermann Schaefer, *Regionale Wirtschaftspolitik in der Kriegswirtschaft. Staat, Industrie und Verbaende waehrend des Ersten Weltkrieges in Baden* (Kohlhammer, Stuttgart, 1983) and Hans Gotthard Ehlert, *Die Wirtschaftliche Zentralbehoerde des Deutschen Reiches 1914 bis 1919. Das Problem der "Gemeinwirtschaft" in Krieg und Frieden* (Steiner, Wiesbaden, 1982).

2. G. Hardach, *First World War*, pp.28-34.

3. Lothar Burchardt, "Walther Rathenau und die Anfaenge der deutschen Rohstoffbewirtschaftung im Ersten Weltkrieg", *Tradition*, vol. 15 (1970), pp.169-

96.

4. Berghahn, *Modern Germany*, p.47.

5. Kocka, *Facing Total War*, p.34.

6. Karl Hardach, *The political economy of Germany in the twentieth century* (University of California Press, Berkeley, Los Angeles and London, 1976), p.13.

7. Michael Geyer, *Deutsche Ruestungspolitik 1860-1980* (Suhrkamp, Frankfurt am Main, 1984) p.104.

8. Feldman, *Army, industry and labour*, p.197.

9. Ulrich Herbert, "Zwangsarbeit als Lernprozess. Zur Beschaeftigung auslaendischer Arbeiter in der westdeutschen Industrie im Ersten Weltkrieg", *Archiv fuer Sozialgeschichte*, vol. 24 (1984), pp.285-304.

10. Geyer, *Deutsche Ruestungspolitik*, p.110; Gunther Mai, *Kriegswirtschaft und Arbeiterbewegung in Wuerttemberg 1914-1918* (Klett-Cotta, Stuttgart, 1983), pp.218-308.

11. Knut Borchardt, "Wachstum und Wechsellagen 1914-1970" in Hermann Aubin and Wolfgang Zorn (eds), *Handbuch der deutschen Wirtschafts- und Sozialgeschichte* (2 vols., Klett, Stuttgart, 1976), vol. 2, p.697.

12. Wolfram Fischer, "Bergbau, Industrie und Handwerk 1914-1970" in Hermann Aubin and Wolfgang Zorn (eds), *Handbuch der deutschen Wirtschafts- und Sozialgeschichte* (2 vols., Klett, Stuttgart, 1976), vol. 2, p.801.

13. Kocka, *Facing Total War*, p.33.

14. Max Rolfes, "Landwirtschaft 1914-1970" in Aubin and Zorn (eds), *Handbuch*, vol. 2, p.741.

15. G. Hardach, *First World War*, p.116.

16. Wolfram Fischer, "Die deutsche Wirtschaft im Ersten Weltkrieg" in Norbert Walter (ed.), *Deutschland. Portraet einer Nation*, vol. 3, *Wirtschaft* (Bertelsmann, Guetersloh, 1985), pp.131-2; Lutz Koellner, *Ruestungsfinanzierung. Daemonie und Wirklichkeit* (Knapp, Frankfurt am Main, 1969), pp.71-2.

17. Carl-Ludwig Holtfrerich, *The German inflation 1914-1923* (de Gruyter, Berlin, New York, 1986), pp.102-19.

Chapter Three

REPARATIONS AND INFLATION

War losses

Under the Versailles Peace Treaty Germany lost 10 per cent of her population and 13.5 per cent of her pre-war territory. She lost her colonies, Upper Silesia, Alsace-Lorraine, the Saar district, most of Posen and part of West Prussia, Schleswig, Danzig, the Baltic part of Memel, the Western frontier districts of Eupen and Malmédy and a small area near Troppau among others. A particular problem was caused by those industries which had earlier formed integrated units, especially Upper Silesia, and by the separation of the Ruhr coal from the rich iron ore deposits of Lorraine. From now on Germany depended to an even greater extent on foodstuffs and raw material imports, because the regions lost were particularly rich in agricultural and industrial resources. Germany lost 15 per cent of her arable land and 75 per cent of her iron ore deposits. Her pig iron production capacity was reduced by 44 per cent, that of steel by 38 per cent and that of coal by 26 per cent.[1]

As far as Germany's development as an industrial state is concerned these territorial losses should, however, not be overrated. The fact that Germany's agricultural and industrial raw material base shrank did not have such a negative effect on the performance of German industry as could have been expected. With her changed economic structure Germany was still integrated into the international division of labour, exporting industrial products and importing foodstuffs and raw materials.[2] Germany could, however, only profit from this, if national trade barriers were abolished. These did create a problem, especially with regard to the transfer of reparations.

Germany's territorial losses affected her balance of payments negatively. This was compounded by the handing over of about 90 per cent of her merchant fleet, the surrender of industrial equipment - mainly railway rolling stock - and the confiscation of almost all her foreign investments including patents and licenses.[3] Germany had to surrender her entire navy and all her armament material to the Allies. In addition, she had to pay all the occupation costs of Allied troops in Germany. Also, the "hole in the west" - duty free trade via the occupied western territories - diminished German revenue.

At the end of the war, about 873,000 prisoners of war and 360,000 foreign civil workers left Germany. But at the same time almost ten million German soldiers entered the labour market with an additional one million German prisoners of war from the summer of 1919 onwards. This large number of people could only partly be employed in spite of emergency work programmes like that of the German railways. At the end of the war, agricultural production was reduced to about 55 to 60 per cent of the 1913 level. Owing to the insufficient supply of phosphoric acid-based fertilizers during the war the soil was worn out and could only recover slowly.[4]

Reparations

Apart from the losses mentioned above, another problem troubled the German economy, reparations. At Versailles, the total amount of the German reparation obligations had been left undetermined because of differing opinions among the Allies. Inter-allied debts amounted to roughly $ 26.5 thousand million with the United States and Britain as the main creditors and France as the principal debtor. In April 1921 the Allied Reparation Commission fixed the sum at 132 thousand million gold marks or roughly $ 33 thousand million, of which France was to receive 52 per cent, Britain 22 per cent, Italy 10 per cent, Belgium 8 per cent and the remaining Allies 8 per cent. This enormous sum, from which payments already made of some 8 thousand million marks were deducted, far exceeded the amount considered feasible and prudent by John Maynard Keynes and by the United States experts on the Reparations Commission. Britain and especially France suggested mixing claims insofar as Germany paid directly to the

United States, thereby releasing the Allies from paying for United States deliveries during the war. The United States' delegates were wise enough to decline this proposal knowing that Germany was much more likely to default on her obligations than the Allies.

The regulations for the payment of reparations were complex. The most significant are that the total reparations sum bore a 6 per cent interest charge and that a schedule of payments provided for the transfer of fixed instalments of gold marks. The first reparation annuities amounted to 2 thousand million gold marks per annum. In addition, a variable payment of 26 per cent of the annual value of German exports had to be paid.[5]

Like those Allied experts who had any economic sense, the German government renounced these figures as too high, but finally had to comply. At the end of 1921 the German government declared itself unable to meet the instalments and early in 1922 asked for a reduction. In March 1922, payments were reduced to 720 million marks for the current year and in August 1922 were suspended for six months.

Already in 1921 Germany found it extremely difficult to pay in kind. Apart from that, cash payments to the Allies contributed to accelerating inflation which caused a depreciation of the currency. This development was enhanced by the fact that the German government increased its borrowing from the central bank to meet its obligations rather than increase taxation. Moreover, there were problems as to the sum Germany should be credited for her deliveries in kind. The German government claimed that the value of those deliveries amounted to about 42 thousand million gold marks whereas the Allies credited only about 10 thousand million. The correct amount is difficult to determine because of differing prices in Germany and the Allied countries, but it must have been somewhere in the middle. Keynes's computation was about 26 thousand million gold marks.[6]

Raising the reparations was complicated enough, but transferring them proved even more difficult. The only feasible way of transfer was by increasing German exports which would enable Germany to earn the necessary foreign currency. This would have meant that the Allies opened their markets to imports of industrial goods from Germany. Because of the similar industrial structures of Germany and the western Allies the national industries of the latter feared increased competition in their home markets with falling sales prospects and rising unemployment.[7] Tensions grew when Germany was in arrears with some rather small deliveries early in 1923. As a consequence, French, Belgian and Italian troops marched into the Ruhr area on 11 January 1923 in order to secure deliveries by exercising direct control of Ruhr industry. Allied mistrust of Germany's intentions of fulfilling her reparation obligations met with German protests and passive resistance. During this *Ruhrkampf* the German currency declined at an enormous speed. In September 1923 the German government called off the passive resistance and suggested that a new currency, the *Rentenmark*, should be introduced. This materialised in November 1923 when the German currency was stabilised at the rate of 1 billion marks for one goldmark. This and the Dawes Plan, which was put into force on 1 September 1924 and provided for more sensible regulations of the reparation question, introduced the German "stabilisation period" of the mid-1920s.

Public Finance

Another prerequisite was the financial reform of the early 1920s. At the end of March 1920 the floating debt of the *Reich* amounted to 96.1 thousand million marks, but with increasing inflation the situation in state finance improved quickly. In 1922 the debt service amounted to only 10 per cent of state expenditure and 32 per cent of the ordinary revenue.[8]

The main incentives for a reorganisation of German public finance came from Mathias Erzberger, who was the *Reich* Minister of Finance from July 1919 until August 1921, when he was murdered. At the end of 1919 he introduced taxes on property gains during the war the most important of which was the "*Reich* emergency contribution".[9]

Following the Erzberger financial reform programme the *Reich* got a fiscal administration of its own and was therefore no longer dependent on the German states. Fiscal sovereignty was transferred from the states to the central government. In March 1920 the income tax, the revenue of which accrued to the states, was replaced by the *Reich* income tax which was supplemented by a corporation tax and a capital-gains tax. In 1922 a tax on property, a transfer tax and a premium tax were added to this.

Although the government extended indirect taxation with an increase in the turnover tax and the tax on semi-luxuries, it shifted the emphasis from indirect towards direct taxation. The *Reich* had all direct taxes at its disposal, particularly the income tax and the tax on property. Erzberger aimed at increasing the government's share of the national product to widen the chances of financial intervention into the economy. The per capita tax load was increased from 9 per cent in 1913 to 17 per cent in 1925.[10]

Erzberger's policy proved partly successful for the *Reich* finances. As a consequence the share of tax revenue relative to national income rose from 15 to 25 per cent. The *Reich*'s share increased from 30 to 39 per cent at the expense of the states and the municipalities the shares of which fell from 30 per cent to 23 per cent and from 40 per cent to 38 per cent respectively.[11] Favourable as inflation was for the public debt it had, however, an extremely negative effect on the real value of tax revenue.

Inflation

The roots of the "Great Inflation" of 1923 are to be found in the First World War. The enormous government expenditure, the resulting national budget deficits and an increase in money supply were prerequisites for the traumatic inflationary experience of 1923. During the war, inflation hardly showed because of price and exchange rate controls. At that time it was curbed and turned into open inflation only after 1919. The financing of reparations and employment programmes intensified the problem, as did the fact that the final reparation sum was not fixed.[12]

In 1918/9 German economic policy aimed at full employment. Taxes were not increased, because the various governments were not strong enough to carry through a strict tax policy in order to avoid inflation. There was a positive aspect to this, because deflation, with negative results for the economy, was avoided.

The "Great Inflation" of 1923 has to be distinguished from the inflationary period between the First World War and the end of 1922. After the First World War inflation assisted the growth of industrial production which was necessary to cope with the large number of demobilised people. Inflation saved the German *Reich* from the effects of the world recession of 1920/1.[13] Whereas in Britain the unemployment rate exceeded 20 per cent in 1921, there was almost full employment in Germany. Apart from this, the German economy helped to overcome the recession by imports from countries such as the United States and Britain. It therefore acted as an "engine of growth" for the world economy. Until the summer of 1922 substantial amounts of foreign, especially United States, short-term capital was invested in Germany which meant that a large part of the losses from inflation were born by foreigners.[14] This is to be understood in the sense that a

Figure 3.1: The development of inflation 1919-1923 (1913 = 1)

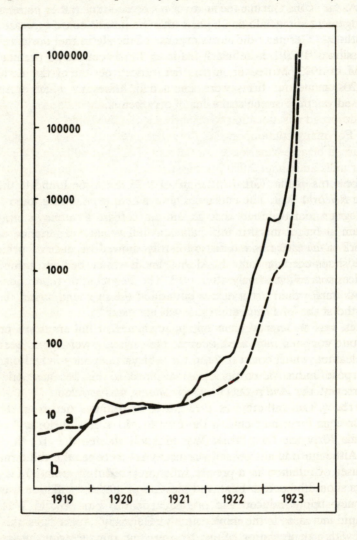

Notes: [a] money circulation; [b] wholesale prices

Source: Knut Borchardt, "Wachstum und Wechsellagen 1914-1970", in Hermann Aubin and Wolfgang Zorn (eds), *Handbuch der deutschen Wirtschafts- und Sozialgeschichte* (2 vols, Klett, Stuttgart 1976), vol. 2, p.699.

large part of German imports were thus financed by Americans and allowed German consumption to have been much higher than would have been otherwise possible and with no later obligation to pay back these devalued debts.

As far as the German economy is concerned, this rather positive judgement about inflation before 1923 should not be exaggerated. Although Germany did not suffer economically in the world recession of 1920/1, it definitely made up for this in the great inflation of 1923. Moreover, in the inflationary period of the early 1920s, numerous firms were founded in Germany which were based on pure speculation, many of which soon collapsed.[15] A widespread misallocation of resources is clearly visible.[16]

For many contemporaries the inflation was a shock, a nightmare, a bizarre experience. At the end of 1923 more than 300 paper mills and about 2,000 printing presses worked continuously to supply the public with *Reichsbank* notes. On 11 November 1923 the *Reichsbank* issued a 1000 billion marks note. At that time a 1 kilogram loaf of bread cost 428 thousand million marks, a kilogram of butter more than 5 billion. After wages had been paid, work in the factories was interrupted, as employees rushed out to the shops carrying large bundles of money to buy goods before prices soared even further.

As during the First World War there was *Ersatz* again, this time in the shape of *Ersatz* money, which, contrary to the war substitutes, was an improvement on the original. In rural areas rye or potato coupons were used as emergency money (*Notgeld*); pieces of leather, which could be used for soling shoes, served the same purpose. Industrial corporations like the BASF issued their own currency, the *Anilin-Dollar*, which was much preferred to state currency. Often there was a return to a primitive barter trade: four eggs for a hair cut, two briquettes for admission to the cinema, forty eggs for a burial (first class with sermon).[17]

Although it is not possible to distinguish between the different causes of inflation in a precise way, three main interrelated factors should be noted. First, and most important, the inflation was money-supply induced and originated in the First World War. Rapid increases in the money supply resulted in a higher price level with a depreciation of the currency.[18] Secondly, according to the balance-of-payments theory of inflation, external deficits, mainly caused by Allied reparation demands, depressed the exchange rate and raised import and domestic prices. This increased the budget deficit and, subsequently, the note issue.[19]

This explanation was a favourite with German politicians, for example Karl Helfferich, who put the blame for inflation at the door of the Allies. The remedy was of course simple, namely a reduction or cancellation of reparations. Another cause of inflation was the substantial wage rises of 1918/9, which triggered off a wage-price spiral.[20] In order to prevent social unrest and realising that increased labour costs could easily be passed on by further inflation, employers often gave in readily to trade union demands.[21]

Examining the consequences of inflation on income distribution there can be no doubt that creditors lost and debtors gained. The greatest debtor was the state. With the year 1913 as a basis the internal debts of the German *Reich,* which had been 154 thousand million marks at the end of the war, amounted to only 15,4 pfennigs on 15 November 1923.[22] Therefore, all those gained from inflation who had to finance the public debt, which meant all German taxpayers. This has to be kept in mind when dealing with the allegedly negative effects of inflation on the German middle class.[23]

Not only the state and the heavily indebted German *Laender* and municipalities gained from inflation but also all those private borrowers who paid back with inflated money the loans they had contracted before the war. Merchants and industrialists benefited from rising prices, because there was a large margin between buying prices of the past and selling prices of the present. This goes especially for the producer-goods industry. "Graspers" (*Raffkes*) and profiteers (*Schieber*) were a species which thrived in the heyday of inflation. The former bought all kinds of goods, factories and real estate on credit which they paid back with inflated money, whereas the *Schieber* made easy gains on the foreign exchange market or on the commodity and stock exchanges. Mortgage debtors, mainly houseowners and especially farmers, also benefited from inflation.

The obvious "losers" were those with contracted incomes like pensions or insurance benefits.[24] Apart from men of private means (*Rentiers*), who held liquid assets in marks, private scholars, artists, writers and many doctors and lawyers who had saved for old age were hit by inflation. A bank account of 60,000 marks, the interest from which would, in 1913, have enabled one to lead a comfortable life in retirement, would not buy a daily newspaper in April 1923. Apart from private persons, insurance organisations, foundations, trade unions and banks were affected by inflation. Although some German banks did make enormous profits during this period their equity capital decreased from 7.1 thousand million marks in 1913 to RM 1.97 thousand million in 1924.[25]

The effects of inflation on workers - including white collar workers - and civil servants are much more difficult to assess than those of the groups mentioned above. It seems clear, however, that the traditional view of an unqualified "destruction of the middle class" is no longer tenable. During inflation the real income of most workers and civil servants rose slightly. Workers' living standards generally exceeded the rise in real incomes if the shorter working day - 48 hours a week from 1919 onwards as compared to 52 to 60 hours in 1913 - better housing and nutrition are taken into consideration.[26]

With both civil servants and white collar workers the trend towards equalisation of wages increased, a tendency which had already been visible before 1914. There was also a trend towards equalisation of wages between skilled and unskilled, male and female and young and old workers.[27] Equalisation meant that, in order to compensate for inflation, the formerly lower income groups had higher wage increases than the higher income groups. As opposed to lower income groups, the higher income groups of employees probably were among the "losers" from inflation, especially if the reduction in value of savings is taken into account. Although the relative position of workers improved, their condition was generally poor indeed owing mainly to food shortages. To attribute savings to particular social groups is a difficult task, but the fact that savings banks' deposits fell from 19 thousand million marks in 1913 to RM 608 million at the end of 1925 is an impressive figure. It is reasonable to assume that this fall affected the higher income groups more than the lower ones.[28]

Notes

1. Derek H. Aldcroft, *From Versailles to Wall Street 1919-1929* (Allen Lane, London, 1977), pp.22-3.

2. Gerd Hardach, "Zur politischen Oekonomie der Weimarer Republik", in Reinhard Kuehnl and Gerd Hardach (eds), *Die Zerstoerung der Weimarer Republik*, 2nd edn (Pahl-Rugenstein, Cologne, 1979), pp.15-6.

3. Karl Hardach, *The political economy of Germany in the twentieth century* (University of California Press, Berkeley, Los Angeles, London, 1980), pp.17-8.

4. Friedrich-Wilhelm Henning, *Das industrialisierte Deutschland 1914 bis 1972* (Schoeningh, Paderborn, 1974), pp.52-4. On demobilisation see Gerald D. Feldman, "Wirtschafts- und sozialpolitische Probleme der deutschen Demobilmachung 1918/19", in Gerald D. Feldman (ed.), *Vom Weltkrieg zur Weltwirt-*

schaftskrise (Vandenhoeck and Ruprecht, Goettingen, 1984), pp.84-99 and Richard Bessel, "Unemployment and demobilisation in Germany after the First World War", in Richard J. Evans and Dick Geary (eds), *The German unemployed. Experiences and consequences of mass unemployment from the Weimar Republic to the Third Reich* (Croom Helm, London, Sidney, 1987), pp.25-43.

5. Aldcroft, *Versailles to Wall Street*, pp.79-83.

6. K. Hardach, *Political economy*, pp.25-6.

7. Dietmar Petzina, *Die deutsche Wirtschaft in der Zwischenkriegszeit* (Steiner, Wiesbaden, 1977), p.78.

8. Hermann Kellenbenz, *Deutsche Wirtschaftsgeschichte* (2 vols., Beck, Munich, 1981), vol. 2, p.445.

9. Fritz Blaich, *Der Schwarze Freitag. Inflation und Weltwirtschaftskrise* (Deutscher Taschenbuch Verlag, Munich, 1985), p.42.

10. Petzina, *Deutsche Wirtschaft*, pp.84-5. See also Peter-Christian Witt, "Finanzpolitik und sozialer Wandel in Krieg und Inflation 1918-1924", in Hans Mommsen, Dietmar Petzina and Bernd Weisbrod (eds), *Industrielles System und politische Entwicklung in der Weimarer Republik* (2 vols., Athenaeum, Droste, Kronberg/Ts., Duesseldorf, 1977), vol.1, pp.395-425.

11. Henning, *Das industrialisierte Deutschland*, p.63.

12. Carl-Ludwig Holtfrerich, *The German inflation 1914-1923* (de Gruyter, Berlin, New York, 1986), pp.192-3.

13. Eberhard Kolb, *Die Weimarer Republik* (Oldenbourg, Munich, 1984), p.178.

14. Holtfrerich, *German inflation*, pp.331-2.

15. Aldcroft, *Versailles to Wall Street*, p.142.

16. Constantino Bresciani-Turroni, *The economics of inflation. A study of currency depreciation in post-war Germany* (Allen and Unwin, London, 1937).

17. Blaich, *Der Schwarze Freitag*, pp.10-14.

18. Peter Czada, "Ursachen und Folgen der grossen Inflation", in Harald Winkel (ed.), *Finanz- und wirtschaftspolitische Fragen der Zwischenkriegszeit* (Duncker and Humblot, Berlin, 1973), p.10.

19. Karsten Laursen and Joergen Pedersen, *The German inflation* (North-Holland Publishing Company, Amsterdam, 1964), pp.36-41; Agnete von Specht, *Politische und wirtschaftliche Hintergruende der deutschen Inflation 1918-1923* (Peter Lang, Frankfurt am Main, Berne, 1982), pp.60-8.

20. Knut Borchardt, "Wachstum und Wechsellagen 1914-1970", in Hermann Aubin and Wolfgang Zorn (eds), *Handbuch der deutschen Wirtschafts- und Sozialgeschichte* (2 vols., Klett, Stuttgart, 1976), vol. 2, p.700.

21. K. Hardach, *Political economy*, p.19.

22. Blaich, *Der Schwarze Freitag*, p.55.

23. Borchardt, *Wachstum*, p.701. See also Otto Buesch and Gerald D. Feldman (eds), *Historische Prozesse der deutschen Inflation 1914-1924: Ein Tagungsbericht* (Colloquium, Berlin, 1978), pp.54-5, 61, 79, 217.

24. K. Hardach, *Political economy*, pp.20-1.

25. Blaich, *Der Schwarze Freitag*, p.56. See also Michael Schneider, "Deutsche Gesellschaft in Krieg und Waehrungskrise 1914-1924. Ein Jahrzehnt Forschungen zur Inflation", *Archiv fuer Sozialgeschichte*, vol. 26 (1986), pp.301-19.

26. Werner Abelshauser, "Verelendung der Handarbeiter?", in Hans Mommsen and Winfried Schulze (eds), *Vom Elend der Handarbeit* (Klett, Stuttgart, 1981), p.470. On the effects of inflation on the workers see also Heinrich August Winkler, *Von der Revolution zur Stabilisierung. Arbeiter und Arbeiterbewegung in der Weimarer Republik 1918 bis 1924* (Dietz Nachf., Berlin and Bonn, 1984), pp.377-92.

27. Andreas Kunz, "Verteilungskampf oder Interessenkonsensus? Zur Entwicklung der Realeinkommen von Beamten, Arbeitern und Angestellten in der Inflationszeit 1914-1924", in Gerald D. Feldman, Carl-Ludwig Holtfrerich,

Gerhard A. Ritter, Peter-Christian Witt (eds), *Die deutsche Inflation. Eine Zwischenbilanz* (de Gruyter, Berlin, New York, 1982), pp.347-84.

28. Gunther Mai, "Wenn der Mensch Hunger hat, hoert alles auf. Wirtschaftliche und soziale Ausgangsbedingungen der Weimarer Republik (1914-1924)", in Werner Abelshauser (ed.), *Die Weimarer Republik als Wohlfahrtsstaat* (Franz Steiner Verlag Wiesbaden, Stuttgart, 1987), pp.33-62, and Robert Scholz, "Lohn und Beschaeftigung als Indikatoren fuer die soziale Lage der Arbeiterschaft in der Inflation", in Gerald D. Feldman and others (eds), *Die Anpassung an die Inflation. Beiträge zu Inflation und Wiederaufbau in Deutschland und Europa 1914-1924* (de Gruyter, Berlin, 1986), pp.278-322.

Chapter Four

RELATIVE STABILISATION

Currency Reform

In order to come to grips with inflation, the chaotic state of the currency had to be remedied. On 15 October 1923 the *Rentenbank* was founded with a registered capital of 3.2 thousand million *Rentenmarks*. This was backed by an internal loan on the basis of real assets.[1] Two mortgages of 1.6 thousand million *Rentenmarks* each were imposed on agricultural lands and on industrial property. The *Rentenbank* notes were redeemable in 5 per cent gold mark bonds; their issue was limited to 2.4 thousand million *Rentenmarks*.[2] For these reasons public confidence in the new currency was high. In November 1923 the *Rentenmark* was fixed at one pre-war gold mark and at one trillion paper marks. *Rentenmark* and paper mark existed side by side.

Increased demand for credit in the spring of 1924 again aroused the fear of inflation. The banking law of 3 August 1924 stipulated the *Reichsbank's* independence of the *Reich* government. The *Reichsmark*, equal in value to the *Rentenmark*, was introduced. This new currency, a gold bullion standard, had to have a 40 per cent backing by gold or foreign exchange with the rest covered by commercial bills of exchange. The reduction of the money supply, an increasing stability of the public finances and an increase in gold and foreign currency reserves were the main monetary and financial prerequisites for the period of relative stabilisation which, according to some writers, comprises the so-called "golden twenties", 1924-1928/9.[3]

44

Dawes Plan and Young Plan

Apart from reforming the currency, the r~paration problem had
to be tackled. In 1923 two international commissions were instituted one of which, chaired by the American Charles G. Dawes,
was the more important. Its purpose was to work out proposals as
to how Germany's economic performance and her financial situation could be improved. It stipulated that in the first year - from 1
September 1924 to 31 August 1925 - RM one thousand million
should be raised by Germany. It was later agreed that this amount
was to be paid annually until 1928/9, plus an additional sum based
on a "prosperity index" which was composed of such heterogenous
items as the consumption of coal, sugar, tobacco, liquor and other
goods. Although the Dawes plan was far superior to the reparation plans of the early 1920s, the fact that neither the duration nor
the aggregate amount of the reparations was fixed caused much
resentment in Germany, and not only in right-wing circles. Of the
annuity of RM 2.5 thousand million the *Reich* had to raise half,
the other half had to be procured by German industry and the
German railways. To ensure that the annuities were duly transferred and to watch over the stability of the German currency the
American Parker Gilbert was appointed as general agent for
reparations. The German railways had to welcome a foreign
commissioner who supervised its management; the *Reichsbank*
had to accept a supervisory "general council" with 14 members,
seven of whom were foreigners.

Whereas the raising of reparations in Germany went according
to plan, transfer was only possible because of a vast influx of foreign capital, especially from the United States. During the period
1924-9 Germany's borrowings were roughly RM 13.5 thousand
million while her reparation obligations only amounted to RM 8.5
thousand million. This was certainly one way to meet her reparation obligations, but it definitely did not square with the ideas of
the Allied reparation experts. The only satisfactory way would
have been to provide the necessary foreign currency by a German
export surplus. As to this, conditions in the mid-1920s had not
changed much from those at the beginning of the decade: because
of various protectionist measures by reparation creditors Germany found it difficult to earn the foreign currency required. Borrowing was an easy way out, which proved to be harmful later. But
even in the mid-1920s reparations were a strain on the German
economy. They contributed to a deflationary policy with de-

celerating effects on capital accumulation and were responsible for Germany's capital exports falling well behind her capital imports.[4]

The Dawes Plan had serious deficiencies, particularly the indefinite reparation sum and the duration of payment. This was remedied by the Young Plan of 20 January 1930, which was made retroactive to 1 September 1929. According to this plan RM 1.6 thousand million were to be paid in 1930/1 with annuities rising to RM 2.3 thousand million in 1987. The final annuity of RM 898 million was due in 1988. The Young Plan was more acceptable to the Germans than its predecessor, because the annuities were not supposed to continue until doomsday, although setting the final date as late as 1988 was rather an ambitious aim, too. Also, the prosperity index was abolished and foreign supervisors were sent home. Still, many problems remained, especially the question of transfer. In June 1931, during the world depression, the Hoover moratorium suspended the Young Plan for a year. On 9 June 1932, at the Lausanne Conference, reparations were reduced to a comparatively modest RM 3 thousand million. Even this sum was not paid. The loan of RM 420 million which had been granted in connection with the Hoover moratorium was repaid, however.

Economic development and business cycles in the 1920s

After the currency reform and the Dawes Plan the German economy quickly recovered from the crisis of the hyperinflation period. From 1924 to 1929 industrial production increased at an annual rate of 7.9 per cent and the economy as a whole grew at about 4 per cent annually. These figures do not imply - at least not as far as the economy is concerned - that this period can be called "the golden twenties". It seems more appropriate to speak of "relative stagnation" with comparatively low investment ratios.[5] Between 1925 and 1929 the average net investment ratio in Germany was only 10 per cent compared to an average ratio of 15 per cent during the period 1910 to 1913.[6] "Relative stagnation" means that economic growth was slower than could have been expected from a theoretical point of view, especially if the substantially reduced growth rates of the immediate post-war period are taken into consideration.

There were really only three years of growth, 1924, 1925, and 1927. Compared to other industrial nations, especially to the United States and Japan, German economic growth rate was well below average. The annual investment ratio of 10 per cent was not high enough to catch up with the figures of the leading industrial nations. Insufficient investment was caused by high interest rates - the *Reichsbank* tried to attract foreign capital into Germany and aimed at preventing any new inflationary tendencies - by the crowding out effects because of increased state spending and possibly because of high wages.[7] In attracting foreign currency the *Reichsbank* was successful. From 1924 to 1929 the balance of capital transactions amounted to RM 17 thousand million in Germany's favour. The fact that a considerable share of this consisted of short-term loans which had been invested long-term posed a major problem at the end of the period.

Cartelisation, industrial concentration[8] and rationalisation[9] increased labour productivity but also created excess capacity. In addition, a trend intensified which had already been visible before the war and which was one of the reasons for the economic stagnation of the European industrial nations: the increasing disparity in growth between the capital goods industries and the consumer goods industries. The former increased at the expense of the latter and created overcapacity. The industrialisation of less developed countries also contributed to the slower growth rates of the consumer goods sector in industrialised states.[10]

Looking at the cyclical development of the German economy in more detail there was a post-war boom between 1920 and 1922 helped by inflation, while, at the same time, the other major industrial nations experienced a recession. From 1919 to 1922 Germany's industrial production doubled, although the low starting point has to be taken into consideration. After the "stabilisation crisis" in the winter of 1923/4 a cyclical upswing began early in 1924, but this was interrupted after a few months, when the *Reichsbank* restricted credits to keep the exchange rate at its current high level. In the autumn of 1924 a new upswing began which turned into a severe "intermediary crisis", the stabilisation crisis of 1925/6, caused mainly by monetary factors: the deflationary policy of the *Reichsbank*, the slowing down of foreign loans and the collapse of several concerns, especially the Stinnes combines, which had been built up during the inflation. In the autumn of 1926 a new cyclical upswing started so that by the summer of 1927 many industries regained pre-war levels of production and some had even surpassed them. But already at the end of 1927 there were signs of a new recession. The stabilising effects of foreign trade mitigated this recession. In 1928 and 1929 exports increased while imports decreased. With the breakdown of the international economy after 1929 recession turned into the great depression.[11]

Industrial production

During the First World War industrial production declined continuously owing to difficulties with raw material supplies, lack of workers because of conscription and insufficient replacement of worn equipment.

Figure 4.1: Growth of German industrial production 1914-1931 [a]

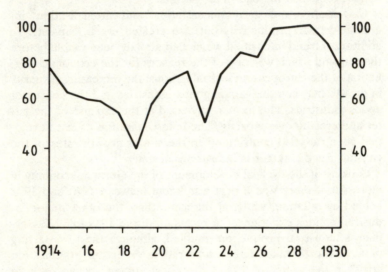

Note: [a] *log. scale, 1928 = 100*

Source: Carl-Ludwig Holtfrerich, *The German inflation 1914-1923* (de Gruyter, Berlin, New York, 1986), p.182.

In 1919, German industrial production sank to the lowest level of the period 1913 to 1931. This was due to the blockade of Germany's foreign trade until mid-1919, insufficient raw material supplies, the loss of territories and industrial capacity, and transport problems owing to the surrender of almost the entire merchant fleet and about 20 per cent of the railway rolling stock to the Allies. To this must be added the introduction of the eight hour working day in November 1918 and strikes and revolutionary disturbances in 1918/9.[12] When, at the beginning of 1920, the do-

mestic political situation in Germany improved, industrial production picked up rapidly and reached a peak in 1922. In spite of
this it was still 29 per cent below the 1913 level. In the autumn of
1922 the industrial boom in Germany petered out and the ensuing
recession was intensified by the occupation of the Ruhr by French
and Belgian troops and German passive resistance.[13] In the
summer of 1923 industrial production amounted to only two-
thirds of its pre-war level.[14]

*Figure 4.2:   German producer goods and consumer goods produc-
tion per capita 1920-1935[c]*

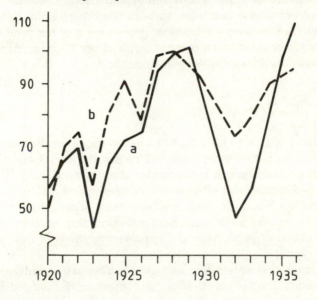

Notes: [a] producer goods; [b] consumer goods, [c] 1928 = 100

Source: Friedrich-Wilhelm Henning, *Das industrialisierte Deutschland 1914 bis
1972* (Schoeningh, Paderborn, 1974), p.104.

During the period of "relative stability" from 1924 to 1929,
industrial production grew steadily in spite of an interruption in
1926. This period is characterised by concentration, cartelisation
and rationalisation. During the world economic crisis, industrial
production in Germany, including mining, declined by 42 per cent
and in 1932 amounted to only 73 per cent of the 1913 figure.[15]

Growth figures in the various industries differ to a considerable
extent, particularly between the producer goods industries and

the consumer goods industries. From 1918 to 1919 output of the producer goods industries fell by more than one-half, mainly because war-related overproduction in some sectors had ended, whereas the consumer goods industries kept up to their previous levels. From 1919 to 1920 output of the producer goods industries doubled while that of the consumer goods industries rose only by 69 per cent.[16]

In the summer of 1923 producer goods output decreased by about 50 per cent, considerably faster than output in the consumer goods industries. Between 1924 and 1928 the ample capacities which the producer goods and capital goods industries had acquired during war and inflation were used more efficiently. In the period of "relative stabilisation" growth rates of the producer and consumer goods sectors were much closer together than at any other time during the Weimar Republic.

Rationalisation

The period of 1924 to 1928/9 is often called the rationalisation period. Rationalisation meant and still means the use of technical innovations and changes in the organisation of production in order to facilitate a more efficient use of labour, raw materials, energy and machinery. It implied a "scientific" organisation of the work process with Taylorism, standardisation, flow production, a simplification of production and improved methods of transport and marketing.[17]

If industrial concentration and cartelisation are considered as rationalisation in its widest sense the latter can be divided into three overlapping stages. During the first, emphasis was on concentration and cartelisation (1924-6), during the second on mechanisation and technical innovation (1926-7) and during the third on changes in the organisation of production (1928-9).[18] The most conspicuous cases of the first stage were the combination of major chemical firms in the *IG Farbenindustrie* (1925) and the formation of the steel trust *Vereinigte Stahlwerke* (1926). Apart from these two there were large concerns in other branches, for example Siemens and *AEG* in the electrical industry. At that time about 2,500 cartels existed in Germany. Rationalisation did not always result in lower prices, however. It is not altogether wrong to call this movement "the art of cutting costs while raising prices".[19]

Mechanisation and technical change had a particular impact in mining[20] and in the iron and steel industry which, by 1927, doubled its output per blast furnace compared to 1913. As a reaction

Table 4.1:   *Growth of output per hour (in constant prices) in selected industrial branches 1926-1930 in per cent*

metal working	25
mining	18
woodwork and timber	16
iron industry	15
construction	15
chemical industry	13
stone and earth	10
paper and printing	10
food and luxury food	10
textiles	9
leather	5
German industry as a whole	17

Source: Wolfram Fischer, "Bergbau, Industrie und Handwerk 1914-1970" in Hermann Aubin and Wolfgang Zorn (eds), *Handbuch der deutschen Wirtschafts- und Sozialgeschichte* (2 vols., Klett, Stuttgart, 1976), vol. 2, p.805.

to fuel shortages after the war[21] and in order to compensate for an ample energy supply in countries like the United States, the German steel industry aimed successfully at the saving of fuel (*Waermewirtschaft*). Productivity increases in the German chemical industry remained modest with only 13 per cent up on the 1913 figures. This is also true of industries such as textiles and leather, in which changes in the organisation of production played a larger role than technical innovation.[22]

An often quoted example of rationalisation is the German automobile industry, although mechanisation and changes in the organisation of production cannot be compared with the American model. In Germany mass production was far less advanced mainly because of a smaller market and different consumer demands.[23]

Although rationalisation was the dominant slogan of German industry in the mid-1920s, its productivity gains should not be overrated. Germany's pre-war productivity level was, indeed, surpassed, but this increase was not sufficient to catch up with the international leaders in industrial productivity such as the United States, or even France, Italy and Britain.[24] In Germany, rationalisation contributed to a sectoral maldistribution of investment with overcapacity in branches such as the heavy industries and textiles.[25] As far as unemployment is concerned, the real problem was not rationalisation but economic stagnation. In the automobile industry, an expanding sector, rationalisation did create employment. In most of the other branches and under the conditions of the Weimar economy it meant, however, that industrial output was produced by fewer workers with the consequence of rising unemployment.[26]

Labour

One of the reasons why output was not higher is insufficient industrial investment. In the literature on Weimar, inadequate profits which were to a large extent due to high wages and unsatisfactory workers' productivity, are sometimes given as an explanation. This question is still highly controversial and obviously difficult to solve.[27] Apart from the problem of providing reliable data it has to remain open to speculation how investment in industry would have behaved if wages had been lower. The high degree of cartelisation even complicates the issue. It is significant, however, that in the late 1920s labour's share of national income was about 10 per cent higher than in the years before the First World War.[28] Between 1924 and 1929 wages rose fast and generally surpassed the growth rates of industrial output. The year 1927 was a reaction to the crisis of 1926 and is an exception.[29] In the period 1927 to 1929 the position of labour improved dramatically.

Table 4.2:   *German industry and artisan production 1925-1932:*
hourly wages and productivity

	% nominal wage increase [a]	% real wage increase [b]	Labour productivity
1925			100
1926	6	6	104
1927	9	5	109
1928	12	10	104
1929	5	4	111
1930	- 3	1	117
1931	- 7	1	118
1932	- 16	5	122

Notes: [a] effective hourly wages
[b] deflated by Reich cost of living index

Source: Harold James, *The German slump. Politics and economics 1924-1936*
(Clarendon Press, Oxford, 1986), p.196.

Five phases can be distinguished in the development of wages in
Germany after the stabilisation of the *Mark*. First, wages moved
up rapidly from their initially very low level (1924-5); during the
recession (mid-1925-6) wages slowed down temporarily. In the
third phase (1927-8) civil service pay increases served as a model
for general wage rises, which continued their upward trend in
1928-30. From 1931 onwards wage rates moved downwards and
fell dramatically in 1932. Whereas the difference between real
wage increases and labour productivity increases had been comparatively small in the years 1926 and 1927, the gap widened dramatically in 1928. Labour productivity increased conspicuously in
1929 and made good some of the previous year's losses.[30]

One of the reasons why workers and their organisations insisted on substantial pay increases in the period of relative stabilisation was that the fears of inflation were by no means over. An expected price increase rate was therefore built into nominal wages increases.[31] Also the issue of net wage levels has to be taken into consideration. During the Weimar Republic social insurance contributions, which had to be paid by labour, especially skilled labour, rose substantially and far exceeded benefits from lower income tax.[32] On the other hand, employers, too, had to pay dramatically increased social insurance contributions for their employees, which probably had a negative effect on investment.[33] The fact that wage rates determined by contract between employers and employees were generally substantially below actual hourly earnings, compounded the problem. In 1928, for example, this "wage drift" amounted to about 80 per cent for skilled workers in rolling mills.[34]

The 48 hour week was introduced into German industry in 1918. In several branches it was, however, invalidated after 1923/4, especially by granting exemptions to work longer. In the mid-1920s numerous workers in the steel industry worked for more than 60 hours a week, but in 1928 the eight hour day became normal again.[35] According to the Weimar constitution, employers and employees had the right of free bargaining. If negotiations were in a deadlock, a government mediator could be called whose arbitration became obligatory upon both management and labour.[36] Frequently, employers complained of biased arbitration in favour of labour. From 1920 onwards workers' councils, which superseded the workers' committees instituted during the First World War, represented workers' interests.

Agriculture

During the Weimar Republic conditions for agriculture were grim. In the first years after the war, production of foodstuffs rose only slightly, because the imports of fodder and fertilizers picked up only slowly.

By 1928 agricultural production came close to the pre-war level. Its increase was mainly due to a more intensive use of agricultural fertilizers. Also, the increase of livestock had, by then, enlarged the supply of natural fertilizers.[37]

Still, during the 1920s, German farmers' complaints did not stop. Some of their problems had external sources. During the

Table 4.3: Agricultural yields in Germany 1913, 1920, 1924 and 1928

Product	yields in 1000 tons			
	1913	*1920*	*1924*	*1928*
rye	10276	4934	5730	8522
wheat	4109	2247	2428	3854
barley	3046	1793	2400	3347
oats	8643	4826	5654	6996
cereals total	26074	13800	16212	22719
potatoes	44650	27877	36402	41269

Source: Friedrich-Wilhelm Henning, *Landwirtschaft und laendliche Gesellschaft in Deutschland* (2 vols., Schoeningh, Paderborn, 1978), vol. 2, 1750 bis 1976, p.189.

war and in the immediate post-war period several English speaking countries overseas and also Argentina had extended their agricultural production significantly. This additional supply caused a price decline on the world market and a structural agricultural crisis in Europe with particularly negative effects on Germany. Between 1913 and 1920 wheat prices on the world market had doubled whereas by 1931 they had fallen to one-third of their 1920 level. The world economic crisis of the early 1930s was preceeded by an agrarian structural crisis.

However, German agricultural problems were not all of foreign origin. Many German agriculturists had not adapted themselves adequately to the requirements of the world market. Compared to countries like the United States, England and the Netherlands, rationalisation, specialisation and modernisation of equipment were insufficient. In most of the Weimar years, agricultural productivity remained below its pre-war level. As employment in industry proved to be more profitable, numerous agricultural workers left the countryside which resulted in increasing wages for farm labour. Other reasons for agricultural problems were the exhaustion of men, materials and soil after the war and the "reagrarianisation", which led to a large increase in agricultural labour with a corresponding decrease in productivity and a change in diet from heavy carbohydrate to more protein-intensive product.[38]

Although there was a trend from farming to stockbreeding, this was only weak. Furthermore, taxes were not adapted to the generally poor economic conditions of farmers, who voiced vehement protests, especially after 1928.[39] Farmers found it hard to cope with the various tax decrees from December 1923 onwards. In the period 1924-30 tax levels on agriculture were about 3.7 times higher than in the period immediately preceding the First World War. To be able to pay taxes or buy seed corn or fertilizers farmers often had to borrow money. Although hyper-inflation had freed many of them from debt this problem emerged again soon enough, particularly because of falling agricultural prices after mid-1927.[40] Farmers' problems were aggravated by rising short-term interest rates at the end of 1927 and the difficulty of obtaining long-term loans in 1928.

The government responded to farmers' difficulties in two ways: by a protectionist agricultural policy after 1925 and by granting subsidies to agriculture. From 1925 onwards protectionist tariffs assisted German farmers. Tariffs rose from RM 35 per ton of wheat in 1925 to RM 50 in 1926, RM 95 in 1930 and RM 250 in 1931.[41] Of course the German consumer, especially the working population in the towns, had to pay the bill.

Apart from increased tariffs state subsidies were granted to farmers, especially in East Prussia. In 1922 the Prussian State and the Reich set up the *Ostpreussenprogramm*, which above all intended to improve the infrastructure in East Prussia. From the mid-1920s onwards various programmes were set up to help agriculture in the East, particularly the *Ostpreussenhilfe* of 1928, the *Osthilfe* of 1930 and the *Osthilfegesetz* of 31 March 1931.[42] The main aim of these programmes was debt relief, especially the conversion of debt by reducing interest rates.

Together with tariff increases and state subsidies agrarian land settlement programmes were an important part of Weimar agrarian policy. From 1919 to 1932 about 60,000 new settlements were created, an achievement which, however, fell well behind the ambitious plans of some politicians.

Foreign trade

Before 1913 Germany was the second largest exporting nation in the world. After the interruption of foreign trade during the First World War Germany coped reasonably well with the stagnation of

Table 4.4: Indices of German export volumes, 1924/5-1928/9 [a]

	1924/5	*1928/9*
foodstuffs	39.1	50.4
grain	31.0	58.9
sugar	37.4	51.1
raw materials	45.2	85.0
coal	23.6	70.4
intermediate goods	47.4	94.8
hardware	37.7	80.2
finished goods	68.6	100.4
textiles	56.9	75.2
metalware and machinery	66.8	113.1
finished chemical goods	56.9	103.2
export goods, total	57.5	93.0

Note: [a] 1913 = 100

Sources: Dietmar Petzina and Werner Abelshauser, "Zum Problem der relativen Stagnation der deutschen Wirtschaft in den zwanziger Jahren", in Hans Mommsen, Dietmar Petzina and Bernd Weisbrod (eds), *Industrielles System und politische Entwicklung in der Weimarer Republik* (2 vols, Athenaeum, Droste, Kronberg/Ts., Duesseldorf, 1977), vol. 1, p.72.

world trade in the 1920s. However, German exports decreased in the first half of the decade. Her export share fell from 17.5 per cent in 1910 to 14.9 per cent in 1924/5, while the import quota fell from 20.2 to 17 per cent. In the second half of the 1920s the trend was reversed.

The increase of German exports was based on industrial finished goods from the engineering, precision engineering, electrical and chemical industries. The export of raw materials, foodstuffs, textiles and consumer goods stagnated or decreased.[43] Industrial finished goods' share of German total exports increased from 53.3 per cent in the period 1910/3 to 59.1 per cent in 1924/9 and 67.7 per cent in 1930/4. This increase was partly due to rising world market prices of finished products.[44]

Although German exporters did well on the world market they were not successful enough to solve the Weimar Republic's economic problems, especially reparations. Even in the "new industries", export difficulties arose. These industries - electrical, chemical, pharmaceutical, optical - were no longer "new". American competition was strong, especially in the electrical industry, and temporary market saturation depressed prices.[45]

With imports, raw materials played the most important role. Although their import share fell from 43.1 per cent in 1910/3 to 38.8 per cent in 1924/9 it later rose to 39.9 per cent in 1930/4. The import of foodstuffs rose until 1924/8 but then fell in the late 1920s and early 1930s while intermediate and finished goods imports rose constantly during the Weimar Republic.

In order to interpret German foreign trade in the 1920s and early 1930s adequately it is necessary to take the development of the terms of trade into consideration.

The terms of trade changed in favour of industrial goods and at the expense of primary goods. For Germany they decreased by 20 per cent between 1890 and 1913 and increased by 7 per cent from 1910/3 to 1924/30 and by more than 30 per cent during the 1930s.[46] From 1931 onwards import prices fell below their pre-war level whereas export prices remained above that level for another two years. In 1924/5 the terms of trade were more unfavourable than in the immediate pre-war period but they improved rapidly. In 1933 they reached their highest point at more than 50 per cent above the 1913 level. Improving terms of trade were, however, a mixed blessing for Germany and other industrial nations. The unfavourable aspect was that in the raw material exporting countries purchasing power for industrial goods decreased rapidly with negative effects on exports from Germany or Britain.

Germany's external economic problems during the Weimar Re-

Table 4.5: Terms of trade 1924-1935 [a]

Year	Exports to imports	Raw materials to raw materials	Finished goods to finished goods	Finished goods to raw materials	Semi-finished goods to raw materials
1924	97.0	104.7	95.2	95.3	94.5
1925	98.6	101.6	112.4	102.4	96.5
1926	104.9	113.4	103.6	112.9	105.7
1927	110.7	123.5	106.9	117.7	116.7
1928	109.2	112.9	108.0	115.1	107.2
1929	105.8	109.2	99.4	116.7	104.2
1930	115.4	116.1	98.4	135.0	120.9
1931	128.8	126.7	93.1	166.0	145.5
1932	147.5	125.1	100.6	195.4	161.0
1933	152.6	120.3	109.1	192.4	168.9
1934	144.8	112.6	111.9	181.7	149.0
1935	128.9	110.7	97.8	161.9	132.3

Note: [a] *1913 = 100*

Source: Dietmar Petzina, Werner Abelshauser, Anselm Faust, *Sozialgeschichtliches Arbeitsbuch, vol. 3. Materialien zur Statistik des Deutschen Reiches* (Beck, Munich, 1978), p.77.

public were not so much due to trade but to international monetary relations. Reparations and especially the transfer problem stand out. Apart from this the *Reichsmark* was overvalued which caused difficulties for German exports. A flexible exchange rate would probably have been a remedy, but the provisions of the Dawes and Young Plan made this choice impossible, at least without major political and economic costs.[47] From 1924 to 1931 Germany had a balance of payments deficit of RM 16.1 thousand million which could only have been adjusted by capital imports, mainly from the United States. The capital imports[48] intensified the propensity to import goods and eased the pressure to export in order to earn the necessary foreign currency to satisfy the reparation creditors.[49]

Notes

1. Derek H. Aldcroft, *From Versailles to Wall Street 1919-1929* (Allen Lane, London, 1977), p.140.

2. Karl Hardach, *The political economy of Germany in the twentieth century* (University of California Press, Berkeley, Los Angeles, London, 1980), p.28. On currency reform and reparations see the short account by K. Hardach, pp.28-30 and Friedrich-Wilhelm Henning, *Das industrialisierte Deutschland 1914 bis 1972* (Schoeningh, Paderborn, 1974), pp.78-81.

3. Henning, *Das industrialisierte Deutschland*, p.81.

4. Gerd Hardach, "Zur politischen Oekonomie der Weimarer Republik" in Reinhard Kuehnl and Gerd Hardach (eds), *Die Zerstoerung der Weimarer Republik*, 2nd edn (Pahl-Rugenstein, Cologne, 1979), p.17.

5. Dietmar Petzina and Werner Abelshauser, "Zum Problem der relativen Stagnation in der deutschen Wirtschaft in den zwanziger Jahren", in Hans Mommsen, Dietmar Petzina and Bernd Weisbrod (eds), *Industrielles System und politische Entwicklung in der Weimarer Republik* (2 vols., Athenaeum, Droste, Kronberg/Ts., Duesseldorf, 1977), vol. 1, pp.57-76.

6. Walther G. Hoffmann, Franz Grumbach and Helmut Hesse, *Das Wachstum der deutschen Wirtschaft seit der Mitte des 19. Jahrhunderts* (Springer, Berlin, Heidelberg, New York, 1965), pp.104-5.

7. Knut Borchardt, "Zwangslagen und Handlungsspielraeume in der grossen Wirtschaftskrise der fruehen dreissiger Jahre: Zur Revision des ueberlieferten Geschichtsbildes", in Knut Borchardt, *Wachstum, Krisen und Handlungsspielraeume der Wirtschaftspolitik* (Vandenhoeck and Ruprecht, Goettingen, 1982), pp.165-82.

8. Ottfried Dascher, "Probleme der Konzernorganisation", in Hans Mommsen, Dietmar Petzina and Bernd Weisbrod (eds), *Industrielles System und politische Entwicklung in der Weimarer Republik* (2 vols., Athenaeum, Droste, Kronberg/Ts., Duesseldorf, 1977), vol. 1, pp.127-34.

9. Robert A. Brady, *The rationalisation movement in German industry* (University of California Press, Berkeley, 1933).

10. Petzina and Abelshauser, "Zum Problem der relativen Stagnation" in Mommsen, Petzina and Weisbrod (eds), *Industrielles System und politische Entwicklung in der Weimarer Republik*, vol. 1, pp.68-75.

11. Gerd Hardach, "Zur politischen Oekonomie", in Reinhard Kuehnl and Gerd Hardach (eds), *Die Zerstoerung der Weimarer Republik*, pp.21-2. On the stabilisation crisis of 1925/6 and attempts to overcome it see Dieter Hertz-Eichenrode, *Wirtschaftskrise und Arbeitsbeschaffung. Konjunkturpolitik und die Grundlagen der Krisenpolitik Bruenings* (Campus, Frankfurt am Main, New York, 1982).

12. Carl-Ludwig Holtfrerich, *The German inflation 1914-1923* (de Gruyter, Berlin, New York, 1986), pp.183-4.

13. Klaus Schwabe (ed.), *Die Ruhrkrise 1923. Wendepunkt der internationalen Beziehungen nach dem Ersten Weltkrieg* (Schoeningh, Paderborn, 1984).

14. Wolfram Fischer, "Bergbau, Industrie und Handwerk 1914-1970" in Hermann Aubin and Wolfgang Zorn (eds), *Handbuch der deutschen Wirtschafts- und Sozialgeschichte* (2 vols., Klett, Stuttgart, 1976), vol. 2, pp.803-4.

15. Hoffmann, Grumbach and Hesse, *Wachstum*, p.393, Wolfram Fischer, *Deutsche Wirtschaftspolitik 1918-1945*, 3rd edn (Leske, Opladen, 1968), p.108.

16. Petzina and Abelshauser, "Zum Problem der relativen Stagnation" in Mommsen, Petzina and Weisbrod (eds), *Industrielles System und politische Entwicklung in der Weimarer Republik*, vol. 1, pp.68-9.

17. Hans-Joachim Braun, "Produktionstechnik und Arbeitsorganisation" in Ulrich Troitzsch and Wolfhard Weber (eds), *Die Technik. Von den Anfaengen bis zur Gegenwart* (Westermann, Braunschweig, 1982), p.407.

18. Juergen Boenig, "Technik und Rationalisierung in Deutschland zur Zeit der Weimarer Republik" in Ulrich Troitzsch and Gabriele Wohlauf (eds), *Technik-Geschichte. Historische Beitraege und neuere Ansaetze* (Suhrkamp, Frankfurt am Main, 1980), pp.398-9.

19. K. Hardach, *Political economy*, p.33.

20. Rudolf Tschirbs, "Der Ruhrbergbau zwischen Privilegierung und Statusverlust: Lohnpolitik von der Inflation bis zur Rationalisierung (1919 bis 1927)" in Gerald D. Feldman, Carl-Ludwig Holtfrerich, Gerhard A. Ritter and Peter Christian Witt (eds), *Die deutsche Inflation: Eine Zwischenbilanz* (Duncker and Humblot, Berlin 1982), pp.308-45.

21. Harold James, *The German slump. Politics and economics 1924-1936* (Clarendon Press, Oxford, 1986), p.149.

22. W. Fischer, "Bergbau, Industrie und Handwerk" in Aubin and Zorn (eds), *Handbuch*, vol. 2, p.805.

23. Many German car buyers still wanted their "taylor-made" car (Fritz Blaich, "Die «Fehlrationalisierung» in der deutschen Automobilindustrie 1924 bis 1929", *Tradition*, vol. 18 (1973), pp.18-33.).

24. Angus Maddison, *Economic growth in the west: Comparative experience in Europe and North America* (Allen and Unwin, London, 1964), p.232.

25. James, *German slump*, p.149.

26. Gerd Hardach, "Zur politischen Oekonomie" in Reinhard Kuehnl and Gerd Hardach (eds), *Die Zerstoerung der Weimarer Republik*, p.24.

27. In 1979 Knut Borchardt published an article which evoked much critical response: "Zwangslagen und Handlungsspielraeume in der grossen Weltwirtschaftskrise der fruehen dreissiger Jahre: Zur Revision des ueberlieferten Geschichtsbildes", *Bayerische Akademie der Wissenschaften, Jahrbuch 1979* (Munich, 1979), pp.87-132. This article has been reprinted several times. In what follows I quote the unchanged version from Knut Borchardt, *Wachstum, Krisen, Handlungsspielraeume der Wirtschaftspolitik. Studien zur Wirtschaftsgeschichte des 19. und 20. Jahrhunderts* (Vandenhoeck and Ruprecht, Goettingen, 1982), pp.165-82. Some of the critical responses to Borchardt's article are given in Eberhard Kolb, *Die Weimarer Republik* (Oldenbourg, Munich, 1984), p.183 and Heinrich August Winkler, *Der Schein der Normalitaet. Arbeiter und Arbeiterbewegung in der Weimarer Republik 1924 bis 1930* (Dietz Nachf., Berlin, Bonn, 1985), pp.46-62. See especially the discerning article by Carl-Ludwig Holtfrerich, "Zu hohe Loehne in der Weimarer Republik? Bemerkungen zur Borchardt-These", *Geschichte und Gesellschaft*, vol. 10 (1983), pp.122-41.

28. Borchardt, "Zwangslagen und Handlungsspielraeume in der grossen Weltwirtschaftskrise der fruehen dreissiger Jahre: Zur Revision des ueberlieferten Geschichtsbildes", p.176.

29. Charles S. Maier, "Die Nicht-Determiniertheit oekonomischer Modelle. Ueberlegungen zu Knut Borchardts These von der «kranken Wirtschaft» der Weimarer Republik", *Geschichte und Gesellschaft*, vol. 11 (1985), p.280.

30. James, *German slump*, pp.195, 213.

31. Theodore Balderston, "The origins of economic instability in Germany 1924-1930. Market forces versus economic policy", *Vierteljahrschrift fuer Sozial- und Wirtschaftsgeschichte*, vol. 69 (1982), p.508.

32. James, *German slump*, p.203.

33. Juergen von Kruedener, "Die Ueberforderung der Weimarer Republik als Sozialstaat", *Geschichte und Gesellschaft*, vol. 11 (1985), p.366.

34. James, *German slump*, p.205.

35. Gerald D. Feldman and Irmgard Steinisch, "Die Weimarer Republik zwischen Sozial- und Wirtschaftsstaat: Die Entscheidung gegen den Achtstundentag", *Archiv fuer Sozialgeschichte*, vol. 18 (1978), pp.353-439. See also Michael Schneider, *Streit um die Arbeitszeit. Geschichte des Kampfes um Arbeitszeitverkuerzung in Deutschland* (Bund-Verlag, Cologne, 1984).

36. Ludwig Preller, *Sozialpolitik in der Weimarer Republik* (Athenaeum, Droste, Kronberg, Duesseldorf, 1978), pp.257-61; Volker Hentschel, *Geschichte der deutschen Sozialpolitik 1880-1980* (Suhrkamp, Frankfurt am Main, 1983), pp.71-8.

37. Friedrich-Wilhelm Henning, *Landwirtschaft und laendliche Gesellschaft in Deutschland* (2 vols., Schoeningh, Paderborn, 1978), vol. 2, 1750-1976, p.188; Willi A. Boelcke, "Wandlungen der deutschen Agrarstruktur in der Folge des Ersten Weltkrieges", *Francia*, vol.3 (1975), pp.498-532.

38. Wolfram Fischer, "Die Weimarer Republik unter den weltwirtschaftlichen Bedingungen der Zwischenkriegszeit", in Hans Mommsen, Dietmar Petzina and Bernd Weisbrod (eds), *Industrielles System und politische Entwicklung in der Weimarer Republik* (2 vols., Athenaeum, Droste, Kronberg/Ts., Duesseldorf, 1977), vol. 1, pp.27-37; Hans Wolfram Graf Finck von Finckenstein, *Die Entwicklung der Landwirtschaft in Preussen und Deutschland 1800-1930* (Holzner, Wuerzburg, 1960); Heinz Haushofer, *Die deutsche Landwirtschaft im technischen Zeitalter*, 2nd edn (Ulmer, Stuttgart, 1972).

39. Gerhard Stoltenberg, *Politische Stroemungen im schleswig-holsteinischen Landvolk 1918 bis 1933: Ein Beitrag zur politischen Meinungsbildung in der Weimarer Republik* (Droste, Duesseldorf, 1962).

40. James, *The German slump*, pp. 254-8; Charles P. Kindleberger, *The world in depression 1929-1939* (Allen Lane, London, 1973), p.88; Ingvar Svennilson, *Growth and stagnation in the European economy* (United Nations, Geneva, 1954), p.92.

41. Henning, *Landwirtschaft*, pp.198-201.

42. Dieter Hertz-Eichenrode, *Politik und Landwirtschaft in Ostpreussen 1919-1930* (Westdeutscher Verlag, Cologne, Opladen, 1969); Max Rolfes, "Landwirtschaft 1914-1970" in Hermann Aubin und Wolfgang Zorn (eds), *Handbuch der deutschen Wirtschafts- und Sozialgeschichte* (2 vols., Klett, Stuttgart, 1976), vol. 2, pp.763-4; Henning, *Landwirtschaft*, pp.198-206.

43. Petzina and Abelshauser, "Zum Problem der relativen Stagnation" in Mommsen, Petzina and Weisbrod (eds), *Industrielles System und politische Entwicklung in der Weimarer Republik*, vol. 1, p.72.

44. W. Fischer, "Weimarer Republik" in Mommsen, Petzina and Weisbrod (eds), *Industrielles System und politische Entwicklung in der Weimarer Republik*, vol. 1, pp.41-2.

45. Volker Hentschel, "Zahlen und Anmerkungen zum deutschen Aussenhandel zwischen dem Ersten Weltkrieg und der Weltwirtschaftskrise", *Zeitschrift fuer Unternehmensgeschichte*, vol. 31 (1986), pp.111-2.

46. Hoffmann, Grumbach and Hesse, *Wachstum*, pp.548-9.

47. W. Fischer, "Weimarer Republik", in Mommsen, Petzina and Weisbrod (eds), *Industrielles System und politische Entwicklung in der Weimarer Republik*, vol. 1, p.44-6.

48. On this topic see especially William C. McNeil, *American money and the Weimar Republic. Economics and politics on the eve of the Great Depression* (Columbia University Press, New York, 1986).

49. Juergen Schiemann, *Die deutsche Waehrung in der Weltwirtschaftskrise 1929-1933. Waehrungspolitik und Abwertungskontroverse unter den Bedingungen der Reparationen* (Haupt, Berne, Stuttgart, 1980), p.93; Gilbert Ziebura, *Weltwirtschaft und Weltpolitik 1922/24-1931. Zwischen Rekonstruktion und Zusammenbruch* (Suhrkamp, Frankfurt am Main 1984), p.91.

Chapter Five

THE GREAT DEPRESSION

Origins

For Germany, not only the economic problems but also - and especially - the political consequences of the great depression were disastrous. The origins of the depression in the United States are still a matter of debate.[1] It seems that not so much monetary but real factors caused it and that the failure of the international economic system contributed to it.

From the mid-1920s onwards the market for consumer durables and housing approached saturation. A restraint on consumer expenditure in 1929 and the temporary exhaustion of investment opportunities as well as the deterioration in business confidence were the main reasons for the turn of the cycle.[2] Once the selling of stocks had started, panic set in, which drove the market down completely.[3] Monetary factors, especially the Federal Reserve's policy of tight money, aggravated the situation.[4]

Already in 1927, investments in Germany, especially in the consumer goods industry, had reached a turning point.[5] From 1928 onwards Germany had to cope with a growing scarcity of credit. US capital imports contracted because of the stock market boom and high interest rates in the United States. A fall of inventory investment in Germany in 1929 compounded the problem.[6]

Generally, the German banks could not cope with the withdrawals of American deposits. According to the "golden bank rule", the ratio between a bank's own funds and capital deposits from outside was to be 1:3. In Germany, however, the ratio was usually 1:10 in 1929 and even 1:15 for the large Berlin banks.[7] Obviously, this ratio made German banks extremely vulnerable to large withdrawals of foreign funds. Although estimates of capital inflow vary, it can be assumed that by the summer of 1930, when indebtedness was at its peak, Germany's external liabilities amounted to about RM 28 thousand million of which RM 16 thousand million were in the form of short-term credit.[8]

In the *Reichstag* elections of 14 September 1930 the National Socialist on 107 seats compared to the 12 seats they had before. In the first weeks after this election more than RM 700 million of foreign deposits and loans were recalled. The *Reichsbank* lost more than RM 1 thousand million of its gold reserves and foreign currency holdings. This withdrawal of funds created severe problems for public construction projects which, together with exports, were a vital prop of the German economy.[9]

Among the different causes of the great depression in Germany the following stand out: a "normal" cyclical recession at the end of the 1920s, an unstable international economy, partly as a legacy of the war, with protectionist policy measures by various governments, the agricultural crisis described above, external account imbalances because of reparations and war debts, excess capacity in industries like steel production, engineering, automobiles, electrical goods, optics and synthetics, deflationary tendencies as a means to fight inflation, attract foreign capital and retain or gain the confidence of investors, overspeculation in securities, long-term investment of short-term credits and international money transfers without corresponding transfers of goods. Moreover, government policies in the late 1920s and early 1930s were not at all suitable to remedy the situation.[10]

Manifestations of the crisis

In Germany there was a recession in the consumer goods industry from 1929 onwards, but this was partially compensated by an increase of publicly financed residential construction and favourable production and export figures in engineering, the electrical and the iron and steel industries.[11] In the autumn of 1929 it was by no means clear that a general economic depression in almost all industrial countries was underway and that the slump would have a duration of several years. In 1929 and 1930 the crisis did not differ significantly from those of the first post-war years. Until 1931 there was still hope that the economy would recover by itself

(*Selbstheilung*), as it had done in 1920, 1924 or 1925/6. When, however, the figures got worse, especially those of unemployment, it became clear that this depression was of a different nature from those experienced before.[12]

There were two main reasons for the deterioration of economic conditions in Germany: the disintegration of international economic relations, especially the decline of international trade and banking, accompanied by protectionism and competitive devaluations, and, possibly, but difficult to establish, the high degree of monopolisation of German industry. Instead of lowering prices, corporations tended to reduce production and dismiss employees. In the depression year of 1932 industrial production in Germany was about 30 per cent below its pre-war level. From 1929 to 1932 consumer goods production declined by 18 per cent, producer goods production by as much as 52 per cent.[13]

In contrast to the mid-1920s, German exports during the great depression could not compensate for the lower demand at home. Still, even in the crisis Germany's foreign trade balance was favourable, with a surplus of RM 1,560 million in 1930, RM 2,780 million in 1931 and RM 1,050 million in 1932. This was not sufficient, however, to compensate for the gold and foreign currency losses by credit withdrawals and capital flight. A bright spot was the trade with the Soviet Union (*Russengeschaeft*) which increased continuously.[14] The Soviet Union was not affected by the great depression and continued to pursue her path of industrialisation. In 1932 German capital goods exports to the Soviet Union amounted to 26 per cent of her total exports. In order to improve her payments position, Germany reduced her imports; a favourable development of the terms of trade eased the situation. After mid-1931, however, foreign trade problems became severe. Protectionist measures by most of Germany's trading partners affected German exports of finished goods negatively and devaluations worsened export conditions for Germany.[15]

In agriculture, the unsatisfactory situation increased in the late 1920s and early 1930s. Falling agricultural prices caused by overproduction and cheap American imports led to a substantial reduction of agricultural incomes. Agricultural value added fell from RM 11.7 thousand million in 1928 to RM 7.3 thousand million in 1932. Although prices had declined even before the great depression, reduced demand increased the crisis. In Germany and in some other countries farmers tried to compensate declining incomes by extending production and increasing supplies, which had the effect of sending prices down even further.[16]

Landowners' debts were high, especially on the large estates in the east. Frequent price fluctuations of rye, the staple crop of farmers in the east, caused severe problems, whereas farmers in the western parts of Germany, relying to a large extent on stock-raising and dairy farming, generally did better. Still, even they were severely hit by the Great Depression and the decreasing demand for agricultural products.[17]

Agricultural policy was high on the agenda of the Weimar governments. The junkers, the gentry east of the Elbe, who still considered themselves as a "pillar of the state", did their best to influence the Weimar politicians. Paul von Hindenburg, the *Reich* President, was a symbol and staunch advocate of their interests. During the depression the Weimar governments continued their policy of agricultural protection which consisted of high import duties, low import quotas or stockpiling in public granaries, as well as granting direct and indirect subsidies, including debt relief.[18]

Although agricultural difficulties were severe, unemployment in industry posed an even greater problem. In 1929 unemployment figures had amounted to 1.9 million but they quickly rose to 5.6 million as a yearly average in 1932 and reached their maximum in the period January to March 1933 with 6 million registered as unemployed. The actual figure was much higher because many people who had given up hope of finding a job or were no longer eligible for unemployment benefits were not registered as unemployed.[19] Although it is difficult to assess the number of unregistered unemployed, the figure probably amounted to 1.7 to 1.8 million at the end of July 1932. Short-time work - in February 1933 24.1 per cent of those employed were on short-time - was another problem. Mainly because of the vast reserve army of unemployed people wages were reduced from 1930 onwards. Between 1929 and 1932 real wages sank by 16 per cent. Civil servants did not have to fear unemployment, but their salaries were particularly affected by the crisis and government policy, falling by 25 to 28 per cent in real terms during the depression years.[20]

The banking crisis of 1931

Although there was a sharp cyclical recession in Germany in the first quarter of 1931, the second quarter already showed signs of recovery. Consumer and producer goods production rose slowly and the unemployment percentage sank from 29.4 to 25.3 per cent. The ensuing collapse of the German capital market in the summer of 1931 turned a "normal" temporary crisis into a crisis of the whole economic and political system.[21] German banks felt the effects of the recession when some of their major debtors defaulted. In order to prevent total collapse the banks provided further loans, which was perhaps understandable in the circumstances, but ran counter to the old banker's wisdom that good money should not be thrown after bad. But this is often easier said than done.[22]

The German banking crisis was triggered off by events in Austria. On 11 May 1931 the *Oesterreichische Creditanstalt*, the largest Austrian commercial bank, published its reports, which showed huge losses. A run on this bank and, subsequently, on other Austrian banks followed. French creditors did not contribute to the crisis by massively withdrawing their loans,[23] but they did nothing to support Austrian banks, either.

The collapse of the *Oesterreichische Creditanstalt* naturally aroused concern about German banks because they, too, were lacking in liquidity. They also had a large amount of foreign debt, about 40 per cent of it American. In the second half of May 1931 RM 288 million of short-term loans were withdrawn from German banks.[24]

At the end of May 1931 the situation worsened when two large German companies, the department store chain *Karstadt* and the large insurance company *Nordstern*, got into difficulty. Foreign credit withdrawals increased again. In early June a *Reich* emergency decree stipulated wage cuts and lower unemployment benefits. *Reich*schancellor Bruening also announced measures to ease Germany's reparation obligations, which aroused the concern of foreign creditors. The *Reichsbank* had to increase its discount rate from 5 to 7 per cent, but this did not help very much, because more bad news was in store: the *Nordwolle* concern had lost RM 200 million in speculative dealings. Two important German banks, the *Danat Bank* and the *Dresdner Bank*, had been heavily involved in financing *Nordwolle's* undertakings. Further withdrawals of deposits caused the *Reichsbank's* gold and foreign currency reserves to dwindle again. In this situation the American President Herbert Hoover on 20 June 1931 announced a one year moratorium on international payments - reparations and war debts - and also provided a $ 150 million credit to the *Reichsbank*. Alas, the moratorium did not come into effect before 7 July, mainly because of French concerns about losses of reparations.[25]

In circumstances like this, swift action would have been necessary. This proved impossible and, consequently, credit withdrawals accelerated. Consecutive rises of the discount rate - in July it reached 15 per cent and later even 20 per cent - did little to stem the tide. On 13 July the *Danat Bank* was closed; a run on the German banks and savings banks followed. After a few hours the banks paid out only 20 per cent of the sums demanded by customers. In this precarious situation the government announced a two day bank holiday.

At the root of the problem was a crisis of confidence, especially foreign confidence, which could not be overcome by German banks or the *Reichsbank*, let alone by government policy.[26] Although contemporary observers made much of American capital withdrawals during the crisis, the important role of German capital flight should not be overlooked. Often German money abroad was re-lent to Germany and appeared in the accounts as a foreign deposit, taxed differently.[27]

One of the greatest problems during the banking crisis was insufficient German gold and foreign currency reserves, which caused alarm to foreign creditors. As a remedy Germany adopted exchange controls in July 1931. All foreign currency in private hands had to be sold to the *Reichsbank*, private dealings in foreign currency were forbidden. Also, in agreement with the American and British governments which wanted to prevent a spreading of the German banking crisis to their countries, the German government issued a six month standstill regulation on foreign short-term debts, which was prolonged later. The general credit squeeze in Germany increased the deflationary tendencies.[28]

Economic and financial policy

According to the Young Plan the German *Reich* was obliged to pay the sum of almost RM 114 thousand million until 1988. The main aims of Bruening's government from 1930 onwards were the reduction and final cancellation of reparations and a balanced budget. Bruening's idea was that as long as the *Reich* tried its best to meet the requirements of the Young Plan its creditors would agree to fresh negotiations if it proved impossible for Germany to meet her obligations.[29] For fear of inflation he tried to avoid government deficits. The means to reach these ends was a deflationary policy. Once the reparations question had been solved he

could start tackling unemployment. If the reparations are regarded as a major cause for the depression in Germany (which,
from the economic point of view, they probably were not), then a
policy which aimed at abolishing reparations could also be looked
upon as suitable to overcome the depression.[30]

The threats of inflation were the reason why a devaluation of
the *Reichsmark*, which was sometimes suggested by contemporaries, did not seem to have been politically feasible. Government
officials thought it highly likely that an exchange depreciation
would have been interpreted as an indication of the impending
collapse of the German currency and economy, and that the withdrawal of foreign capital from German industry and the real burden of foreign claims against Germany would have increased.[31]
Besides, the Young Plan stipulated that the exchange rate of the
Reichsmark should be left unaltered. By a policy of deflation
Bruening also tried to improve the competitiveness of German industry. Wages and salaries, interest rates and rents as well as
cartel prices and prices of branded articles were lowered by an
emergency decree of 8 December 1931. This policy developed
into a state-interventionist strategy, which can be interpreted as a
substitute for devaluation.

However, there were fundamental contradictions in Bruening's
policy. A policy of retrenchment and deflation did not square at
all with costly subsidies for agriculture and the export industries.[32] Apart from agricultural subsidies which aimed at preserving the property of the German rural elite, export industries
received a large share of the government's subsidies, much more
than industrial firms producing mainly for the domestic market.[33]
In spite of the favourable foreign trade balance the actual gains
from foreign trade were rather modest because of the continuously shrinking world trade. On the whole the contractive effects
of retrenchment by far outweighed the comparatively weak
growth effects of foreign trade stimulation.[34]

The Bruening government based its restrictive financial policy
on the implicit presupposition that a liberal economic system still
existed. The problem was that the elements of that system, flexible
wages and prices, unrestricted international trade and capital
movements had disappeared a long time ago. It was wrong to assume that in spite of constant interference the German economy
would still react like a free market economy.[35]

There had been budget deficits almost during the whole period
1926 to 1928,[36] whereas budgets from 1930 to 1932 were more or

less balanced. From the spring of 1930 onwards this was only possible by pursuing a deflationary policy. The general trend was to
increase taxes and decrease spending. Increasing income tax rates
and turnover taxes as well as tariffs and unemployment insurance
contributions kept revenue high. During the last years of the
Weimar Republic, especially under *Reichskanzler* Bruening, the
government reduced expenditure by cutting civil servants' salaries,
pensions and unemployment benefits.[37] From 1929/30 to 1931/2
public spending on house construction fell by more than 60 per
cent. The *Laender* and municipalities increased the commercial
tax rates (*Gewerbesteuern*) thus making up for lower *Reich* tax
transfers.[38]

By the spring of 1932 it seemed unlikely that the Bruening government would be able to overcome the economic and financial
crisis. Many German citizens had little confidence in the Republic
and demanded a strong government led by a strong *Fuehrer*.
Apart from this there was staunch opposition from East German
estate owners against Bruening's agrarian settlement programme,
his alleged "agrarian bolshevism" and his plans to expropriate rural estates which could not be cleared from debt. These problems
were compounded by his disagreements with General Kurt von
Schleicher, an influential officer and politician, and by right-wing
protests against the government's restrictions on the National Socialist SA and SS. On 29 May 1932 *Reichspraesident* von Hindenburg, who always had an open ear for the *Junker's* wishes, strongly
recommended Bruening's resignation. Bruening resigned a day
later.[39]

Attempts at overcoming the crisis

The huge unemployment figure in Germany gave rise to various
job creation plans, some of them sensible, others less so. To the
latter category belonged a programme worked out by the "*Reich*
association for the reform of male clothing", founded in Munich in
1931, which was of the opinion that an economic recovery could
be effected by producing large quantities of men's clothing.[40]
During the years 1931 and 1932 the Bruening, Papen and Schleicher governments set up various employment programmes. Bruening appointed a commission headed by the former *Reichsminister*
for employment, Heinrich Brauns, and several economists,
government officials and trade union representatives. In May 1931
the Brauns commission proposed an emergency work creation

programme, consisting of agricultural improvements as well as road and canal construction and settlements.[41] In May 1932 the government decided to launch an employment programme.

In view of the severe employment situation this programme was very meagre indeed. The *Reichskanzler* pursued the idea in a rather half-hearted way. A successful job creation programme would have meant an economic recovery in Germany which would, however, have been quite unwelcome before the reparations problem had been solved. There was also the danger of new inflation if the programme was financed by an extension of the money supply.[42] Under these circumstances the programme was not put into effect. Under Bruening the *Reichsbank* did, however, pursue a policy of a "silent" extension of credit, especially in connection with the trade with Russia.[43] In the summer of 1931 economic decline in Germany ended, but a real improvement took place only a year later.[44]

A few days after the cancellation of reparations at the Lausanne conference which took place from 16 June 1932 to 9 July 1932, Bruening's RM 135 million job creation programme was put into operation by the Papen government, which had succeeded Bruening. Early in September 1932 Franz von Papen increased the funds available for a public works programme by another RM 167 million to a total of RM 302 million. He emphasized "indirect" job creation measures, which meant that entrepreneurs received tax incentives to employ workers and expand production. A main incentive was tax credit certificates which they received for 40 per cent of the taxes they paid during the period 1 October 1932 to 30 September 1933. These certificates, which were negotiable and could be discounted by the *Reichsbank*, amounted to RM 1.5 thousand million and could be used for paying taxes during the period 1934-1938. For the firms which made use of the government's offer this device amounted to a year's tax rebate. In addition to the tax certificates, the Papen government, in order to provide a "first spark" to increase employment, undertook public works based on bills of exchange to government organisations. These could also be discounted at the *Reichsbank*.[45] Because of an unstable political situation in which entrepreneurs refrained from additional investments, inappropriate timing - for the construction industry investments at the end of the summer came too late - a ponderous bureaucracy, and the limited size of the programme the effects of the Papen government's efforts were rather small.[46]

Most of these reasons also apply to the employment programmes of Kurt von Schleicher who succeeded von Papen as
Reichskanzler on 3 December 1932. Contrary to Papen, Schleicher
was of the opinion that only a government employment programme, not private investment, could bring about an economic
upswing. In general he favoured direct state intervention in the
economy[47] and on 3 December 1932 he appointed Guenther
Gereke as *Reich* commissioner for job creation. The Schleicher
government continued Papen's employment efforts and supplemented them by a new RM 500 million programme for emergency
measures, of which RM 100 million were earmarked for armament contracts. The rest was assigned to several German states
and municipalities for improvements and repair of already existing installations, especially roads, canals, public utilities and agricultural improvements. In order to employ as many people as
possible, machinery had to be used sparingly and the maximum
working time per week was fixed at 40 hours.[48] The programme
was financed by exchange bills which became the model of
Schacht's *Mefo* bills used to finance the National Socialist rearmament policy.[49] After Hitler's seizure of power the National Socialists made use of the instruments of economic stimulation provided by the Papen and Schleicher governments. They managed
to reduce unemployment quickly in an overall economic situation
which was more favourable to growth than the one in 1932.

Notes

1. See for example Derek H. Aldcroft, *From Versailles to Wall Street
1919-1929* (Allen Lane, London, 1977), pp.268-84; Peter Fearon, *The origins and
nature of the great slump 1929-1932* (Macmillan, London, 1979), pp.13-44; Volker
Hentschel, "Grosse Depression und Wirtschaftspolitik. Sachzwaenge und
Handlungsspielraeume der Grossmaechte", in Wolfram Fischer (ed.),
*Sachzwaenge und Handlungsspielraeume in der Wirtschafts- und Sozialpolitik der
Zwischenkriegszeit* (Scripta Mercaturae, St. Katharinen, 1985), pp.9-115.
2. Aldcroft, *Versailles to Wall Street*, pp.273-4.
3. John K. Galbraith, *The Great Crash, 1929* (Hamish Hamilton, London, 1955); Fearon, *Great slump*, p.133.
4. Aldcroft, *Versailles to Wall Street*, pp.273-4.
5. Fritz Blaich, *Der schwarze Freitag. Inflation und Wirtschaftskrise*
(Deutscher Taschenbuch Verlag, Munich, 1985), p.76.
6. This is particularly maintained by Peter Temin, who rejects the
common explanation that the decline of American capital exports started the
Great Depression in Germany. In his view, credit contraction was too small and
too late to account for the turning point. (Peter Temin, "The beginning of the
depression in Germany", *Economic History Review*, 2nd. ser., vol. 24 (1971),

pp.240-8, and, by the same author, *Did monetary forces cause the great depression?* (Norton, New York, 1976). Temin's view is challenged by M.E. Falkus, "The German business cycle in the 1920's", *Economic History Review*, 2nd ser., vol. 28 (1975), pp.451-65; T. Balderston, "The German business cycle in the 1920's: a comment", *Economic History Review*, 2nd ser., vol. 30 (1977), pp.159-61 and, by the same author, "The beginning of the depression in Germany 1927-1930: investment and the capital market", *Economic History Review*, 2nd ser., vol. 36 (1983), pp.395-415. See also Andrea Sommariva and Giuseppe Tullio, *German macroeconomic history, 1880-1979. A study of the effects of economic policy on inflation, currency depreciation and growth* (St. Martin's Press, New York, 1987), pp.173-6.

7. Blaich, *Der schwarze Freitag*, p.78; Karl Hardach, *The political economy of Germany in the twentieth century* (University of California Press, Berkeley, Los Angeles, London, 1980), p.40.

8. Aldcroft, *Versailles to Wall Street*, p.255.

9. Blaich, *Der schwarze Freitag*, p.13.

10. Karl Erich Born, *Geld und Banken im 19. und 20. Jahrhundert* (Kroener, Stuttgart, 1977), p.480; K. Hardach, *Political economy*, p.39; Aldcroft, *Versailles to Wall Street*, pp.282-4.

11. Gerd Hardach, "Zur politischen Oekonomie der Weimarer Republik" in Reinhard Kuehnl and Gerd Hardach (eds), *Die Zerstoerung der Weimarer Republik*, 2nd edn (Pahl-Rugenstein, Cologne, 1979), pp.27-8.

12. Friedrich-Wilhelm Henning, *Das industrialisierte Deutschland 1914 bis 1972* (Schoeningh, Paderborn, 1974), p.96.

13. G. Hardach, "Zur politischen Oekonomie" in Reinhard Kuehnl and Gerd Hardach (eds), *Die Zerstoerung der Weimarer Republik*, pp.26-30.

14. Hans-Juergen Perrey, *Der Russlandausschuss der deutschen Wirtschaft. Die deutsch-sowjetischen Wirtschaftsbeziehungen der Zwischenkriegszeit* (Oldenbourg, Munich, 1985), pp.128-202. See also Werner Beitel and Juergen Noetzold, *Deutsch-sowjetische Wirtschaftsbeziehungen in der Zeit der Weimarer Republik. Eine Bilanz im Hinblick auf gegenwaertige Probleme* (Nomos, Baden-Baden, 1979) and Hartmut Pogge von Strandmann, "Grossindustrie und Rapallopolitik: Die deutsch-sowjetischen Handelsbeziehungen in der Weimarer Republik", *Historische Zeitschrift*, vol. 222 (1976), pp.265-341.

15. Verena Schroeter, *Die deutsche Industrie auf dem Weltmarkt 1929 bis 1932. Aussenwirtschaftliche Strategien unter dem Druck der Weltwirtschaftskrise* (Lang, Frankfurt/Main, Berne 1984), pp.54-9.

16. Friedrich-Wilhelm Henning, *Landwirtschaft und laendliche Gesellschaft in Deutschland* (2 vols, Schoeningh, Paderborn, 1978), vol. 2, pp.192-4.

17. Dieter Gessner, *Agrardepression und Praesidialregierungen in Deutschland 1930-1933: Probleme des Agrarprotektionismus am Ende der Weimarer Republik* (Droste, Duesseldorf, 1977); K. Hardach, *Political economy*, p.43.

18. Harold James, *The German slump. Politics and economics 1924-1936* (Clarendon Press, Oxford, 1986), pp.265-7; Richard Bessel, "Eastern Germany as a structural problem in the Weimar Republic", *Social History*, vol. 3 (1978), pp.199-218.

19. Albin Gladen, *Geschichte der Sozialpolitik in Deutschland* (Steiner, Wiesbaden, 1974), pp.97-101; Ludwig Preller, *Sozialpolitik in der Weimarer Republik* (Athenaeum/Droste, Kronberg, Duesseldorf, 1978), pp.165-9; G. Hardach, "Zur politischen Oekonomie", in Reinhard Kuehnl and Gerd Hardach (eds), *Die Zerstoerung der Weimarer Republik*, p.26. On unemployment see especially Peter D. Stachura (ed.), *Unemployment and the great depression in Weimar Germany* (Macmillan, Basingstoke, London, 1986).

20. Blaich, *Der schwarze Freitag*, pp.68-71.

21. Gottfried Plumpe, "Wirtschaftspolitik in der Weltwirtschaftskrise.

Realitaet und Alternativen", *Geschichte und Gesellschaft*, vol. 11 (1985), p.341.

22. Born, *Geld und Banken*, p.482.

23. There had been plans of a German-Austrian customs union which French businessmen and politicians rejected. Harold James, "The causes of the German banking crisis of 1931", *Economic History Review*, 2nd ser., vol. 37 (1984), pp.68-87.

24. Friedrich-Wilhelm Henning, "Die Liquiditaet der Banken in der Weimarer Republik", in Harald Winkel (ed.) *Waehrungs- und Finanzpolitik der Zwischenkriegszeit* (Duncker and Humblot, Berlin, 1973), pp.43-92.

25. S. Weyerhoff, "Das Stillhalteabkommen 1931-33: Internationale Versuche zur Privatschuldenregelung unter den Bedingungen des Reparations- und Kriegsschuldensystems" (Diss. rer.pol., Munich, 1982); Werner Link, *Die amerikanische Stabilisierungspolitik in Deutschland 1921-1932* (Droste, Duesseldorf, 1970); S.A. Schuker, "American «Reparations» to Germany 1919-1933", in Gerald D. Feldman (ed.), *Die Nachwirkungen der Inflation auf die deutsche Geschichte* (Oldenbourg, Munich, 1985), pp.335-83; K. Hardach, *Political economy*, p.42.

26. On this see especially Rolf E. Lucke, *Von der Stabilisierung zur Krise* (Polygraphischer Verlag, Zurich, 1958); Karl Erich Born, *Die deutsche Bankenkrise 1931: Finanzen und Politik* (Piper, Munich, 1967); Gerd Hardach, *Weltmarktorientierung und relative Stagnation. Waehrungspolitik in Deutschland 1924-1931* (Duncker and Humblot, Berlin, 1976); James, *German slump*, p.291.

27. James, *German slump*, p. 299. See also Alice Teichova, *An economic background to Munich. International business and Czechoslovakia 1918-1938* (Cambridge U.P., Cambridge, 1974).

28. K. Hardach, *Political economy*, p.42.

29. There is a controversy in the literature about whether Bruening risked or even engineered a deterioration of the economic situation in Germany with the aim of first solving the reparations problem and then pursuing an active employment policy to overcome the crisis. See, on the one hand, Wolfgang J. Helbich, *Die Reparationen in der Aera Bruening. Zur Bedeutung des Young-Plans fuer die deutsche Politik 1930 bis 1932* (Colloquium Verlag, Berlin, 1962); Plumpe, "Wirtschaftspolitik in der Weltwirtschaftskrise"; Eckhard Wandel, *Hans Schaeffer. Steuermann in wirtschaftlichen und politischen Krisen* (Deutsche Verlags-Anstalt, Stuttgart, 1974); Werner Jochmann, "Brunings Deflationspolitik und der Untergang der Weimarer Republik", in Dirk Stegemann, Bernd-Juergen Wendt, Peter Christian Witt (eds), *Industrielle Gesellschaft und politisches System. Beitraege zur politischen Sozialgeschichte. Festschrift für Fritz Fischer zum siebzigsten Geburtstag* (Verlag Neue Gesellschaft, Bonn, 1978), pp.97-112, and on the other Knut Borchardt, "Wachstum und Wechsellagen 1914-1970", in Hermann Aubin and Wolfgang Zorn (eds), *Handbuch der deutschen Wirtschafts- und Sozialgeschichte* (2 vols, Ernst Klett, Stuttgart, 1976), vol. 2, p.709; Horst Sanmann, "Daten und Alternativen der deutschen Wirtschafts- und Finanzpolitik in der Aera Bruening", *Hamburger Jahrbuch für Wirtschafts- und Gesellschaftspolitik*, vol. 10 (1965), pp.109-40. Eberhard Kolb, *Die Weimarer Republik* (Oldenbourg, Munich, Vienna, 1984), p.205 is probably right in his view that it is unlikely that Bruening purposefully aggravated the crisis to solve the reparations problem. But he used the difficult economic and social situation of the early 1930s as a means for having the reparations revised.

30. Knut Borchardt, "Zwangslagen und Handlungsspielraeume in der grossen Weltwirtschaftskrise der fruehen dreissiger Jahre. Zur Revision des ueberlieferten Geschichtsbildes" in Knut Borchardt, *Wachstum, Krisen, Handlungsspielraeume der Wirtschaftspolitik. Studien zur Wirtschaftsgeschichte des 19. und 20. Jahrhunderts* (Vandenhoeck and Ruprecht, Goettingen, 1982), footnote 45.

31. Juergen Schiemann, *Die deutsche Waehrung in der Weltwirt-*

schaftskrise 1929-1933. Waehrungspolitik und Abwertungskontroverse unter den Bedingungen der Reparationen (Haupt, Berne, Stuttgart, 1980), pp.166-251; K. Hardach, *Political economy*, p.44.

32. Tilmann P. Koops, "Zielkonflikte der Agrar- und Wirtschaftspolitik in der Aera Bruening", in Hans Mommsen, Dietmar Petzina and Bernd Weisbrod (eds), *Industrielles System und politische Entwicklung in der Weimarer Republik* (2 vols, Athenaeum, Droste; Kronberg/Ts., Duesseldorf, 1977), vol. 2, pp.852-68.

33. For the latter see Fritz Blaich, "«Garantierter Kapitalismus». Subventionspolitik und Wirtschaftsordnung in Deutschland zwischen 1925 und 1932", *Zeitschrift für Unternehmensgeschichte*, vol. 22 (1977), pp.50-70.

34. Dietmar Petzina, *Die deutsche Wirtschaft in der Zwischenkriegszeit* (Steiner, Wiesbaden, 1977), p.105. See also by the same author "Staatliche Ausgaben und deren Umverteilungswirkungen. Das Beispiel der Industrie- und Agrarsubventionen in der Weimarer Republik", in Fritz Blaich (ed.), *Staatliche Umverteilungspolitik in historischer Perspektive. Beitraege zur Entwicklung des Staatsinterventionismus in Deutschland und Oesterreich* (Duncker and Humblot, Berlin, 1980), pp.59-105.

35. See Petzina, *Deutsche Wirtschaft*, p.102.

36. Claus-Dieter Krohn, *Stabilisierung und oekonomische Interessen. Die Finanzpolitik des Deutschen Reiches 1923-1927* (Droste, Duesseldorf, 1974).

37. Manfred Nussbaum, *Wirtschaft und Staat in Deutschland waehrend der Weimarer Republik* (Topos, Vaduz/Liechtenstein, 1978), pp.291-95; Peter-Christian Witt, "Die Auswirkungen der Inflation auf die Finanzpolitik des Deutschen Reiches 1924-1933", in Gerald D. Feldman and Elisabeth Mueller-Luckner (eds), *Die Nachwirkungen der Inflation auf die deutsche Geschichte 1924-1933* (Oldenbourg, Munich, 1985), pp.43-95.

38. James, *German slump*, pp.66, 71.

39. Karl Dietrich Bracher, *Die Aufloesung der Weimarer Republik. Eine Studie zum Problem des Machtverfalls in der Demokratie* (Ring Verlag, Villingen, 1957), pp.481-517.

40. Willi A. Boelcke, *Die deutsche Wirtschaft 1930-1945. Interna des Reichswirtschaftsministeriums* (Droste, Duesseldorf, 1983), p.13.

41. On the problem of work creation programmes under Bruening see Michael Wolffsohn, *Industrie und Handwerk im Konflikt mit staatlicher Wirtschaftspolitik? Studien zur Politik der Arbeitsbeschaffung in Deutschland 1930-1934* (Duncker and Humblot, Berlin, 1977), pp.45-77; Carl-Ludwig Holtfrerich, "Alternativen zu Bruenings Wirtschaftspolitik in der Weltwirtschaftskrise", *Historische Zeitschrift*, vol. 235 (1982), pp.605-31; Knut Borchardt, "Noch einmal: Alternativen zu Bruenings Wirtschaftspolitik", *Historische Zeitschrift*, vol. 237 (1983), pp.67-83.

42. Knut Borchardt, "Inflationsgefahren in der Weltwirtschaftskrise? Zu den Spielraeumen der Brueningschen Wirtschaftspolitik 1930-1932", in Wolfram Engels, Armin Gutowski and Henry C. Wallich (eds), *International capital movements, debt and monetary system. Essays in honour of Wilfried Guth* (v. Hase and Koehler, Mainz, 1984), pp.21-42. See also Gerhard Schulz, "Inflationstrauma, Finanzpolitik und Krisenbekaempfung in den Jahren der Wirtschaftskrise, 1930-1933", in Gerald D. Feldman and Elisabeth Mueller-Luckner (eds), *Die Nachwirkungen der Inflation auf die deutsche Geschichte 1924-1933* (Oldenbourg, Munich, 1985), pp.261-96.

43. Wolffsohn, *Industrie und Handwerk*, p.77; Hans Luther, *Vor dem Abgrund 1930-1933. Reichsbankpraesident in Krisenzeiten* (Propylaeen, Berlin, 1964), pp.255-61.

44. See, however, Friedrich-Wilhelm Henning, "Die zeitliche Einordnung der Ueberwindung der Weltwirtschaftskrise in Deutschland" in Harald Winkel (ed.), *Waehrungs- und Finanzpolitik der Zwischenkriegszeit* (Duncker

and Humblot, Berlin, 1973), pp.135-73.

45. Charles Kindleberger, *The world in depression 1929-1939* (University of California Press, Berkeley, Los Angeles, 1973), p.177.

46. Friedrich-Wilhelm Henning, *Das industrialisierte Deutschland 1914 bis 1972* (Schoeningh, Paderborn, 1974), p.138.

47. Dietmar Petzina, "Hauptprobleme der deutschen Wirtschaftspolitik 1932/33", *Vierteljahrshefte für Zeitgeschichte*, vol. 15 (1967), p.26. On *Arbeitsbeschaffung* see also Michael Wolffsohn, "Arbeitsbeschaffung als Wohlfahrtspolitik? Die Endphase der Weimarer Republik" in Wolfgang J. Mommsen and Wolfgang Mock (eds), *Die Entwicklung des Wohlfahrtsstaates in Grossbritannien und Deutschland 1850-1950* (Klett-Cotta, Stuttgart, 1982), pp.213-51.

48. K. Hardach, *Political economy*, p.48.

49. Boelcke, *Deutsche Wirtschaft*, p.28.

Chapter Six

THE NATIONAL SOCIALIST ECONOMY

Economic ideology

Although the National Socialists had some economic concepts it would be an exaggeration to speak of a coherent economic doctrine or even a theory.[1] The ideas and principles put forward were vague - and deliberately so. They were designed to give everything to everybody; they changed their meaning like a chameleon changes its colours if representatives of pressure groups insisted on demanding clear definitions of national socialist slogans. In spite of the "unalterable 25 points" of the economic programme of 1920 Hitler took some pride in declaring: "the basic feature of our economic theory is that we have no theory at all."[2]

Still, until 1933, and even after the National Socialists' "rise to power", Gottfried Feder's 25 points were often referred to as a guideline for economic policy. Feder, an engineer by training, had prepared a curious but - as was shown later - dangerous mixture of slogans that were geared to attract the different groups which comprised German society. A point which found wide acclaim was the demand for a complete confiscation of profits from the First World War and the immediate post-war period. Usury and profiteering were particular targets with the demand for the death penalty for usurers, profiteers and traitors. Small farmers were wooed with the demand for the abolition of land rents and speculation in land, small traders with the nationalisation of trusts, the state's profit sharing of large corporations and the communalisation of department stores.[3]

Two points were of particular importance: the abolition of income not earned by work and toil and the acquisition of land to feed the German people, with the underlying idea of the extension of German "living space". The first point has to be seen in the context of the distinction between "rapacious" and "productive" capital. Within the former came international finance and stock market capital, capital for non-productive purposes, which the National Socialists often termed "Jewish capital". "Productive capital" on the other hand was capital invested for socially beneficial ends.[4]

The "unalterable points of 1920" were speedily altered as soon as they irritated important social and economic interests. This applies, for example, to point 13, which envisaged the socialisation of incorporated trusts. In 1923 Feder set up a 39 point programme to replace and modify the old one.

Ideas on social and economic matters differed to quite an extent among members of the National Socialist Party. People on the party's left, like Gregor Strasser, had a strict anti-capitalist bias.[5] On several occasions the National Socialist Party in the Weimar Reichstag sided with the Communists when, for example, both parties voted against increases in indirect taxes, which would mainly have affected people in the lower income brackets. This, however, was definitely not the way in which National Socialist parliamentarians were to behave in the future. The social revolutionaries in the NSDAP were a minority with little or no backing from the party leadership. It was not at all in Hitler's interest to antagonise the leaders of industry, whom he later needed for putting his rearmament programme into reality. Already in the late 1920s he made it clear that the revolutionary jargon of the *Kampfzeit* was a thing of the past and that a "second revolution" with an anti-capitalist restructuring of the economic system was not intended.[6]

In 1930, Hans Buchner, economic editor of the *Voelkischer Beobachter*, published a book in which he set forth a new version of National Socialist economic doctrine. Borrowing old corporatist ideas from Mussolini's Italy and from various German writers of the late nineteenth and early twentieth century he stressed the importance of estates (*Staende*), which Feder had already mentioned in his programme. The idea was that the state organised all productive units into estates, which corresponded with the various branches of the economy. Representatives of both capital and labour were to represent their estates in chambers at regional and national levels. By working together for the common aim of reaching the goals set by the state, class struggle would be avoided.

Although the estate system played not only a theoretical but also an important practical role in the social organisation of Germany under National Socialist rule, its advocates no longer tried to put it into effect in industry after September 1933. On 6 June 1933 Hitler had already made it clear that practical experience should prevail over the *Staendeideologie*. As far as industry is concerned he considered this ideology unsuitable for achieving the aims in the desired armament effort. Hitler stressed the importance of private property and on several occasions expressed his respect for the "daring entrepreneur", who incurred great risks and overcame many obstacles by his ingenuity and perseverance. He told industrial leaders that he was not in favour of a planned economy and that free enterprise and competition were necessary for a high industrial output.[7] On the other hand, there are remarks of a completely different nature, which not only show that his attitude towards entrepreneurs was ambivalent, but that much depended on whom he was addressing. On appropriate occasions he referred to German industrialists as "dividend-hungry businessmen", denounced their greed and ruthlessness - although ruthlessness was generally a virtue to him - and called them "rogues and cold-blooded money grabbers". He had never met an industrialist, he said, who, on catching sight of him, had not put on a woebegone pleading expression in the hope of obtaining something.[8]

Big business and the National Socialist rise to power

Hitler and many National Socialist leaders counted on industry for assistance in the rearmament effort. However, it is not correct to speak of industry as a uniform entity. There were important branches, like coal, iron and steel, machinery and the chemical industry which had much to gain from rearmament, especially after the second Four Year Plan of 1936. Others, like the manufacturers of consumer goods and the export-oriented firms, were in quite a different position. The National Socialist drive towards autarky with its preference for investment and producer goods industries and the drastic curtailment of international trade made their position difficult.[9]

Having derived enormous profits from rearmament after the National Socialist rise to power the question is, whether big business or vital parts of it were instrumental in this process. First, it has to be made clear that although various branches of industry benefited from National Socialist policy this did not necessarily mean that they were the driving force behind rearmament.[10] There are, indeed, several instances in which leading German businessmen supported Hitler and his party with quite substantial contributions.[11] Members of the *Ruhrlade*, an informal body of West German heavy industrialists founded in 1928 and consisting of twelve prominent coal and iron and steel industrialists, supported the National Socialist party at elections. However, these industrialists assisted other parties, too, and it seems to be justified to call the funds handed over to the National Socialists "protection money".[12] Besides, some anti-capitalist rhetoric by the party's leftwingers and Hitler's often "uncivilised" demeanor were not conducive to turning the iron and steel barons of the Ruhr into enthusiastic National Socialist followers. Most of them were more inclined to give Franz von Papen their support, a politician with whom they felt they had more in common and who was likely to serve their interests better than the upstart Hitler.

It would, however, be shortsighted indeed to reduce the problem of heavy industry's support for Hitler and his party to matters of financial assistance. Generally speaking, the role of big business in the National Socialist rise to power was more indirect than direct. By not supporting the democratic system of the Weimar Republic to a sufficient degree big business certainly has its share of responsibility.[13] By having Hitler give speeches at several of their meetings big business contributed to making him socially acceptable. Although the effect of these speeches cannot be put into figures, factors like this should not be discarded lightly.

In the period 1933 to 1939, and especially after the Four Year Plan of 1936, several industrial branches in Germany, mainly chemical engineering, iron and steel and machinery, benefited from rearmament to a considerable extent. The producers of consumer goods and those branches depending on exports were less successful. Still, even in the case of branches heavily involved in rearmament and war preparation there was not always an identity of interest between industry and the state. In the much publicised case of the BRABAG (Lignite-Gasoline Company, *Braunkohle-Benzin AG*), for example, the government forced reluctant lignite producers to finance the production of synthetic fuels and lubricants.[14] The lignite producers were forced into a compulsory partnership (*Pflichtgemeinschaft*), similar to that of the cellulose industry. Another case in point is the government-owned *Reichswerke Hermann Goering*. The National Socialist official Paul Pleiger founded this concern in the summer of 1937 as a reaction to the iron and steel industrialists' refusal to enlarge their capacity by mining and smelting the inferior iron ores of the Salzgitter area. This was meant to warn the iron and steel corporations that, if necessary, the National Socialist government would pursue its goals without private capital.[15]

For some time there has been a debate among historians on the relationship between state and private industry during the Third Reich.[16] It seems that neither a "primacy of politics" nor a "primacy of economics" does full justice to the complex relationship between state and economy. Much can be said in favour of Peter Huettenberger's model of a complex and changing multi-dimensional ("polycratic") power structure in the Third Reich.[17] According to this model there was an unwritten "pact" or "alliance" between different but interdependent blocs in a "power cartel". As far as the relationship between the National Socialist state and industry is concerned this model may be disappointing for those who look for a clear-cut causal relationship between industry and state. For all we know at present about this topic, however, the polycratic model may be regarded as a suitable interpretative device for a complex relationship, although the key point in the relationship was a growing *dirigisme*.

Economic policy 1933-1935

The National Socialist government benefited from the economic effects of the work creation programmes of von Papen and von Schleicher and successfully pursued this idea further. Already on 1 February 1933, just after the *Machtergreifung*, Hitler announced a rather vague sounding programme with two main objectives: first, saving the German peasant and preserving the nation's means of subsistence, and, secondly, saving the German worker by fighting unemployment. To achieve these aims, support for the agricultural sector and a work creation programme for industry were necessary. In the following months, government officials discussed the particulars of a work creation programme with several industrial leaders.[18] Two main areas of activity were chosen, construction, which can be looked upon as a key growth sector, and motorisation. The latter is not only to be associated with the motor vehicle industry, but comprised the whole infrastructure, particularly road building.[19] Hitler placed the construction of motorways into the context of his foreign policy plan which envisaged that, as a first step, Germany should be consolidated and made fit for war. Later, by means of a skillful diplomacy and foreign policy followed by military action, Germany's chief adversary on the European continent, France, was to be eliminated and, finally, "living space" in the east was to be gained.[20]

On 1 June 1933, the "Reinhardt Programme", a work creation programme, became law. This programme was set up by Fritz Reinhardt, the state secretary in the Ministry of Finance. It combined indirect incentives, especially tax concessions, with direct public investment expenditures. The main aims were the improvement of the infrastructure - waterways, railroads, highways - and the redevelopment of residential housing and public buildings.

The Second Reinhardt Programme following shortly afterwards, which Hitler called "a general attack on unemployment", was more ambitious and more effective than the first. It provided subsidies of RM 500 million for the repair and reconstruction of residential and agricultural buildings during the winter of 1933/4 and made available funds for investment in the railways and postal services.[21] Looking on work creation projects as a whole, a total of RM 5,250 million was spent on the various programmes between 1932 and 1935, which was about 4 per cent of the annual GNP.[22]

There is no doubt that these programmes, at least to a large extent, achieved the desired ends. By the end of 1933 unemployment was already down by about one-third, with only four million instead of six million people still without work. It has to be stressed, however, that the effects of the National Socialist work creation programmes should not be overrated. A particular feature of the early years of National Socialist rule in Germany was the overlapping of a "normal" cyclical upswing in the economy and an upswing based on government economic policy (*Staatskonjunktur*).[23]

By 1934 car production was almost 50 per cent higher than in 1929. During the period 1932-7 Germany caught up in motorisation with the other industrialised countries. New construction (mainly residential housing and road construction) totalled RM 2 thousand million in value in 1932, by 1934 it had reached RM

5,700 million and by 1936 RM 9 thousand million. Of the various construction activities residential housing had the largest share (28 per cent), followed by road construction (21 per cent). Linkages with the economy as a whole were significant and the employment effects were also important: in 1933 only 666,000 people worked in the construction industries; by 1936 the figure had gone up to two million.[24]

Looking at public expenditure in Germany the following picture emerges.

Table 6.1: Public expenditure in Germany by category 1928-1938 [a]

	1932	1933	1934	1935	1936	1937	1938
total expenditure (central, local)	17.1	18.4	21.6	21.9	23.6	26.9	37.1
construction	0.9	1.7	3.5	4.9	5.4	6.1	7.9
rearmament	0,7	1.8	3.0	5.4	10.2	10.9	17.2
transportation[b]	0.8	1.3	1.8	2.1	2.4	2.7	3.8
work creation	0.2	1.5	2.5	0.8	-	-	-

Notes: [a] *RM thousand million.* There is some overlap between the categories. Work-creation included some expenditure on roads; construction also includes some rearmament expenditure.

[b] Figures for national expenditure on roads and waterways. Local expenditure averaged 600 million to 800 million *Reichsmark* 1933-5.

Source: Richard J. Overy, *The Nazi economic recovery 1932-1938* (Macmillan, London, 1982), p.50.

In spite of the overlapping categories and a "normal" cyclical upswing, it seems safe to say that construction and motorisation played the major role in generating the growth necessary for economic recovery. In 1936, for the first time, military expenditures exceeded 10 per cent of GNP, a level not reached by Britain until after 1938, or by the United States until 1941. Military investment alone - excluding basic industry and transportation - exceeded civilian investment from 1936 on. Also, from 1936 onwards, armaments dominated government expenditures for goods and services as well as total investments in the sense that expenditure on armaments was absolutely larger than all other government expenditure.[25]

The National Socialist Four Year Plan

When examining the origins of the Four Year Plan[26] it is necessary to distinguish between the medium and long term aims on the one hand and the short term aims on the other. The latter were responses to immediate problems and thus influenced the timing of the plan. The former were expressed in Hitler's memorandum of August 1936, when he set the Four Year Plan the task of procuring the prerequisites for the self-defence of the German people by providing the necessary armament materials. This was to enable Germany to prepare herself for future military conflicts. Connected with this was the expansion of "living space" in the east which included the extension of food and raw material resources.[27]

There were also several reasons why, according to Hitler and other National Socialist leaders, the introduction of a Four Year Plan was inevitable in 1936: domestic agricultural problems had turned into a crisis with rapidly increasing imports of agricultural products and the consequent loss of foreign currency.[28] The main reason for this was recurring crop failures in the first half of the 1930s. Between 1933 and 1935 harvest yields decreased by up to 20 per cent. The National Socialists took up notions of agricultural autarky, which had a long tradition in economic policy and remodelled them according to their political purposes.

Secondly, there were raw material and fuel problems which were particularly urgent in view of rearmament and war preparation. Germany was and is comparatively poor in natural resources. This the National Socialists tried to remedy by exploiting inferior grades of iron ores or substituting mineral oil by synthetic fuel.[29]

Thirdly, the development of the terms of trade has to be mentioned. Whereas during the Great Depression of the late twenties and especially early thirties there had been a fall in world raw material prices from which Germany benefited, conditions changed after 1933. Raw materials, foodstuffs and semi-finished products became dearer on the world markets, whereas manufactured goods, on which Germany's exports to a large extent relied, became cheaper. This meant that Germany ran into balance of payments problems which were quite severe considering the fact that on average, import prices increased by 9 per cent while export prices decreased by the same amount.[30]

A fourth problem concerned inflation. By 1936 the economy was approaching full employment. Beneficial as this was for the economy and society there was a risk involved. If the government pursued its policy of dramatically increasing armament production and not cutting down consumer goods production, there would be the danger of inflation.[31]

In his memorandum of August 1936 Hitler made it clear that the German army had to be ready for war in four years time so that "living space" in the east could be gained. These targets were to be reached by striving for raw material autarky - by which means foreign currency could also be saved - by developing synthetic fuels, rubbers and synthetic fibres and by the extension of the German iron ore base.

This policy met with opposition in several quarters. The German Ministry of Economic Affairs under Hjalmar Schacht was critical of Hitler's autarky plans, which, to him, were based on illusions and would cut Germany off from the world market. In the spring of 1936 a "raw material and foreign currency staff" (*Rohstoff- und Devisenstab*) under Hermann Goering was founded, an institution independent of the Ministry of Economic Affairs, and on 18 October 1936 Goering was made plenipotentiary of the Four Year Plan.

To make the Four Year Plan work, various instruments of control were applied. Most of them were not new and had been in use from 1933 onwards. However, in the context of the Four Year Plan, they were applied in a systematic way to achieve the desired ends.[32]

Raw material control has to be mentioned first. This had been in use since 1934 and was probably the most important means of steering the economy towards rearmament. Connected with and complementary to raw material control was investment control, which was based on the "Statute to establish compulsory syndicates" (*Gesetz zur Errichtung von Zwangskartellen*) of 15 July 1933. By this, the *Reich* Ministry of Economic Affairs, in order to cope with the Great Depression, was granted power to decree company mergers and control investment. Now, a reorientation of this statute took place in order to direct investment into armament. There were similar controls over consumption, of employees and of wages and prices. A statute of 15 May 1934, the "Statute for the regulation of the employment of labour" (*Gesetz zur Regelung des Arbeitseinsatzes*) forbade the migration of labour into branches of the economy not favoured by the government and tied agricultural workers to rural areas. In line with the purposes of the Four Year Plan the statute of 1934 was remodelled to provide sufficient labour for the armament effort.

As far as price and wage policy is concerned there had already been a "*Reich* price commissioner" (*Reichspreiskommissar*) from 1931 onwards[33] and in 1933 the government decreed a wage freeze. At the end of October 1933 a "*Reich* commissioner for price formation" (*Reichskommissar fuer die Preisbildung*) was instituted. The first important political measure in relation to the Four Year Plan was the price freeze decree of 26 November 1936. The wage freeze which existed complementary to the price freeze, was only partly effective, because employers, who had a high demand for labour, often evaded it.

It is possible to identify three different phases of the Four Year Plan. During the first phase from autumn 1936 to summer 1938 the extension of the raw material base and technical innovations, agricultural reforms and the various measures of economic and social control were in the forefront. The second phase from summer 1938 to August 1939 was dominated by synthetic products of the chemical industry and by light metals and armament materials, whereas the chemical industry and especially *IG Farben* played the major role in the Four Year Plan's third phase from September 1939 to spring 1942.[34]

In answering the question, whether the Four Year Plan fulfilled the intentions of the National Socialist leaders, the table given below is helpful.

It shows that with aluminium, synthetic fibre and explosives - and also with electric energy, zinc and lignite not mentioned here - the requirements of the plan were met or even surpassed. The greatest failure was mineral oil, but there were also serious shortcomings with steel, various metals and fats.[35]

The Four Year Plan had a prominent position in the economy

Table 6.2:   *The production of selected goods under the Four Year Plan*

Product	Planned[a]	Produced[a] in 1938	Produced in 1942[a]	Fulfillment of plan in 1942 in per cent
mineral oil	13,830	2,340	6,260	45
aluminium	273	166	260	98
magnesium	36	13	30	83
buna	120	5	96	80
synthetic fibres	-	53.4	119.3	-
cellulose	146.5	154	300	206
explosives	223	45	300	135
steel	24,000	22,656	20,480	80
lead	218.5	185.2	148.9	68
copper	75.9	68.8	41.1	54

Notes: [a] in 1000 tons

Source: Dietmar Petzina, *Die deutsche Wirtschaft in der Zwischenkriegszeit* (Steiner, Wiesbaden, 1977), p.137.

of National Socialist Germany during the period 1936 to 1942. The total output of the plan was RM 13.25 thousand million, amounting to about half of all industrial investment. However, having a plan did not mean having a planned economy without any entrepreneurial room to manoeuvre. This room did exist, although the extent depended on the particular branch of industry and period of time.[36]

Finance

From 1933 onwards National Socialist financial policy was characterised by two main trends: the elimination of the German states from financial decision making processes which implied a trend towards centralisation of the legislative and executive functions and second, the curbing of the Minister of Finance's authority by transferring important powers to the *Fuehrer* or to special commissioners (*Sonderbevollmaechtigte*). This happened in other areas of policy in a similar way and often led to a rivalry between the established institutions and the recently created ones and to effects which Hitler intended: competition between institutions and functionaries in a social-darwinistic way. The seemingly well-organised "totalitarian" system, which historians of the 1950s detected when interpreting National Socialism, was really more of a fascist "un-system", meaning both "no-system" and "destructive system".[37]

From 1933 onwards the capital market was at the *Reich's* disposal. In 1933 the government decreed capital issue restrictions for the private business sector which, however, were disregarded in 1936, when Four Year Plan investments had to be financed in a private form. To reserve a large share of the capital market for public bonds the government decreed the capital stock law (*Anleihestockgesetz*) of 4 December 1934, which restricted dividend payments to 6 per cent.

During the years of National Socialist rule public finance was increasingly used for rearmament and war preparation, which is reflected in the statistics given below.

Generally speaking, there was a large expansion of government expenditure, which exceeded government revenue, especially tax revenue, by far, and resulted in a dramatically rising budget deficit. Government expenditure rose from about 25 per cent of the average net national income of the period 1925-7 to 33 per cent in 1936 and almost 45 per cent in 1938. A third of this rise can probably be attributed to the secular trend. Of an estimated total of RM 80 thousand million "extraordinary" government expenditure between 1933 and 1939, about 56 per cent was financed by non-borrowed income (taxes and revenue from public enterprises), 24 per cent was borrowed on long term and 12 per cent on short term capital markets. The remaining 8 per cent was financed by monetary expansion with an inflationary effect, but this occurred only at the end of the 1930s. Between 1928 and 1939 GNP increased by only 16 per cent whereas the money supply increased by 80 per cent in the period 1933 to 1939 and the total debt rose almost three and a half times. Still, the relation between public debt and national income, which had been comparatively low in

Table 6.3: Statistics on German finance 1932/3-1938/9 [a]

Year	Government revenue	Government expenditure	Total debt	Money supply
1932/3	6.6	9.2	12.3	13.4
1933/4	6.8	8.9	13.9	13.9
1934/5	8.2	12.6	15.9	15.7
1935/6	9.6	14.1	20.1	16.7
1936/7	11.4	17.3	25.8	18.1
1937/8	13.9	21.4	31.2	20.0
1938/9	17.7	32.6	40.7	23.7

Note: [a] In RM thousand million. Fiscal year beginning 1 April for column 1 and 2. End of fiscal year for column 3. End of calender year for column 4.

Source: Richard J. Overy, *The Nazi economic recovery 1932-1938* (Macmillan, London, 1982), p.46.

Germany before 1933, became similar to that of the other major industrial nations. To many National Socialist leaders, and especially to Hitler, inflation and a rising public debt were a constant worry. Goebbels' claim that budget deficits were nothing to worry about, since there had never been a nation which had perished because of deficits, but only because of lack of weapons, could not allay the fears.[38]

Government deficits from 1932 to 1934 tended to be hidden from the public by being called "anticipation of future revenue". Part of the work-creation programmes was financed through tax certificates (*Steuergutscheine*), which the owner could use to pay for several taxes in the future, and which in the meantime could be discounted by the banking system. From 1934 onwards a second way of veiled financing of deficits was used, the "Mefo-bill". Already under Chancellor Bruening the *Reich* had pre-financed work-creation projects in anticipation of future revenue.[39]

In the period from 1934 to 1936 about half of the expenditure on rearmament was financed by the *Mefo-Wechsel*. Mefo was an acronym for *Metallurgische Forschungs-GmbH* (Metal Research Ltd.), a straw firm with Siemens, *Deutsche Werke*, Krupp and *Rheinmetall* as stockholders. Mefo bills were a three-monthly paper, which could be extended to six months, drawn by firms with limited capital supplying material to the Armed Forces, "accepted" by the Mefo and then discounted at the *Reichsbank* or sold to the capital market. Thus the Mefo remained debtor to the *Reichsbank* and the *Reich* could delay paying for up to five years. In 1936, the paper outstanding amounted to RM 12 thousand million, but it was reduced to 6 thousand million at the end of March 1938. Obviously, there were inflationary tendencies in this way of financing public spending.

From 1 April 1938, another kind of short-term paper was issued, the *Lieferschatzanweisungen* ("supplier treasury bills"). By the outbreak of the war they amounted to RM 4 thousand million. Supplementary to the *Lieferschatzanweisungen* were the *Steuergutscheine* (tax-anticipation bonds) issued from May 1939 until October 1939.[40] Long-term interest-bearing *Reich* loans (*Li-Anleihen*) and treasury bonds were another pillar of National Socialist financial war preparation. Banks, savings banks, cooperative societies and insurance companies lost their function as negotiators of credit for industry and became mainly agents for the indirect creation of state finance.[41]

Industrial development and productivity, 1933-1939

The index of industrial production, which in 1932 had fallen to 50 per cent of the level of 1928, rose to 66 in 1933, 83 in 1934 and 96 in 1935. In 1936 it already exceeded the level of 1928 and in 1938 was about 22 per cent higher.[42]

At the height of the Great Depression, in 1932, the statistics show almost 6 million people out of work in Germany. The real figure was probably considerably higher, because after several years of unemployment, many people no longer received unemployment benefits and were therefore not recorded in the unem-

Table 6.4: Economic recovery in Germany 1932-1938

	1932	1933	1934	1935	1936	1937	1938
GNP[a]	57.6	59.1	66.5	74.4	82.6	93.2	104.5
GNP (1928 prices)	71.9	73.7	83.7	92.3	101.2	114.2	126.2
national income[a]	45.2	46.5	52.8	59.1	65.8	73.8	82.1
industrial production[b]	58	66	83	96	107	117	122
unemployment[c]	5.6	4.8	2.7	2.2	1.6	0.9	0.4

Notes: [a] in RM thousand million; [b] 1928 = 100; [c] in million

Source: Richard J. Overy, *The Nazi economic recovery 1932-1938* (Macmillan, London, 1982), p.29.

ployment statistics. In 1932, probably every third person in the workforce was unemployed.

The rise of national income between 1933 and 1939 exceeded even the spectacular growth in the first decade of the Federal Republic of Germany. It was triggered off by work creation programmes and sustained by the rearmament policy of the National Socialist government. Until 1936/7 quite a large share of that growth can be attributed to a "normal" cyclical upswing after the slump of the Great Depression, but government rearmament policy played the key role thereafter.[43]

Whereas production in the construction and the iron and steel industries rose considerably, the rise in mining (about 80 per cent between 1932 and 1938) was lower. The motor car industry and shipbuilding were above average - the growth of the tractor industry was particularly significant - while the textile, paper and leather industries and consumer goods in general showed only a moderate rise. Between 1932 and 1938 the production increase in the textile industry amounted to only 60 per cent. There was a marked shift from consumer goods industries to industrial raw materials and capital goods.

With the statistical material available, productivity is difficult to assess, but the average increase was about 1.3 per cent, a conspicuously low figure. There are several reasons for this modest rise: already in the 1920s the German economy had experienced a "rationalisation drive" which affected various branches of industry. Secondly, and compared with a country like the USA, demand was not high enough to make standardisation and mass production pay in many fields in the period before 1938. Thirdly, and more important, many of the projects financed by the National Socialists were labour intensive. Especially in the early phase of National Socialist rule, until 1936, the government was not at all keen on saving labour, because the reduction of unemployment had a high priority. Sometimes firms were even granted government subsidies to take on additional workers. As the state assumed increasing responsibility for the economy, normal market pressures for innovations and improved efficiency were often nonexistent. The fact that the state provided contracts on a fixed cost-plus basis did not encourage efficiency within the corporations. In the fourth place, labour often used defensive tactics vis-à-vis the demands made on it by the National Socialist party. These tactics implied veiled strikes, absenteeism and the reluctance to adopt new production methods and contributed to a less efficient utilisation of labour.[44]

When analysing armament production in the period 1933-1939 several authors have credited the National Socialist government with giving "guns" *and* "butter" to the German people and thereby fulfilling a promise often made in speeches and in writing.[45] Looking at the figures available and at the development of the living standard in Germany it soon becomes obvious that this claim is unjustified. In spite of propaganda slogans and Hitler's desire not to antagonise the workers by impairing their living standard too much, the National Socialists pursued, although partly under cover, an austerity policy, which put armament production first.

Labour

Spectacular as the success of the National Socialists in bringing down the unemployment rate was - unemployment had decreased to 1 million by September 1936 and in 1937 and 1938 there was already overemployment - the available statistics should be taken with a grain of salt. From 1933 onwards those only temporarily employed were no longer counted as being out of work. Against the National Socialists' claim that by mid-1934 3.5 million people had found jobs it has to be pointed out that among these were about 600,000 emergency workers (*Notstandsarbeiter*), who worked for a very low wage indeed. There was also a tendency among some firms to shorten working hours and divide work among as many employees as possible.[46] The introduction of universal compulsory military service (March 1935), the transformation of the originally voluntary labour service into the obligatory Reich Labour Service (*Reichsarbeitsdienst, RAD*) in June 1935 and the propaganda against the gainful employment of women, contributed to a reduction of male unemployment.[47]

Taken as a whole the dramatic recovery of the labour market was, in spite of the *caveats* mentioned above, much more than a statistical conjuring trick. It was based on a revival of economic activity, which turned the problem of unemployment round to the similarly severe problem of overemployment.[48]

Mobilisation of labour for the preparation of war took place in several stages. Trade unions were made illegal on 2 May 1933 and replaced four days later by a new compulsory corporate organisation, the German Labour Front (*Deutsche Arbeitsfront, DAF*). The "Law on the Organisation of National Labour" (*Gesetz zur Ordnung der nationalen Arbeit*) of 20 January 1934 became the framework for industrial relations.[49] The basic unit of industrial relations was to be the "shop community" (*Betriebsgemeinschaft*) with a "leader" (*Betriebsfuehrer*) and "followers" (*Gefolgschaft*). The elected factory council (*Betriebsrat*) was replaced by the *Vertrauensrat*, an advisory body with no executive functions whatever. The wage agreement, formerly worked out between employers and trade unions, was now the responsibility of the "trustees of labour" (*Treuhaender der Arbeit*) appointed by the Labour Front as mediating agents between employers and employees.[50] To win the workers over to their cause the National Socialists introduced "Strength through Joy" holidays and the "Beauty of Work" movement for decorating factories, which was but a poor substitute for having to give up free bargaining.[51]

By 1934 immigrants to urban areas of concentration needed a permit. In February 1935 a work book was introduced which was to be retained by the employer for the duration of the labour contract and intended to tie the workers to the job and prevent them from moving because of higher wages offered elsewhere. A further objective was the total statistical investigation into the available labour reserves and their control. In June 1938 about 400,000 workers were needed to build the Western border fortifications (*Westwall*). Between June and October 1938 partial, and in February 1939 comprehensive, labour conscription was introduced as a reaction to the growing shortages on the German labour market. In May 1939 the militarisation of the labour market was completed by making intended changes of jobs dependent on a labour exchange permission.[52]

Table 6.5: Wages and wage shares 1933-1939 [a]

Year	Nominal hourly wages		Real hourly wages	Effective weekly nominal wages	Real weekly wages	Percentage share of wages in national income
	con-trac-tual	effec-tive				
1933	97	97	99	102	104	56.0
1934	97	99	99	110	109	55.5
1935	97	101	99	112	110	54.6
1936	97	102	100	.17	112	53.5
1937	97	105	101	121	115	52.7
1938	97	108	104	126	119	52.4
1939	98	111	107	131	123	51.8

Note: [a] 1932 = 100

Source: Dietmar Petzina, *Autarkiepolitik im Dritten Reich. Der nationalsozialistische Vierjahresplan* (Deutsche Verlagsanstalt, Stuttgart, 1968), p.167.

Although National Socialist propaganda never stopped pointing out an allegedly enormous rise in the workers' living standards since 1933 the statistics show that the rise was rather modest.

The nominal hourly wages fixed by the trustees of labour do not give the real picture, because the nominal wages, i.e. those not adjusted for prices, which were actually paid between 1933 and 1939, rose only at a yearly average of 2 per cent. Real wages rose only by 1.3 per cent, while weekly wages rose by 2.8 per cent. This is because the weekly working hours were gradually extended as labour shortages became more and more acute in various branches of the economy. In view of the yearly rise of national income (8.2 per cent) and the rise of undistributed net profits of business corporations (36.5 per cent) this increase was modest indeed. The wage share actually declined in the period 1933-1939. National Socialist wage policy took away an increasing share of the national production from private consumption and made it available for rearmament purposes.[53]

Contrary to the official average of 46 to 47 working hours per week, an 80 hour week was not uncommon in 1938, especially in aircraft production. There were complaints about a decreasing labour performance and a too slow transition to multiple shift operation.[54]

Because of the wage freeze from 1933 onwards there were no official wage rises between 1933 and 1939. In "bottleneck industries" like construction and metal, employers after 1936 introduced quite an ingenious variety of veiled wage rises in the shape of workers' benefits, thus circumventing state policy. These were cost free meals and medical assistance, cheap company dwellings, subsidies to building costs, motorcycles for commuters or refunds of travelling expenses, payments during leave or allowances in kind. There are also absurd stories about employers chasing for labour and a builder carrying a whole bus-load of workers from a competitor at night.[55] Between 1935 and 1938 employers supported the construction of 112,000 company dwellings by an allowance of about RM 250 million.[56]

According to National Socialist ideology the place assigned by nature to women was at home as a wife and a mother.[57] Politically this ideology was supported by marriage loans and by forbidding gainful employment of husband and wife. To stall both university enrolment and female pressure on the labour market, a "home economics year" (*Hauswirtschaftliches Jahr*) was introduced in 1935 by which participants were engaged in domestic service without payment, although they were given pocket money, board and keep. After the introduction of general military service for men in March 1935 and the obligatory *Reichsarbeitsdienst* in June of the same year problems of procuring sufficient labour for the armament effort arose. Ball bearing production was a case in point with operations demanding manual dexterity which until then had been done almost exclusively by women.

The same goes for other industries linked to the arms drive and self-sufficiency programme such as the manufacture of rubber or chemical and electrical goods. It is not surprising that in October 1937 the government revoked its stipulation that only those women who did not enter the labour market, would qualify for marriage loans. Here again we find the gap between National Socialist ideology and practical economic requirements.

As, after 1937, there was a tendency for female labour to look for better paid jobs in the cities and the commercial sector, the government early in 1938 decreed a compulsory "duty year" for all unmarried girls or women under twenty-five entering the labour market. During this time they had to do either agricultural or domestic work or, alternatively, two years as auxiliary nurses or social welfare workers. Resulting from this there were almost 200,000 women in the labour service.[58]

Agriculture

From the beginning, agriculture and farmers played an important role in National Socialist ideology. The preservation of a large farm population as the "blood-well of the nation" (*Blutquell der Nation*) has to be seen in the context of autarky and war preparation and as an attempt to stop the rural exodus. The National Socialists regarded agriculture as a stabilising element in society. Already before the *Machtergreifung* of 1933 protection for agriculture was one of the more prominent issues in National Socialist political agitation. This was one of the reasons which in September 1932 led the Papen government to give in to demands of agricultural pressure groups like the "Green Front": foreclosure was made extremely difficult for creditors, agricultural interest rates were lowered by 2 per cent and a quota system for some agricultural import products was introduced. Shortly after the National Socialist "seizure of power", on 14 February 1933, the government enacted protection against foreclosure valid until October of the same year. Accompanying measures in favour of agriculture were a substantial rise of agricultural import duties and grain subsidies, which were particularly beneficial for the large estates in eastern Germany. This early period of agrarian policy under Alfred Hugenberg, the Minister of Agriculture and a member of the *Deutsch-Nationale Volkspartei* (*DNVP*, German-National People's

Party), ended with the "Statute for the regulation of agricultural contractual obligations" (*Gesetz zur Regelung der landwirtschaftlichen Schuldverhaeltnisse*) of 1 June 1933, which provided for the financial reorganisation of indebted estates by lowering debts, interest and sometimes selling land. The creditors had to pay the bill.[59]

At the end of June 1933, Walther Darré replaced Hugenberg as Minister of Agriculture. He started the period of National Socialist agricultural policy with the foundation of the Reich Food Estate (*Reichsnaehrstand*) and the Entailed Farm Law (*Reichserbhofgesetz*). The *Reichsnaehrstand* inaugurated an all-embracing national cartel to regulate food production and distribution. Its purpose was to ensure stable food prices.[60] It was a gigantic corporation comprising Germany's total of more than 3 million farms, 500,000 food and drink retail stores, and 300,000 food-processing enterprises. The Reich Food Estate with its enormous bureaucracy of 20,000 full-time and 113,000 honorary officials fixed all agricultural prices and wages, set production quotas and determined what crops were to be sown. By the Entailed Farm Law some 600,000 medium-sized farms with an average of thirty acres in 1933 became *Erbhoefe*, hereditarily entailed holdings between 7.5 and 12.5 hectares, which were not to be mortgaged, could not be sold, were indivisible and passed from father to eldest son.[61] Apart from the economic aspects, the National Socialists did their best to make the *Erbhof*-peasant socially acceptable. Only they could call themselves *Bauern*, whereas large estate owners and smallholders without an *Erbhof* were called *Landwirte*.[62]

When, in 1936, increasing agrarian imports caused further foreign currency exchange problems and made rationing of basic victuals unavoidable, Hermann Goering, plenipotentiary of the Four Year Plan, took charge of agrarian policy. Goering brought agricultural policy into line with armament policy. He decreed lower prices for fertilizers, guaranteed farmers higher incomes from their products, intensified agricultural improvement and accelerated land consolidation. The "decree to secure the cultivation of land" (*Gesetz zur Sicherung der Landbewirtschaftung*) of 23 March 1937 granted public authorities the power to regulate the use of agricultural areas under cultivation, if farmers did not comply with the government's ideas of securing the people's subsistence. The "decree to secure bread grain requirements" (*Verordnung zur Sicherung des Brotgetreidebedarfs*) of 22 July 1937 made all agrarian producers deliver their complete rye and wheat yields. For storing these grain provisions the government could, if necessary, requisition gymnasiums or dance halls.[63]

In line with National Socialist policy the government tried to exclude "unproductive wholesale and intermediate trade", which was mainly intended to affect Jewish businessmen. Cheap adolescent labour (an agrarian "ninth year" for poor schoolchildren, the girls' "land service year", Hitler Youth and student harvest camps) and the Reich Labour Service were mobilised to meet the National Socialists' objectives. Even so, in the late 1930s, agricultural labour became increasingly scarce. By lowering prices for machinery, especially tractors and electric motors, and electricity rates, the government provided incentives for mechanisation and rationalisation. Although there was some success the National Socialists also created obstacles to a successful agricultural policy, which were partly rooted in their ideology and in their politically motivated striving for autarky: agricultural production on German soil to make the German population independent of foreign imports regardless of cost was not a sensible economic proposition. Also the *Reichserbhofgesetz*, by limiting unit sizes, often hindered efficient cultivation. Whereas British farmers deployed one tractor for every 310 acres of land, the German used one for every 810 acres and the daily area ploughed by a German farmer ranged from a fifth to a quarter of the American average. The drive for self-sufficiency promoted an intensification of agriculture, but it also put into operation the law of diminishing returns. The most efficient means of raising yields was to lower the cost of artificial fertilizers, especially nitrogen, the price of which was reduced by 70 per cent from 1934/5 to 1938/9 and potassium (53 per cent price reduction in the same period).[64]

From 1927/8 to 1938/9 there was an increase of agricultural production in Germany by about one-fifth. This and the fact that the degree of self-sufficiency had increased from 68 to 83 per cent was a considerable achievement of National Socialist agrarian policy.

On the other hand, there were various deficiencies. The notorious "fat gap" remained and thirty per cent of meat and milk production was still based on imported fodder. During the period 1935/6 to 1938/9 rising demand caused a quantitative increase of agrarian imports in the range of 40 per cent. Thus the foreign exchange savings of agrarian policy remained insignificant. Taken as a whole, the dependence on imports could only be decreased by a small degree. Therefore, neither the goal of becoming independent of agricultural imports in case of war nor a significant improvement of the foreign exchange balance was accomplished by National Socialist agrarian policy.[65]

Table 6.6: *Degree of self-sufficiency in the agricultural sector 1927/8-1938/9* [a]

Foodstuff	1927/8	1933/4	1938/9
bread grains	79	99	115
pulse (without lentils)	62	50	71
potatoes	96	100	100
vegetables	84	90	91
sugar	100	99	101
meat	91	98	97
eggs	64	80	82
fat	44	53	57
foodstuff total	68	80	83

Note: [a] in per cent, yearly averages

Source: Dietmar Petzina, *Autarkiepolitik im Dritten Reich. Der nationalsozialistische Vierjahresplan* (Deutsche Verlags-Anstalt, Stuttgart, 1968), p.95.

Farmers' incomes developed favourably. Although there was an increase of 39 per cent in the period 1925 to 1939, problems remained. Especially from 1938 onwards wages in armament production tended to be higher than in agriculture. At the end of 1939, for example, a dairy worker received about RM 60 a week, whereas a bricklayer's helper doing piecework earned up to RM 150. This considerable gap caused a rural exodus with which, in spite of various decrees and much propaganda, the National Socialists never really came to grips.[66]

Foreign trade

One of the consequences of the Great Depression was a tendency towards the formation of economic areas with a reduction of exports and imports and internal deflation. The foreign-trade balance, which from 1888 onwards had been generally unfavourable, showed an export surplus. Still, in spite of these factors, the service of capital to foreign countries, especially reparations, caused a rapid fall of German foreign exchange reserves. Already in July 1932 there were the beginnings of a "bilaterialisation" of German foreign trade, when the commercial treaty with Sweden was revoked and the treaty with the Netherlands was not renewed at the end of the same year.[67]

Although endeavours to achieve autarky were soon visible after the National Socialists came to power, Hitler told the *Reichstag* on 23 March 1933 that he was aware of the fact that the geographical location of Germany and her lack of raw materials made complete autarky impossible. Therefore commercial links with other countries had to be maintained. In order to use its inadequate foreign currency reserves as effectively as possible, the National Socialist government from the start applied state interventionist measures of import and export controls, although at the beginning this was done rather cautiously.[68] On an institutional level the functions of the chambers of commerce were transferred to the newly created "foreign trade bureaus" (*Aussenhandelsstellen*).

As a whole, National Socialist foreign trade policy was, in its early phase, characterised by a system of bilateral preferences, foreign-exchange controls, import quotas and export subsidies. This phase was completed by the "New Plan" (*Neuer Plan*) of 19 September 1934, which had been designed by Hjalmar Schacht, Minister of Economic Affairs from 2 April 1934 onwards.[69] With the "New Plan" foreign trade policy was secondary to full employment and rearmament with the latter becoming dominant after 1936.

The plan was based on a simple-sounding principle: "do not buy more than you can pay for and buy only really necessary goods". "Really necessary" was, of course, subject to interpretation; the National Socialists meant mainly raw materials for armaments. The "New Plan" envisaged a shift of foreign trade to raw material exporting countries avoiding foreign-exchange cash payments and substituting them by a clearing system. The implied aims were to become independent of imports and develop raw materials production - often synthetic - at home. Although Schacht was the author of the plan, he made it clear that he sacrificed his economic principles of free international trade to National Socialist economic and political aims and to political expediency. In a speech in Weimar on 29 October 1934 he said: "This «New Plan», which we introduced, is repulsive to me. But we cannot do without it."[70]

The New Plan generally implied a shift of trade from Western Europe and North America to Southern and Eastern Europe and South America with the objective of having agrarian and industrial raw material resources as close by as possible. The commercial treaty with Yugoslavia of 1 May 1934 can be regarded as a model of a bilateral treaty, which already anticipated *Grosswirtschaftsraum* ("greater economic area") policy.[71] There were similar treaties with Hungary and Greece.

As the 1930s progressed the aims of foreign trade policy were to create an economic area around Germany, which could not be afflicted by a blockade, a *cordon économique* consisting of a number of friendly or neutral states to be made dependent on Germany. In this the National Socialist government had considerable success: by 1938, Yugoslavia, Hungary, Roumania, Bulgaria and Greece transacted 50 per cent of their foreign trade with Germany.[72] In March 1938, by the annexation of Austria, another vital corner-stone on the way to a National Socialist *Grosswirtschaftsraum* was added. Not every National Socialist leader realised that the states of the "greater economic area" were independent and not German colonies.

The treaty with Roumania on 23 March 1938 marked a new phase in National Socialist foreign trade policy. Max Ilgner, member of the board of directors of *IG Farben*, expressed its aims like this: "Export increase by playing an active role in the industralisation of the world". The treaty was based on a German-Roumanian Five Year Plan according to which Roumania was to deliver agricultural products and raw materials, for example mineral oil, to Germany, for the production and processing of which Germany provided the necessary plants and machinery.[73]

The table below shows that under National Socialist rule foreign trade was characterised by a marked stagnation. Until 1937 the value of exports remained below the figure for 1932, the height of

Table 6.7:   *Germany's foreign trade 1930-1939. Foreign trade, gold- and foreign-exchange movements*[a]

Year	Value	Ex-ports	Im-ports	Balance (ex-im), current prices	Gold- and foreign ex-change in-flows (+) or out-flows (-)	Gold- and foreign exchange holdings (Ø)
1930	22.4	12.0	10.4	+1.64	-0.12	2.80
1931	16.3	9.6	6.7	+2.87	-1.65	1.91
1932	10.4	5.7	4.7	+1.07	-0.02	0.97
1933	9.1	4.9	4.2	+0.66	-0.44	0.52
1934	8.6	4.2	4.4	-0.28	-0.42	0.16
1935	8.4	4.2	4.2	+0.11	-0.03	0.09
1936	8.9	4.7	4.2	+0.55	-	0.07
1937	11.3	5.9	5.4	+0.44	-	0.07
1938[b]	11.7	6.1	5.6	+0.5	-	-
1938[c]	10.7	5.3	5.4	-0.1	-	-
1939[b]	10.9	5.7	5.2	+0.5	-	0.5

Notes: [a] in RM thousand million; [b] including Austria; [c] excluding Austria

Source: Eckart Teichert, *Autarkie und Grossraumwirtschaft in Deutschland 1930-1939. Aussenwirtschaftliche Konzeptionen zwischen Wirtschaftskrise und Zwei-tem Weltkrieg* (Oldenbourg, Munich, 1984), p.349.

depression. From 1933 to 1936 average exports reached only about 40 per cent of the figures for 1928. As far as imports are concerned the contraction was even bigger. The rise from 1937 onwards was due to gearing the economy to war.

Notes

1. Ludolf Herbst, *Der totale Krieg und die Ordnung der Wirtschaft. Die Kriegswirtschaft im Spannungsfeld von Politik und Propaganda 1939-1945* (Deutsche Verlags-Anstalt, Stuttgart, 1982), pp.26-7. See also Peter Krueger, "Zu Hitlers «nationalsozialistischen Wirtschaftserkenntnissen», *Geschichte und Gesellschaft*, vol. 6 (1980), pp.262-3.

2. Edward R. Zilbert, *Albert Speer and the Nazi Ministry of Arms. Economic institutions and industrial production in the German war economy* (Fairleigh Dickinson University Press, Rutherford, London, 1981), p.54.

3. On department stores see Heinrich Uhlig, *Die Warenhaeuser im Dritten Reich* (Westdeutscher Verlag, Cologne, Opladen, 1956), and Helmut Genschel, *Die Verdraengung der Juden aus der Wirtschaft im Dritten Reich* (Musterschmidt, Goettingen, 1966).

4. Karl Hardach, *The political economy of Germany in the twentieth century* (University of California Press, Berkeley, Los Angeles, London, 1980), p.54.

5. Henry Ashby Turner, Jr., *German big business and the rise of Hitler* (Oxford University Press, Oxford, New York 1985), pp.60-71.

6. Dietmar Petzina, *Die deutsche Wirtschaft in der Zwischenkriegszeit* (Steiner, Wiesbaden, 1977), pp.124-5.

7. Hans-Erich Volkmann,"Die NS-Wirtschaft in Vorbereitung des Krieges", in Militaergeschichtliches Forschungsamt (ed.), *Ursachen und Voraussetzungen der deutschen Kriegspolitik. Das Deutsche Reich und der Zweite Weltkrieg* (Deutsche Verlags-Anstalt, Stuttgart, 1979), vol. 1, p.219.

8. Turner, *German big business*, p.75.

9. Richard J. Overy, *The Nazi economic recovery 1932-1938* (Macmillan, London, 1982), p.9.

10. Turner, *German big business*, p.354. See, however, from a Marxist point of view, Eberhard Czichon, *Wer verhalf Hitler zur Macht? Zum Anteil der deutschen Industrie an der Zerstoerung der Weimarer Republik* (Pahl-Rugenstein, Cologne, 1967).

11. Examples are, *inter alia*, in Henry Ashby Turner Jr., *Faschismus und Kapitalismus in Deutschland* (Vandenhoeck and Ruprecht, Goettingen, 1972). But see Dirk Stegmann, "Zum Verhaeltnis von Grossindustrie und Nationalsozialismus 1930-1933. Ein Beitrag zur Geschichte der sogenannten Machtergreifung", *Archiv fuer Sozialgeschichte*, vol. 12 (1973), pp.399-482. Also Dick Geary, "The industrial elite and the Nazis in the Weimar Republic", in Peter D. Stachura (ed.), *The Nazi Machtergreifung* (Allen and Unwin, London, 1983), pp.85-100 and George W.F. Hallgarten and Joachim Radkau, *Deutsche Industrie und Politik von Bismarck bis in die Gegenwart* (Rowohlt, Reinbek near Hamburg, 1981), pp.180-236.

12. The term is Turner's (*German big business*, p.347).

13. Thomas Trumpp, "Zur Finanzierung der NSDAP durch die deutsche Grossindustrie. Versuch einer Bilanz", in Karl Dietrich Bracher, Manfred Funke and Hans-Adolf Jacobsen (eds), *Nationalsozialistische Diktatur 1933-1945. Eine Bilanz* (Droste, Duesseldorf, 1983), pp.152-3 and Gerald D. Feldman, "Aspekte deutscher Industriepolitik am Ende der Weimarer Republik 1930-1932", in Karl Holl (ed.), *Wirtschaftskrise und liberale Demokratie. Das Ende der Weimarer Republik und die gegenwaertige Situation* (Vandenhoeck and Ruprecht, Goettingen, 1978, pp.103-125.

14. Wolfgang Birkenfeld, *Der synthetische Treibstoff 1933-1945. Ein Beitrag zur nationalsozialistischen Wirtschafts- und Ruestungspolitik* (Musterschmidt, Goettingen, Berlin, Frankfurt am Main, 1964).

15. Mathias Riedel, *Eisen und Kohle fuer das Dritte Reich. Paul Plei-gers Stellung in der NS-Wirtschaft* (Musterschmidt, Goettingen, Frankfurt am Main, Zurich, 1973).

16. Ian Kershaw, *The Nazi dictatorship. Problems and perspectives of interpretation* (Edward Arnold, London, 1985), pp.42-50; Wolfgang Wippermann, *Faschismustheorien. Zum Stand der gegenwaertigen Diskussion* (Wissenschaftliche Buchgesellschaft, Darmstadt, 1980), pp.138-48 and Arthur Schweitzer, *Big Business in the Third Reich* (Eyre and Spottiswoode, London, 1964).

17. Peter Huettenberger, "Nationalsozialistische Polykratie", *Geschichte und Gesellschaft*, vol. 2 (1976), pp.417-42; see, however, Bernd-Juergen Wendt, *Grossdeutschland. Aussenpolitik und Kriegsvorbereitung des Hitler-Regimes* (Deutscher Taschenbuch Verlag, 1987), p.230.

18. Petzina, *Die deutsche Wirtschaft*, p.109-10; on the transition from the Weimar to the National Socialist economy see Volker Hentschel, "Wirtschafts-und sozialhistorische Brueche und Kontinuitaeten zwischen Weimarer Republik und Drittem Reich", *Zeitschrift fuer Unternehmensgeschichte*, vol. 28 (1983), pp.39-80.

19. Richard J. Overy, "Cars, roads and economic recovery in Germany 1932-8", *Economic History Review*, Second Series, vol. 28 (1975), pp.466-83. By the same author: "Transportation and rearmament in the Third Reich", *Historical Journal*, vol. 16 (1973), pp.389-409. See also Karl Laermer, *Autobahnbau in Deutschland 1933 bis 1945. Zu den Hintergruenden* (Akademie-Verlag, Berlin (GDR), 1975); the controversial dissertation by Juergen Stelzner, *Arbeitsbeschaffung und Wiederaufruestung 1933-1936. Nationalsozialistische Beschaeftigungspolitik und Aufbau der Wehr- und Ruestungswirtschaft* (Diss., Tuebingen, 1976) and Hansjoachim Henning, "Kraftfahrzeugindustrie und Autobahnbau in der Wirtschaftspolitik des Nationalsozialismus 1933-1936", *Vierteljahrschrift fuer Sozial- und Wirtschaftsgeschichte*, vol. 65 (1978), pp.217-42.

20. Karl-Heinz Ludwig, "Strukturmerkmale nationalsozialistischer Aufruestung bis 1935", in Friedrich Forstmeier and Hans-Erich Volkmann (eds), *Wirtschaft und Ruestung am Vorabend des Zweiten Weltkrieges* (Droste, Duesseldorf, 1975), p.50.

21. K. Hardach, *Political economy*, pp.58-9.

22. Harold James, *The German slump. Politics and economics 1924-1936* (Clarendon Press, Oxford, 1986), p.379.

23. Gerhard Kroll, *Von der Weltwirtschaftskrise zur Staatskonjunktur* (Duncker and Humblot, Berlin, 1958).

24. R. Overy, *Nazi economic recovery*, p.49 for this and the following.

25. Berenice H. Carroll, *Design for total war. Arms and economics in the Third Reich* (Mouton, The Hague, Paris, 1968), pp.185-8.

26. In what follows I shall be dealing with the "Second Four Year Plan" in National Socialist parlance, although there was no proper "First Four Year Plan" (See Arthur Schweitzer "Der urspruengliche Vierjahresplan", *Jahrbuecher fuer Nationaloekonomie und Statistik*, vol. 16 (1956), pp.348-96.

27. Wilhelm Treue, "Hitlers Denkschrift zum Vierjahresplan 1936", *Vierteljahrshefte fuer Zeitgeschichte*, vol. 3 (1955), pp.184-210.

28. For this and the following see Petzina, *Die deutsche Wirtschaft*, pp.126-29; by the same author: *Autarkiepolitik im Dritten Reich. Der nationalsozialistische Vierjahresplan* (Deutsche Verlags-Anstalt, Stuttgart, 1968).

29. Birkenfeld, *Der synthetische Treibstoff*, and Matthias Riedel "Die Rohstofflage des Deutschen Reiches im Fruehjahr 1936", *Tradition. Zeitschrift fuer Firmengeschichte und Unternehmerbiographie*, vol. 14 (1969), pp.310-34.

30. Arthur Schweitzer, "The foreign exchange crisis of 1936", *Zeitschrift fuer die gesamte Staatswissenschaft*, vol. 118 (1962), pp.243-77.

31. Fritz Blaich, "Wirtschaft und Ruestung in Deutschland 1933-1939", in Wolfgang Benz and Hermann Graml (eds), *Sommer 1939. Die Grossmaechte*

und der Europaeische Krieg (Deutsche Verlags-Anstalt, Stuttgart, 1979), p.47.

32. Petzina, *Autarkiepolitik*, pp.153-77 for this and the following.

33. Kroll, *Weltwirtschaftskrise.*

34. Petzina, *Die deutsche Wirtschaft*, p.132. Critical of Petzina is Peter Hayes, *Industry and ideology. IG Farben in the Nazi era* (Cambridge University Press, Cambridge, 1987).

35. Petzina, *Autarkiepolitik*, p.181.

36. See Michael Geyer, *Deutsche Ruestungspolitik 1860-1980* (Suhrkamp, Frankfurt am Main, 1984).

37. On this general problem see, among others, Martin Broszat, *Der Staat Hitlers* (Deutscher Taschenbuch Verlag, Munich, 1969).

38. James, *German slump*, p.372. See also René Erbe, *Die nationalsozialistische Wirtschaftspolitik 1933-1939 im Lichte der modernen Theorie* (Polygraphischer Verlag, Zurich, 1958), p.54.

39. James, *German slump*, pp.373-7.

40. Charles P. Kindleberger, *A Financial history of Western Europe* (Allen and Unwin, London, 1984), p.393; Wolfram Fischer, *Deutsche Wirtschaftspolitik 1918-1945 (Leske, Opladen, 1968), pp.68-9. On taxation see Fritz Blaich, "Die «Grundsaetze nationalsozialistischer Steuerpolitik» und ihre Verwirklichung", in Friedrich-Wilhelm Henning (ed.), Probleme der nationalsozialistischen Wirtschaftspolitik (Duncker and Humblot, Berlin, 1976), pp.99-117.*

41. Willi A. Boelcke, "Probleme der Finanzierung von Militaerausgaben", in Friedrich Forstmeier and Hans-Erich Volkmann (eds), *Wirtschaft und Ruestung am Vorabend des Zweiten Weltkrieges* (Droste, Duesseldorf, 1975), p.32. Also Willi A. Boelcke, *Die Kosten von Hitlers Krieg. Kriegsfinanzierung und finanzielles Kriegserbe in Deutschland 1933-1948* (Schoeningh, Paderborn, 1985).

42. Wolfram Fischer, "Bergbau, Industrie und Handwerk 1914-1970", in Hermann Aubin and Wolfgang Zorn (eds), *Handbuch der deutschen Wirtschafts- und Sozialgeschichte*, 2 vols. (Klett, Stuttgart, 1976), vol. 2, p.818.

43. Petzina, *Die deutsche Wirtschaft*, pp.16-8.

44. Overy, *Nazi economic recovery*, pp.37, 55-60.

45. For example Burton H. Klein, *Germany's economic preparations for war* (Harvard University Press, Cambridge, Mass., 1959), p.79.

46. Timothy W. Mason, *Sozialpolitik im Dritten Reich. Arbeiterklasse und Volksgemeinschaft*, 2nd edn (Westdeutscher Verlag, Opladen, 1978), pp.126-31. Also Richard J. Overy, "Unemployment in the Third Reich", *Business History*, vol. 29 (1987), pp.253-81.

47. Henning Koehler, *Arbeitsdienst in Deutschland. Plaene und Verwirklichungsformen bis zur Einfuehrung der Arbeitsdienstpflicht 1935* (Duncker and Humblot, Berlin, 1967); Wolfgang Benz, "Vom freiwilligen Arbeitsdienst zur Arbeitsdienstpflicht", *Vierteljahrshefte fuer Zeitgeschichte*, vol. 16 (1968), pp.317-46.

48. James, *German slump*, p.371.

49. Timothy W. Mason, "Zur Entstehung des Gesetzes zur Ordnung der nationalen Arbeit vom 20. Januar 1934; Ein Versuch ueber das Verhaeltnis «archaischer» und «moderner» Momente in der neuesten deutschen Geschichte", in Hans Mommsen, Dietmar Petzina and Bernd Weisbrod (eds), *Industrielles System und politische Entwicklung in der Weimarer Republik* (2 vols., Athenaeum, Droste, Kronberg/Ts., Duesseldorf 1977), vol. 1, pp.322-51.

50. David Schoenbaum, *Hitler's social revolution. Class and status in Nazi Germany 1933-1939* (Weidenfeld and Nicolson, London, 1967), pp.91-2.

51. Overy, *Nazi economic recovery*, p.59.

52. Schoenbaum, *Hitler's social revolution*, pp.97-99. See also Juergen Kuczynski, *Darstellung der Lage der Arbeiter in Deutschland von 1933-1945* (Akademie-Verlag, Berlin (GDR), 1964), pp.218-26.

53. Petzina, *Autarkiepolitik*, pp.167-8. See also Ruediger Hachtmann, *Industriearbeiter im Dritten Reich* (Vandenhoeck and Ruprecht, Goettingen, 1989), pp.71-7.

54. Timothy W. Mason, *Arbeiterklasse und Volksgemeinschaft. Dokumente und Materialien zur deutschen Arbeiterpolitik 1936-1939* (Westdeutscher Verlag, Opladen, 1975), pp.379-81.

55. Mason, *Arbeiterklasse*, p.404.

56. Blaich, "Wirtschaft und Ruestung in Deutschland 1933-1939", p.41.

57. Jill Stephenson, *Women in Nazi society* (Croom Helm, London, 1975); Claudia Koonz, *Mothers in the Fatherland. Women, the family and Nazi politics* (Jonathan Cape, London, 1987); Dorothee Klinksiek, *Die Frau im NS-Staat* (Deutsche Verlags-Anstalt, Stuttgart, 1982).

58. Richard Gruenberger, *A social history of the Third Reich* (Penguin, Harmondsworth, 1974), p.325.

59. Horst Gies, "Die nationalsozialistische Machtergreifung auf dem agrarpolitischen Sektor", *Zeitschrift fuer Agrargeschichte und Agrarsoziologie*, vol. 16 (1968), pp.210-32; by the same author "Aufgaben und Probleme der nationalsozialistischen Ernaehrungswirtschaft 1933-1939", *Vierteljahrschrift fuer Sozial- und Wirtschaftsgeschichte*, vol. 66 (1979), pp.466-99 and Petzina, *Die deutsche Wirtschaft*, pp.114-15.

60. Horst Gies, "Die Rolle des Reichsnaehrstandes im nationalsozialistischen Herrschaftssystem", in Gerhard Hirschfeld and Lothar Kettenacker (eds), *The "Fuehrer State": Myth and reality. Studies on the structure and politics of the Third Reich* (Klett-Cotta, Stuttgart, 1981), pp.270-340; K. Hardach, *Political economy*, p.67.

61. Friedrich Grundmann, *Agrarpolitik im "Dritten Reich". Anspruch und Wirklichkeit des Reichserbhofgesetzes* (Hoffmann and Campe, Hamburg, 1979).

62. Gruenberger, *Social history*, p.202-4.

63. Petzina, *Die deutsche Wirtschaft*, p.149. See also on the general problem Juergen von Kruedener, "Zielkonflikte in der nationalsozialistischen Agrarpolitik. Ein Beitrag zur Leitungsproblematik in zentralgelenkten Wirtschaftssystemen", *Zeitschrift fuer Wirtschafts- und Sozialwissenschaften*, vol.4 (1974), pp.335-61.

64. Blaich, "Wirtschaft und Ruestung in Deutschland 1933-1939", pp.52-3; Gruenberger, *Social history*, pp.199-216.

65. John E. Farquharson, *The Plough and the Swastika: The NSDAP and Agriculture in Germany 1928-45* (SAGE, London, 1976), pp.221-48; Petzina, *Autarkiepolitik*, p.95.

66. Blaich, "Wirtschaft und Ruestung in Deutschland 1933-1939", p.53.

67. Eckart Teichert, *Autarkie und Grossraumwirtschaft in Deutschland 1930-1939. Aussenwirtschaftliche Konzeptionen zwischen Wirtschaftskrise und Zweitem Weltkrieg* (Oldenbourg, Munich, 1984), p.38.

68. Doerte Doering, *Deutsche Aussenwirtschaftspolitik 1933-35. Die Gleichschaltung der Aussenwirtschaft in der Fruehphase des nationalsozialistischen Regimes* (Diss. rer.pol., Berlin, 1969), pp.56-70. See also Joachim Radkau, "Entscheidungsprozesse und Entscheidungsdefizite in der deutschen Aussenwirtschaftspolitik 1933-1940, *Geschichte und Gesellschaft*, vol. 2 (1976), pp.33-65.

69. Heinz Pentzlin, *Hjalmar Schacht. Leben und Wirken einer umstrittenen Persoenlichkeit* (Ullstein, Berlin, 1980).

70. Willi A. Boelcke, *Die deutsche Wirtschaft 1930-1945. Interna des Reichswirtschaftsministeriums* (Droste, Duesseldorf, 1983), p.109.

71. Teichert, *Autarkie und Grossraumwirtschaft*, p.27; Roland Schoenfeld, "Deutsche Rohstoffsicherungspolitik in Jugoslawien 1934-1944", *Vierteljahrshefte fuer Zeitgeschichte*, vol. 24 (1976), pp.215-58; Wolfgang Schumann, "Aspekte und Hintergruende der Handels- und Wirtschaftspolitik Hitlerdeutsch-

lands gegenueber Jugoslawien 1933 bis 1945" in *Bulletin des Arbeitskreises "Zwei-ter Weltkrieg"*, No. 3 (1973), pp.5-38.

72. See on the controversy on aims and results of German foreign trade policy in the late 1930s Alan S. Milward, "The Reichsmark Bloc and the international economy", in Gerhard Hirschfeld and Lothar Kettenacker (eds), *The "Fuehrer State": Myth and reality. Studies on the structure and politics of the Third Reich* (Klett-Cotta, Stuttgart, 1981), pp.377-413 and Bernd-Juergen Wendt, "Suedosteuropa in der nationalsozialistischen Grossraumwirtschaft", in the same volume, pp.414-28. See also Alfred Kube, "Aussenpolitik und «Grossraumwirtschaft». Die deutsche Politik zur wirtschaftlichen Integration Suedosteuropas 1933 bis 1939", in Helmut Berding (ed.), *Wirtschaftliche und politische Integration in Europa im 19. und 20. Jahrhundert* (Vandenhoeck and Ruprecht, Goettingen, 1984), pp.185-211; Bernd-Juergen Wendt, "Deutschland in der Mitte Europas. Grundkonstellationen der Geschichte", *Deutsche Studien*, vol. 76 (1981), pp.220-75; Larry Neal, The economics and finance of bilateral clearing agreements: Germany 1934-8", *Economic History Review*, Second Series, vol. 32 (1979), pp.391-404; Norbert Schausberger, "Oesterreich und die nationalsozialistische Anschluss-Politik", in Manfred Funke (ed.), *Hitler, Deutschland und die Maechte. Materialien zur Aussenpolitik des Dritten Reiches* (Athenaeum, Droste, Kronberg/Ts., Duesseldorf, 1978), pp.728-58; Alice Teichova, "Ueber das Eindringen des deutschen Finanzkapitals in das Wirtschaftsleben der Tschechoslowakei vor dem Muenchener Diktat. Ein Beitrag zur oekonomischen Geschichte des Imperialismus", *Zeitschrift fuer Geschichtswissenschaft*, vol. 5 (1957), pp.1160-80.

73. Hans-Erich Volkmann, "Aussenhandel und Aufruestung in Deutschland 1933 bis 1939", in Friedrich Forstmeier and Hans-Erich Volkmann (eds), *Wirtschaft und Ruestung am Vorabend des Zweiten Weltkrieges* (Droste, Duesseldorf, 1975), pp.101-9.

Chapter Seven

THE SECOND WORLD WAR

August 1939

As the development of production and the results of the Four
Year Plan showed, the German economy was inadequately prepared for war. The food and raw materials situation was sufficient
for a short, but by no means for a long war. Leading *Wehrmacht*
officers argued that, at the outbreak of the Second World War,
the German economy was not as strong as it had been in 1914.
Enemies with a weak economic base could be overcome, but if
one or more of the leading powers entered the war, insurmount-
able problems could arise.[1]

The British historian Tim Mason put forward the thesis that
there were irreconcilable contradictions in the German economy
and society in 1938/9, which were mainly caused by an armament
policy ruining the economy. In a situation of full employment this
policy put unbearable strains on the labour market. These strains,
in combination with raw materials and foreign exchange problems
as well as inflationary tendencies, increased alarmingly. The only
way out was a war to aquire more resources, a *Raubkrieg*. To ease
the tensions within Germany, the invasion of Poland was a des-
perate attempt to forestall civil unrest at home which might en-
danger the National Socialist government. Mason argues that at
least the timing of the attack on Poland and the outbreak of the
Second World War was to large extent due to these socioeconomic problems.[2]

Indeed, several of Hitler's statements point in this direction. In
a monologue to the leaders of the armed forces in November 1937

Hitler mentioned expansionism as the only solution to Germany's otherwise gloomy economic prospects. He repeated these remarks in a speech to the armed forces' commanders in August 1939, a few days before the attack on Poland, when he said that "there is only the choice of going through with it or losing."[3]

Considering the issue of the relationship between economic and social problems in Germany and the outbreak of the Second World War it seems, however, that Mason's thesis has more against than in favour of it. It is hard to show that the National Socialist economy was in a greater state of crisis in August 1939 than, for example, in 1936. Besides, the term "crisis" is very difficult to come to grips with. Another interpretation comes much closer to reality than the one given above: the financial and economic crisis of 1938/9 was not the prerequisite for war but the outcome of a decision to go to war, a decision which had been made earlier.[4]

A *Blitzkrieg* economy?

The first three years of the Second World War have often been described as the *Blitzkrieg* period based on German "armament in width" (*Breitenruestung*) as opposed to the British or United States' "armament in depth" (*Tiefenruestung*). In Germany, Colonel - later General - Georg Thomas also favoured a comprehensive development of the basic industries on which armament production was founded, leading to armament in depth.[5] This type of war preparation, in which intensive research and development of new weapons were to play a major role, aimed at total war.

According to the historians who stress the role of *Blitzkrieg* and "armament in width", Hitler and the National Socialist leadership did not follow Thomas's suggestions. They preferred the more flexible concept of *Blitzkrieg* which was particularly well suited to the domestic political structure. Hitler tried to achieve his political objectives by short campaigns which took the enemies by surprise. Between these campaigns, there were breathing spaces, in which the armed forces prepared for their next enemy. By this, an uninterrupted long-term armament effort could be avoided. Also, by exploiting the conquered and occupied territories, the German military potential could be replaced continuously and the German people saved from a total exertion of their own powers. Germany had a high degree of armament readiness, but a low degree of armament-producing potential. Only from late 1941 onwards did the National Socialist government change its *Blitzkrieg*-concept.[6]

It cannot be denied that *ex post* this interpretation seems plausible. The problem, however, is whether the intentions and goals of the National Socialist government are correctly described by it. This does not seem to be the case. *Blitzkrieg* was not a strategy based on rational calculations and Hitler's intentions were probably not to wage a short war in the late 1930s and early 1940s, but a great war in the mid-1940s. If there was a *Blitzkrieg*, then it was *Blitzkrieg* by default.[7] By invading Poland he ran the risk of a large war resulting from it.

Germany's war preparations cannot be described as "limited armament"; they suggest that a total war was intended. Although there were deficiencies in armament research and development the naval plans - especially the Z-Plan - and also plans for aircraft production lead to the conclusion that the economy was geared towards total war. The same goes for the huge investments of the late 1930s, like hydrogenation plants and aircraft factories.[8] As far as German military expenditure is concerned, no break is discernible between a "*Blitzkrieg*" period with "limited armament" up to the end of 1941 and a "Total War period" thereafter. Military spending rose constantly between 1940 and 1944. Not only was there no abrupt change in 1942 but the greatest percentage increase took place in the years 1939-1941.[9]

Government and industry 1939-1945

Similar to the problem of the role of big business in the National Socialist rise to power, the relationship between state policy and industry during the Second World War has been the subject of a lively debate among historians.[10] One of the results is that a clear-cut distinction between "state" or "government" on the one hand and "industry" on the other is difficult to make. Interests were often similar and institutions developed in which both state officials and industrialists were represented.

The view that the National Socialist government in general and Hitler in particular were merely puppets in the hands of "big business" and "monopoly capitalism"[11] is not tenable. Without being apologetic to big business it has to be pointed out that state owned companies like the *Reichswerke Hermann Goering* played

Figure 7.1:   National income and government expenditure of the "Greater German Reich" 1940-1944 [a]

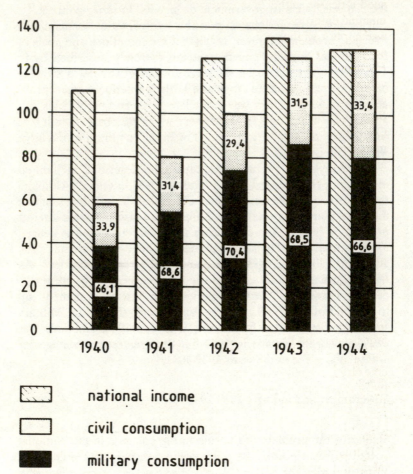

national income

civil consumption

military consumption

Note: [a] In RM thousand million (current prices). The figures denote the share of civil and military expenditure in total government expenditure (in per cent).

Source: Willi A. Boelcke, "Kriegsfinanzierung im internationalen Vergleich", in Friedrich Forstmeier and Hans-Erich Volkmann (eds), *Kriegswirtschaft und Ruestung 1939-1945* (Droste, Duesseldorf, 1977), p.56

an important role in National Socialist economic and foreign policy from 1937/8 onwards. The *Reich* or, to be exact, the *Reich* Ministry of Economic Affairs, held more than 90 per cent of the

Reichswerke's ordinary shares. In the west Hermann Goering, in order to get the Lorraine industry going again, early in 1941 issued a decree authorising a trustee system and allocating the remaining enterprises to the *Reich*. Paul Pleiger, head of the *Reichswerke*, put together a list of firms to be taken over by the *Reichswerke* and reorganised under a general holding company, the *Huettenverwaltung Westmark*.[12] In the east there were similar developments in the mining and iron and steel sector. At the beginning of 1941 Pleiger set up an iron and steel monopoly called *Berg- und Huettenwerksgesellschaft Ost* (Mining and Iron and Steel Company East), which had a monopoly of coal, iron ore and manganese. This company forced local labour to work in its mines and iron and steel works and compulsorily transferred skilled personnel to the east. There was a monopoly in the oil industry, the *Kontinentale Oel*, and in textiles, the *Ostfasergesellschaft* (Textile Fibre Company East). In the case of the *Huettenwerksgesellschaft* Goering made several large Ruhr firms take over Russian installations and run them as trustees, a method similar to that practised in Lorraine. The Ruhr companies were anything but enthusiastic about the idea of investing money in this firm and sending engineers there who could be better employed at home.

However, to generalise from cases like this would yield a distorted picture. It is certainly not correct to assume that reluctant industrialists had generally to be forced by state officials to invest capital in countries belonging to the *Grosswirtschaftsraum*. The contrary is usually true. There were often converging interests between government and industry. It seems that by the end of the 1930s a substantial part of German industry had decided to support the National Socialist government in its objective to expand economically and politically into the east.

During the Second World War the distinction between government and industry became increasingly blurred. German industrialists assumed administrative functions or became members of committees set up by the state. On a regional basis, economic chambers (*Gauwirtschaftskammern*) developed with economic advisors (*Gauwirtschaftsberatern*), who were normally industrialists. On a state level research institutions, financed by industry and its federations, worked out the foundations of political decisions for the *Reich* Ministry of Economic Affairs. Although it is true that the industrial autonomy was sometimes impaired by the National Socialist state, German industrialists often had a sphere of "relative autonomy" during the Second World War.[13]

Finance

To finance the Second World War income and excise taxes were raised shortly after the outbreak of the war, in contrast to the First World War, when taxes were not raised until 1916. Another dissimilarity was "indirect finance", the continuous funding of short- into long-term debt by secret negotiation with banks, savings banks and insurance companies. During 1914-18 war finance in Germany had also been characterised by periodic public fundings with bonds sold to the public.[14]

Tax increases on income and consumption were comparatively moderate during the Second World War. The top marginal tax rate for yearly incomes of RM 10,000 was 13.7 per cent in 1941 compared to 23.7 per cent in Great Britain.[15] Additional war charges were levied on income and corporation taxes from late 1939 onwards as well as additions to indirect taxes (tobacco, alcoholic beverages). In order to keep the German population in reasonably good humour, these surcharges were rather modest, but there were still numerous complaints about them. About one-third of the *Reich's* total expenditures during the Second World War, which amounted to about RM 1.471 thousand million, were financed by taxes or other internal revenue. The government received roughly one-fifth from long- and medium-term loans, which banks and related organisations had to make available to the *Reich*. By this "noiseless war finance" the saver or insurance policy holder became a creditor of the *Reich* without, in most cases, being aware of it. Another third was covered by credits from the *Reichsbank* in exchange for treasury bills and other short-term *Reich* securities. The rest - about an eighth - came from war contributions and occupation costs. It has to be pointed out, however, that during the Second World War the defeated nations' burden exceeded war contributions and occupation costs. They had to export low-priced commodities which were sold in Germany at considerably higher prices. Thus the *Reich* received revenues to pay for her debts, which by the end of April 1945 had reached the enormous amount of almost RM 388 thousand million as compared to about 31 thousand million at the outbreak of the war.[16]

Contrary to the First World War there was no systematic consolidation of the floating short-term debt and also no subscription to loans by the public.[17] Apart from the dramatic increase of the total debt and the stagnation of the funded debt during the last

Table 7.1: Development of the public debt 1939-1945 [a]

	Fun-ded debt[b]	In per cent	Floa-ting debt	In per cent	Total	Yearly increase
31 Dec. 1939	26.96	65.6	14.13	34.4	41.10	13.86
31 Dec. 1940	43.04	56.7	32.79	43.3	75.84	34.74
31 Dec. 1941	64.23	51.4	60.63	48.6	124.87	49.03
31 Dec. 1942	87.62	47.7	95.97	52.3	183.59	58.72
31 Dec. 1943	110.3	43.6	143.2	56.4	253.5	69.9
31 Dec. 1944	131.8	37.9	216.3	62.1	348.1	94.6
31 Mar. 1945	138.4	37.6	229.7	64.4	368.1	
21 Apr. 1945	41.3	36.4	246.6	63.6	387.9	

Notes: [a] In RM thousand million. The debts of the German postal services, railways and motorway administration are not included. The same goes for tax-anticipation bonds issued until 1940 and the Mefo exchange bills until 1938.
  [b] Medium- and long-term Reich loans and treasury bonds partly placed in foreign countries.
  To the total given above has to be added the sum of roughly RM 63.8 thousand million consisting mainly of clearing obligations, payments for wages, salaries etc., which had not been made by the end of the war, loans by countries like Italy, Denmark and Norway, Mefo exchange bills and tax-anticipation bonds.

Source: Willi A. Boelcke, "Kriegsfinanzierung im internationalen Vergleich", in Friedrich Forstmeier and Hans-Erich Volkmann (eds), *Kriegswirtschaft und Rue-stung 1939-1945* (Droste, Duesseldorf, 1977), p.52.

war years, the increase of the floating debt from 1943 onwards is particularly striking. It shows that in the last three war years public finance had gone completely out of control.

The main means of public finance which had been used already before the war were interest bearing *Reich* loans with a maturity of 20 to 30 years, interest bearing treasury bonds (maturity first 5 then 22 years), the no interest bearing treasury bonds (*U Schaetze*,

6 months maturity), and finally the no interest bearing *Reich* bills of exchange (*Reichsschatzwechsel*), which, from 1942 onwards, played a prominent role. Also, "iron saving" (*eisernes Sparen*) has to be mentioned: interest on such deposits, which had been paid into an "iron saving account" were, up to a certain amount, not subject to taxation. During the Second World War interest rates gradually decreased (for *Reich* loans from 4.5 per cent in 1939 to 3.5 per cent in 1941) with the *Reich* practically the only borrower. The government made use of the funds available to it thus curbing private investment and purchasing power. From 1939 to 1944 private consumption was reduced by about 50 per cent.[18]

Another means of war finance was the "national credit offices" (*Reichskreditkassen*), which issued *Reichskreditkassenscheine* (special bank notes) for use in occupied territories. These notes, the "fast troops of the *Reichsbank*", were issued and used by German authorities and troops in anticipation of "occupation costs" and clearing arrangements. This "occupation money" was changed by the central banks into the currency of the respective occupied country and later deducted from the "occupation costs". The National Socialist government charged Belgium, for example, occupation costs of 1 thousand million Belgian francs a month and raised this sum to 1.5 thousand million in 1941. There was a German deficit in the clearing that reached 1 thousand million Belgian francs a month in the second half of 1941 and rose further to 2.5 thousand million by March 1942. While *Reichskreditkassenscheine* were used in occupied countries at overvalued rates, *Wehrmachtsbeihilfegeld* (Army emergency money) was issued to German troops in friendly or satellite countries like Hungary or Roumania. This was denominated in marks and could be spent locally at regular exchange rates equal to those in the clearing. How much Germany gained from occupied territories during the war is difficult to estimate. A figure of RM 85 thousand million - not including war booty - might be realistic.[19]

During the Second World War prices rose only slightly. In spite of an increasing surplus of spending power the cost of living index increased by only 12 per cent from 1939 to 1944. Bank note circulation rose from RM 8.7 thousand million in mid-1939 to 24.4 thousand million by late 1942 and 52.8 thousand million by 1945. This shows that, apart from additional taxation, loans from the public and the exploitation of occupied territories, expansion in the money supply was a major method of National Socialist war finance. Only at the end of the war, however, was there an "open inflation". Until 1944 price and wage controls were, in spite of "grey" and "black" markets, fairly effective and inflationary tendencies were curbed.[20]

Trade and economic exploitation in the "European war economy"

"The basic problem of the German people is", Hitler said in March 1939, "to make sure that the sources, from which the raw materials so important for Germany's welfare can be obtained are always available." Therefore German rule had to be extended to Poland to secure the delivery of Polish agrarian products and coal. The same applied to Hungary and Roumania. After the Polish surrender they, as well as Yugoslavia, were to be made subject to Germany's wishes and to supply agricultural products and mineral oil.[21]

According to several computations, "Greater Germany" was only able to provide 84 per cent of its foodstuffs, but, together with the *Generalgouvernement* (part of Poland), the Protectorate Bohemia and Moravia and Slovakia, this figure increased to 87 per cent. If some central European states and the Soviet Union are added, the figure amounted to 96 per cent. Also, the supply situation of coal, iron and light metals was quite favourable. The agrarian countries in the European south-east possessed many of the natural resources which "Greater Germany" needed most. Roumania and Hungary supplied mineral oil; manganese for alloyed steel production was available in most of the countries in south-eastern Europe. There were extensive antimony deposits in the Hungarian-Slovakian border mountains, and chromium ores, needed for the production of special steels, in Yugoslavia, Greece and Turkey.

In spite of these assets several shortcomings have to be mentioned. As the war went on, it became clear that the iron ore, non-iron metals and energy supplies would hardly be sufficient for the German war economy. After the occupation of Denmark, Norway, Belgium, the Netherlands and parts of France many National Socialist leaders and especially Hitler regarded the raw material supplies of the Soviet Union as the ultimate way out of these problems.[22]

By the spring of 1940 the German foreign trade area extended to Central and South-Eastern Europe, Italy, Switzerland, Eastern Europe and parts of Asia, the states bordering on the Baltic as well as Belgium and Holland. In this trading area Germany played the key role as a supplier of industrial products and a buyer of foodstuffs and raw materials.[23] However, it is misleading to call the occupied areas Germany's trading partners, because they usually had to deliver their goods to Germany without proper compensation and were often obliged to negotiate a bilateral trading agreement with Germany from a weak position. The balance of trade was kept in clearing accounts. The German government often overvalued its own currency and ascribed arbitrarily low prices to exports from other countries. At the centre of all transactions was the *Deutsche Verrechnungskasse* (German clearing office) in Berlin.[24]

In 1939 and 1940 various trade agreements were concluded with Roumania. The agreement of March 1939 was followed by the "Mineral Oil - Arms Pact" of 29 May 1940, which envisaged the exchange of Roumanian mineral oil deliveries for German weapons. Raw material supplies in the Soviet Union were equally extensive with mineral oil, grain and phospates particularly attractive for Germany. German officials proposed to send engineering experts to the Soviet Union in order to assist in increasing production. Germany also needed the Soviet Union as a transit country for maintaining and intensifying German economic relations with the Middle and Far East, especially Iran, Afghanistan, Japan and Manchukuo.[25] After the German-Russian trade agreement of 11 February 1940 it soon became clear, however, that German-Soviet trade was beset with problems. The Soviets compiled a "list of wishes" which comprised items of the most recently developed and most sophisticated German war material. *IG Farben* were not at all keen on the idea of handing over any of their secret production technologies to the Soviets, especially the process of toluol production needed for producing aircraft gasoline. Apart from this, Germany found it difficult to let the Soviet Union have machinery which she needed badly herself.

Also, there was the danger of becoming dependent on supplies from Russia. German politicians complained about the Soviet Union's "special position" in the "Greater Economic Area" dominated by Germany. The economic power of the Soviet Union, the economic pressure she could exercise on the nations bordering on the Baltic and - last but not least - the "spirit of Bolshevism" were, they argued, a danger to Europe, which Germany had to eliminate one way or another. Already before the outbreak of the Second World War Hitler had emphasised the importance of Soviet grain supplies for Germany when he said: "I need the Ukraine so that it is not possible to starve us as happened to Germany in the First World War."[26]

For the National Socialist war economy France was of particular importance. She had to pay occupation costs originally fixed at RM 20 million a day. The value of the franc was fixed at 20:1 against the *Reichsmark*, which meant an over-valuation of the latter of about 50 per cent.

There was a rising trend of imports and exports in the period September 1939 to September 1941. The longer the war progressed the more were exports exceeded by imports.

By the end of 1940 16 countries already belonged to the central clearing agreement. Some German politicians intended to extend central clearing and make it the basis of a European trade system with the *Reichsmark* as a sort of key currency and Berlin as the international financial centre. However, the consumption of war material, especially after the winter of 1941, made it impossible for Germany to provide the goods necessary for export. There was also the problem of transport facilities - railway engines and carriages, lorries - which the *Wehrmacht* required. All this resulted in a growing clearing deficit for the *Reich*. At the end of 1940 it amounted to "only" 953 million *Reichsmark*, but with the beginning of the campaign against the Soviet Union it rose dramatically and had reached well over RM 3.251 thousand million one year later and about RM 28 thousand million in mid-1944.[27]

The National Socialist government had hoped to obtain vast amounts of foodstuffs and raw materials from an invaded and conquered Soviet Union. Apart from the grains in the Ukraine, mineral oil of the Caucasus, the iron ore and manganese deposits of Krivoi Rog and Nikopol attracted the invaders.[28] After the invasion the results were somewhat disappointing, because of the Soviet scorched earth policy. The Germans did a lot of reconstruction work to make the plants and installations usable again, but these efforts were only partly successful because of the lack of raw materials and tools. Only 10 to 20 per cent of the regular coal production from the coalfields east of the Dnieper could be obtained. The case with manganese was different: during the German occupation of the Soviet Union roughly 90 per cent of the manganese used in Germany came from there.[29]

The occupied countries in Western Europe but also those in Scandinavia made the largest contribution to the German war economy. France was of particular importance: two-thirds of the goods carried there in trains were destined for the German econ-

Figure 7.2: Germany's foreign trade, September 1939 to September 1941 (in RM million)

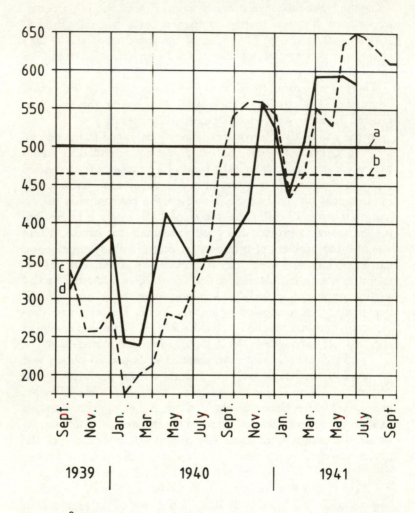

Notes: [a] Average monthly total imports 1938;

[b] Average monthly total exports 1938;

[c] Total imports;

[d] Total exports.

Source: Hans-Erich Volkmann, "NS-Aussenhandel im geschlossenen Kriegswirt-schaftsraum (1939-1941)", in Friedrich Forstmeier and Hans-Erich Volkmann (eds), *Kriegswirtschaft und Ruestung 1939-1945* (Droste, Duesseldorf, 1977), p.132.

omy. The figures for Belgium, the Netherlands and Luxembourg were not much lower. Norway lost about 25 per cent of her national income in 1940 and about 40 per cent in 1943.

The decree of 2 August 1940 issued by the Four Year Plan office stipulated that German ownership of foreign enterprises was to be increased. Whereas industrialists' plans to acquire firms and capital in the occupied territories of Western Europe received state support only when strategic interests were at stake, the policy towards Eastern Europe aimed at transferring assets to German ownership. In order to increase industrial output the Ministry of Armament and Munitions headed by Albert Speer in 1943 ordered an increase of production in the occupied territories. In September 1943 an agreement was reached between Speer and Jean Bichelonne, the French Minister of Industrial Production, to extend the production committees and rings, which controlled war production in Germany, into France. By that time several German industrialists had been appointed as trustees to control firms in France.

German, as well as some Belgian and French industrialists, too, found the idea of creating a European Customs Union (*Wirtschaftsunion*) attractive. There were plans to set up a unified system of transportation and to found several European multinational corporations. Many French, Dutch, Belgian and Luxembourg entrepreneurs found it profitable to do business in "New Order Europe". There were agreements on the foundation of a Franco-German dyestuff monopoly headed by IG Farben and of a synthetic fibre consortium with French and German producers.[30]

Labour

During the first two years of the Second World War new institutions and laws to regulate labour were few, because these had already been created in the second half of the 1930s. The mobilisation of labour did not increase significantly until the beginning of 1942, when a new, intensified stage of labour mobilisation was reached. During the first war year the National Socialist government benefited from its *Blitz*-victories which strained Germany's economic resources, and especially labour, only to a limited degree.[31]

Table 7.2: Mobilisation of labour 1939-1944[a]

Year[b]	German labour		Total	Foreign labour and prisoners of war	Total (German and foreign labour and prisoners of war)
	male	female			
1939	24.5	14.6	39.1	0.3	39.4
1940	20.4	14.4	34.8	1.2	36.0
1941	19.0	14.1	33.1	3.0	36.1
1942	16.9	14.4	31.3	4.2	35.5
1943	15.5	14.8	30.3	6.3	36.6
1944	14.2	14.8	29.0	7.1	36.1
1944[c]	13.5	14.9	28.4	7.5	35.9

Notes: [a] In million. Territory as by 31 December 1937, including Austria and the Sudeten- and Memel region; [b] End of May; [c] End of September

Source: Rolf Wagenfuehr, *Die deutsche Industrie im Kriege 1939-1945* (Duncker and Humblot, Berlin, 2nd ed. 1963), p.139

There was a steady decline of German male labour, due mainly to recruitment for the Armed Forces (1.4 million recruited by 1939, 5.7 million by 1940, 11.2 million by 1943). This drain could not be compensated by female German labour the mobilisation of which remained more or less constant. As in the pre-war period the social ideas of the National Socialists prevented any fuller mobilisation. Also, social allowances for wives of servicemen were comparatively high.

The National Socialist regime tried to compensate these deficiencies by integrating a rapidly rising number of foreign workers into the German war economy. By 1944 their share was about 21 per cent of the total labour force in Germany. After the armistice with France on 22 June 1940 roughly one million French prisoners of war were retained in Germany. An even higher number was recruited from the 5.1 million Russian prisoners of war. As with German workers, mobilisation of foreign labour was comparatively low until the beginning of 1942. In May 1940 Poles constituted by far the majority of foreign workers.[32]

In May 1942 about 45 per cent of the foreign civilian workers and 54 per cent of the prisoners of war were employed in agriculture.[33] With the need for substantial increases in armament production this picture changed, however, during the next two years. Civilian foreign labour worked increasingly in armament manufacture with a share of 30 per cent in November 1944. Airframe factories with repetitive assembly-line operations were considered particularly suitable for foreign labour.[34] With increasing labour shortages, even foreign prisoners of war worked in German armament factories. There were, however, security problems and cases of sabotage which increased after mid-1943.[35]

On 21 March 1942 Fritz Sauckel was appointed Plenipotentiary-General for Labour. In a series of notorious "Sauckel-actions" he recruited labour - often by force - from the whole European continent. In 1942 alone more than 1.5 million foreign workers arrived in Germany and Sauckel even tried to increase this figure during the next two years.[36] The National Socialists graded foreign labour according to their origin with workers from Western Europe at the top and workers from Eastern Europe at the bottom of the scale. People from the East were often treated cruelly by the members of the "master race". More than three million Russian soldiers died as prisoners of war; the survivors had to work in German factories, often under appalling conditions.[37] More than 50 per cent of the workers from Poland and the Soviet Union were women. German industrialists employed them willingly, because their work achievement was generally above average, their wages were conspicuously low and the benefits of German social legislation did not apply to them.[38]

Foreign workers could be made to work hard by an extension of control in the factories, by harsh disciplinary methods or by tight food rationing. The execution of offenders was to serve as a deterrent for others. However, from the second half of 1942 onwards, cases of flights from factories were quite frequent and increased rapidly after 1943. The workers fled because of extremely hard working conditions, lack of food and - from 1943 onwards - air attacks. In the last two war years the National Socialist administration was definitely overtaxed in coping with the problem. Many of those who stayed in the factories often went on a "go slow" and, from 1944 onwards, did not appear for work in the factories at all. There were some strikes, politically motivated opposition and several cases of sabotage, but these did not occur frequently.[39]

The use of foreign labour is closely linked to concentration camps and the SS. The SS controlled a separate economic empire with several large concerns run on concentration camp labour, especially the "German Earth and Stone Works" (*Deutsche Erd- und Steinwerke, DEST*), which had numerous small assembly plants for bombs, rifles and aircraft parts, and the "German Equipment Works" (*Deutsche Ausruestungswerke, DAW*), which produced various armaments.[40] After the bombing of the Messerschmitt aircraft works at Regensburg the SS untertook aircraft production with concentration camp labour at their factories in Flossenbuerg and Mauthausen. Jet engines were produced in the SS plants Nordwerk and Mittelwerk, which operated underground in the Harz mountains with workers from concentration camps.[41] During the last two war years the infamous SS economic empire developed from an organisation engaged in war production to a body which took over control of complete sectors of the economy.[42]

There was constant competition for skilled labour between the armament industry and the Armed Forces. The war situation made it imperative to attempt a "total mobilisation" of the German population. A secret *Fuehrererlass* of 13 January 1943 decreed a "comprehensive mobilisation of men and women for the defense of the *Reich*" with compulsory registration of all males not yet registered from the age of sixteen to sixty-five and females from seventeen to fourty-five years of age. The government also had the right to close plants not considered necessary for the war economy and could send unemployed labour to the battlefields. The *Fuehrererlass* was particularly geared to female labour, but, for ideological reasons, only in a half-hearted way. Females often found it unattractive to take up employment because of wage discrimination - their male colleagues earned considerably more - and because of the comparatively good sustenance granted to wives of soldiers. For these reasons the results of Hitler's decree proved anything but satisfactory.[43]

Looking at employment as a whole during the Second World War, a structural change between the various branches of the German economy becomes visible. The share of labour employed in industry rose from 27.8 to 30.2 per cent; there was a rise espe-

cially in the capital goods industries. The share of artisan undertakings, the building industry and the consumer goods industries,
however, declined, the latter two from 13 to 7 per cent and from
33 to 21 per cent respectively.[44]

It is extremely difficult to make a reliable statement about the
development of real wages in the German war economy. Wage
rates rose only by 1.8 per cent in total between 1939 and 1944.
Weekly earnings rose by 9.6 per cent; and the rate of increase of
hourly and weakly earnings fell after 1941 compared to the
decade before. After 1943 there was probably an actual decline in
earnings. In view of the fact that workers in several industries, especially the aircraft industry, faced a dramatic increase of working
hours, the real wage concept is extremely difficult to apply.[45]

The issue of labour productivity is equally difficult. From the
middle of 1941 onwards officials discovered a decrease in the
performance of German labour due to long working hours,
insufficient nourishment and alarms at night. In the winter of 1941
much time was spent in obtaining food, clothes, coal and other
goods for daily use, which were in short supply. From 1942 onwards qualified workers, especially in the metal and chemical industries, had to join the armed forces in increasing numbers.
Generally, productivity of foreign workers was lower than that of
German labour.

Tentative statements about labour productivity can be made
only for specific branches of the economy. In the primary sector,
especially in mining, labour productivity declined from 1942 onwards. It stagnated in the consumer goods industry and increased
in the armaments industry after 1942. For industry as a whole,
there seems to have been a gradual rise especially in 1943. Increases in productivity were mainly due to rationalisation, attempts at mass production, but also to *Entfeinerungen*, the production of lower quality goods.[46]

Agriculture

In line with its autarky policy the National Socialist government
had, by the beginning of the Second World War, set up extensive
stocks of grain provisions. Bread grain stocks increased from 2.3
million tons in the years 1937-8 to 6.4 million in 1939; feed grain
supplies amounted to 2.4 million tons. If conditions of agricultural
output had remained similar to those of the immediate pre-war
period, only about 1 million tons of grain would have had to be

imported annually. By extending the cultivation of oil seeds, the "fat gap" was to be narrowed.[47]

In spite of well-sounding speeches and National Socialist rallies agricultural production in Germany during the Second World War declined steadily. Grain and potato production decreased by about 10 per cent, livestock production even more. From 1938/9 to 1943/4 the consumption of meat in Germany fell by about 40 per cent.

The main reason for this unsatisfactory development was insufficient labour. At the beginning of the war, agricultural workers from Poland and later numerous prisoners of war and civilian prisoners could not make good the rural exodus. Also, exemptions from military service were not as common in the agricultural sector as in the various branches of industry, especially in the armament industry.

Insufficient supplies of phosphorous and nitrogenous fertilizers, a relatively low degree of agricultural mechanisation and an inadequate number of livestock also created problems.[48] Military demands prevented an increase in tractor production; draught horses were moved away from the farms. Still, until 1944 no real famines occurred as during the First World War. Only at the end of the war were food rations lowered to subsistence levels and many people had to find additional food in order not to starve.

The comparatively adequate supply of food for the German population until 1944 was only made possible because large parts of the population in occupied territories and the prisoners of war in Germany had to be content with smaller rations. There were large differences - mainly on racial grounds - between the way Scandinavians or people from Western Europe on the one hand and Eastern Europeans on the other were treated.[49] The high hopes which the National Socialists had put on the grain supplies from the Ukraine did not materialise. In 1943 the Soviet Union's total contribution to the *Grossraumwirtschaft* was smaller than that of France or Denmark and even smaller than food imports from Italy. In the Soviet Union, the decline in the productivity of land and labour far exceeded that of the Western and Northern European countries. Those, too, had their agricultural problems, however: labour drafts by the occupying forces in France caused a decline of the pre-war French agricultural labour force by about 400,000 people. Also shortages of fertilizers, machinery and horses made themselves felt. A similar situation prevailed in Norway and other occupied countries.[50]

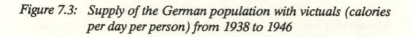

Figure 7.3: Supply of the German population with victuals (calories per day per person) from 1938 to 1946

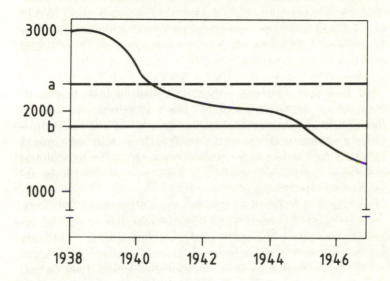

Notes: ^{a} basic requirements
^{b} subsistence level

Source: Friedrich-Wilhelm Henning, *Landwirtschaft und laendliche Gesellschaft in Deutschland* (2 vols., Schoeningh, Paderborn, 1976), vol. 2, p.228.

The organisation and development of armament production, 1940-1941

During the first three years of the war, the German economy was controlled by four organisations independent of each other: the Ministry of Economic Affairs, the War Economy and Armament Office, the Four-Year Planning Office, and the Ministry of Armament and Munitions.[51] By the Defense Law of May 1935 Schacht's Ministry of Economic Affairs had been made responsible for the preparation of the German economy for war. The Armed Forces' "War Economy and Armament Office" (*Wehrwirtschafts- und Ruestungsamt*) was founded in 1934 as an economic planning staff of the Ministry of War. As the three military branches resisted the foundation of a central procurement agency, the Office's powers were confined to gathering statistical data or pre-

127

paring economic intelligence on foreign countries. When the Ministry of War was abolished in 1938 the Supreme Command of the Armed Forces (*Oberkommando der Wehrmacht, OKW*) took over the War Economy and Armament Office. After the outbreak of the war the office's functions became more important, although its success in coordinating the procurement activities of army, navy and air force was still limited.

Additional to Goering's office of the Four-Year Plan founded in 1936, Hitler, in February 1940, established another agency, the Ministry of Armament and Munition (*Reichsministerium fuer Bewaffnung und Munition*), because he was dissatisfied with the military's handling of economic matters. The new ministry was responsible to him alone. Its foundation is typical of the National Socialists' - especially Hitler's - endeavour to overcome difficulties by establishing new institutions. Seldom were the leaders of the various institutions on amicable terms with each other. They considered themselves as rivals and quite often friction and partial paralysis resulted, instead of "healthy competition" and Darwinian "survival of the fittest".

Fritz Todt, the new Minister of Armament and Munitions, had a civil engineering background. He had been put in charge of the construction of the *Autobahnen* (superhighways) in the 1930s as Inspector General for Roads. Apart from this he was also Inspector General for Water and Power, Plenipotentiary for Building and head of the *Organisation Todt*, which, among other things, built western fortifications.[52] On 23 February 1940 Goering appointed Todt to a new post as "Inspector-General for Special Tasks in the Four-Year Plan".[53] His first task was to find ways of reducing consumption of scarce metals, especially copper, and to deal with problems of munitions production. Shortly afterwards, on 17 March 1940, Hitler appointed Todt as *Reichsminister* of Armament and Munitions.

Todt was of the opinion that engineers and businessmen, not civil servants or officers of the armed forces, were best suited for overcoming difficulties in industrial production by introducing new production techniques, substitutes for scarce commodities or rationalisation. His main innovation was in the organisation of armament production. Early in April 1940 he introduced a new structure of industrial organisation for manufacturers of munitions. All plants which produced similar types of munitions had to join in compulsory "working associations". The chairmen of these associations combined to form regional "munitions committees" and the chairmen of these participated in a central "main munitions committee". Todt's objective was to increase the "self-responsibility of industry". Industrialists, not state officials, had to distribute materials like steel and even munitions contracts.

Todt seems to have been an appropriate choice for the new post. Shortly after having taken office as Munitions Minister, production of army munitions increased by 40 to 70 per cent in the second quarter of 1940 compared to the autumn of 1939. In the third quarter it increased even more, reaching 60 to 90 per cent above the 1939 level.

However, Todt should not be given too much credit for these increases. The increase in the spring quarter came too soon after Todt's appointment to credit him for the success. Production of munitions decreased in the last two quarters of 1940 and the early autumn of 1941, whereas production of army weapons continued its upward trend.

It was clear to Todt as it was to Hitler that an increase of armament and munitions output was necessary. On 3 December 1941 Hitler decreed further rationalisation of production under military contracts. This was to be achieved by three methods: new mass production methods and simpler designs for equipment, concentration of production in plants with the best and most economical working methods and the construction of additional floorspace in order to replace losses of military equipment in the Soviet Union.[54]

On 22 December 1941 Todt ordered additional organisational changes with the introduction of "main committees" to organise the work of "special committees", which dealt with special types of munitions, armament or equipment. Five main committees were established: munitions, armament, armoured cars and tractors, *Wehrmacht* equipment and machinery. With the increasing need for armament mainly due to the losses in the Soviet Union and the beginning of the battle in the Atlantic, the *Fuehrerbefehl "Ruestung 1942"* (*Fuehrer* order "Armament 1942") of 10 January 1942 decreed further increases in armament, aircraft, flak, light alloys, mineral oil and *buna*.

At that time Todt was the central figure of German war production. On 6 February 1942 he invited the chairmen of the new production rings and committees to an inaugural meeting to establish a central control mechanism over the German war economy. Two days later he died in an airplane crash and was succeeded in all his important posts by Albert Speer. After his fatal accident there were rumours of sabotage, which, in view of the available evidence, were probably unfounded.

Growth and collapse of the German war economy, 1942-1945

Albert Speer, an ambitious and capable technocrat, followed Todt as munitions minister on 18 February 1942. Apart from this ministry, the Four-Year Plan organisation, the "War Economy and Armament Office", the Ministry of Economic Affairs, the Ministry of Labour, and the SS Main Office of Economics and Administration held independent power over German war production.[55]

As Munitions Minister Speer extended Todt's system of committees. Naval production was included by creating a main committee for shipbuilding. On 20 April 1942 Speer issued a decree which ordered the application of the committee system not only to armament and munitions but also to "end products important for war" (*kriegswichtige Fertigungszweige*) generally and to the production of component parts (*Zulieferungsproduktion*). Producers of end products were organised in main committees, special committees, and working committees, producers of component parts became members of main rings, special rings and working rings. Industrial rings could give orders to all firms in their line of production. Tank or lorry production, for example, would be organised by a committee, the production of cog-wheels by a ring. Speer called the thirteen main committees the "pillars of war production", which were held together by thirteen main rings.[56] Speer introduced development committees (*Entwicklungskommissionen*) which consisted of armed forces' officers and engineers in industry and had the task of organising, controlling and rationalising new technical developments and improving construction. There were no scientists in these development committees and too much emphasis was placed on production.

According to Speer, Walther Rathenau, who organised the German war economy in the First World War, was the real author of "industrial self-responsibility". This is to an extent true, but other roots must also be mentioned.[57] Walther Schieber, a senior official in Speer's ministry, traced the development of main committees and rings back to the business and trade groups (*Wirtschafts- und Fachgruppen*) of German industry in the 1920s. Also, an organisation for industrial rationalisation, the *Reichskuratorium fuer Wirtschaftlichkeit*, was active in the 1930s trying to improve industrial efficiency. Further models may have been the *Organisa-*

tion Todt with its various commissions in the armament field and industrial managers' responsibility for the production of war equipment or the *Industrierat des Reichsmarschalls fuer die Fertigung von Luftwaffengeraet* (Industrial Council of the Reich Marshall for the Production of Air Force Equipment) which General Ernst Udet had created in the spring of 1941.

Through the rings and committees which were extended throughout manufacturing industry *Zentrale Planung* (central planning) enforced its decisions.[58] In the spring of 1942 Speer had formed a central planning board which Hitler decreed officially on 15 April 1942. It consisted of only three members: Speer himself, Paul Koerner for the Four-Year Plan Office and the Ministry of Economic Affairs and Field Marshall Erhard Milch for the Armed Forces, especially the Air Force. The new institution's objective was to improve the direction of the war economy and the utilisation of material, above all raw material. It exerted a tight control of raw material allocation throughout the economy and thereby enforced a system of economic priorities. Each industrial branch had to justify its raw material demands before the *Zentrale Planung*.

Apart from occasional problems the system worked reasonably well. By the summer of 1942 general armament production was increased by fifty per cent with higher increases later. Still, the success of *Zentrale Planung* varied very much from industry to industry. Several industrial sectors were rather difficult to control, and Fritz Sauckel's operations in the labour market, which he did not coordinate with Speer's ministry, were not conducive to successful planning.

According to Speer's reports after the war, long-term planning was introduced in the spring of 1942. In May 1942 the "War Economy and Armament Office" was transferred from the High Command of the armed forces to his ministry.[59] From June 1942 onwards he controlled all naval production, in September 1943 he took over the complete responsibility for war production with the title of *Reichsminister fuer Ruestung und Kriegsproduktion* (Reichsminister for Armament and War Production).

As a reaction to increasing air attacks in 1943 and especially after February 1944 fighter production received a high priority. Speer and Milch agreed to form the *Jaegerstab* (Fighter Staff) on 1 March 1944 in order to increase fighter production substantially. If necessary and possible the working day for skilled labour was extended to 72 hours a week. After the introduction of the Fighter

Staff the output of fighters rose dramatically, as the following table shows.

Table 7.3: Fighter production in 1944 ª

	Newly produced	Repaired	Total
1943 July-December (monthly average)	1369	521	1890
1944:			
January	1340	419	1759
February	1323	430	1753
March	1830	546	2376
April	2034	669	2703
May	2377	647	3024
June	2760	834	3594
July	3115	935	4050
August	3051	922	3973
September	3538	776	4314

Note: ª Figures from Speer Ministry

Source: Alan S. Milward, *The German economy at war* (Athlone Press, London, 1965), p.146.

On 1 August 1944 the Fighter Staff was dissolved and the direction of aircraft production taken over by the newly-formed Armament Staff.

One of the reasons why armament production figures in Germany were lower than various planners had envisaged was the constant alterations and modifications. Although those were necessary in order to achieve the - largely imaginary - goal of "qualitative superiority", the only hope in turning the outcome of the war in Germany's favour was a substantially higher output of weapons and armament by mass manufacture. On 19 June 1944 Hitler decreed his "Concentration Order" (*Konzentrationserlass*), according to which modifications of mass produced weapons and equipment were forbidden. Only those development projects were to be continued which could be brought to a successful conclusion within six months. In July 1944 this production drive was followed by Goebbels' appointment as "Plenipotentiary-General for Total War", when all available labour was mobilised.

Goebbels' appointment and the new moves towards mass production were partly a result of the continuous bombing attacks by the British and American Air Forces. British bombing mainly aimed at destroying the major German industrial centres and cities. By attacking German residential areas at night the British bomber command aimed at demoralising the German population, an objective which was achieved only to a limited degree.[60] American strategy preferred daylight precision attacks against the vital parts of the German economy, especially power plants, refineries and the means of transport and communication. In October 1943 the highly concentrated ball-bearing works at Schweinfurt were attacked.

German officials and industrialists used mainly three measures to cope with these attacks: reconstruction, dispersion - also called "decentralisation" - and underground dispersal. Reconstruction was often successful to a degree which astonished the Allies, whereas dispersion proved difficult, especially in view of the transport and communication networks, which were vulnerable to Allied attacks. Underground production was practically the last resort. Although too many projects were started with too few workers, the results were far from negligible: by the beginning of April 1945 more than 700 - mainly small - factories operated underground.[61] In the Harz mountains, for example, two SS factories produced jet engines and parts for the V2.

In the second half of 1944 Allied bombers increasingly attacked synthetic fuel plants and the transportation system. In August 1944 the production of aviation gasoline was reduced to only 10 per cent of the March 1944 figures with the result that many German fighters were unable to take off. In their devastating attack on Dresden in February 1945 the Allied bombers met hardly any opposition, because the German fighters were grounded through lack of fuel.

As large parts of the transport system were destroyed, delivery of weapons and ammunition to the front became difficult indeed. Numerous junctions, stations and tunnels were out of order and the number of available freight cars and locomotives shrank steadily. Goering, showing his lack of technical expertise, suggested in all earnest building locomotives out of concrete, because of the severe lack of iron and steel.[62] Coal supplies, which to a

133

large extent depended on railway transportation, broke down, rivers were often not navigable because destroyed bridges blocked transport.

Another factor contributing to Germany's economic collapse was the shortage of labour, mainly of qualified workers. Because of the armed forces' demand for soldiers, the draft age was reduced from seventeen and a half to sixteen years of age, which cut the available labour force by 1.1 million between May and December 1944. The working week was extended from 48 to 60 hours with substantial effects on the quality of the work produced and on the workers' morale. This declined rapidly in view of the fact that the war was obviously lost for Germany. Highly qualified engineers, who so far had been exempted from fighting in the war, were now called to arms with negative consequences for armament production. The continuous loss of territory compounded the difficulties. Vital raw material supplies, like iron ore from Sweden or chrome from the Balkans, declined rapidly.

From the end of 1944 onwards even Hitler realised that the war was lost for Germany. If the enemy's advance could not be stopped, Germany should perish. This meant the demolition of military installations, transport and communication systems, factories and public utilities: the enemy should be prevented from making use of them. On 19 March 1945 Hitler decreed what was later called the "Nero Order", which commanded that the above measures should be taken.[63] Speer objected to this and modified the scorched earth policy (*Zerstoerung*) to one of paralysis (*Laehmung*) which meant that factories and power plants were not destroyed, but made unusable by taking away parts vital for their operation. By watering down the "Nero Order", numerous plants were preserved virtually intact.

Even so, at the end of the war the economic situation in Germany was severe enough. About 8 million Germans had been killed - the total number of victims in Europe was about 35 to 40 million people - the economic capacity of what was left to Germany had shrunk to about 70 to 75 per cent of the 1937 figures, industrial capacity to only 30 to 35 per cent.[64]

War production, technology and productivity

In the first years of the war German production was based on the concept of "qualitative superiority". After December 1941 it became obvious that in sheer quantity the Allies' armament output could not be equalled. Qualitative superiority meant that German engineers always had to be one step ahead in technological innovation and it rested on the idea that a very small qualitative advantage in military technology can have enormous strategic consequences.[65] Although German military technology was in several instances superior to that of the Allies, the advantage was not significant. There are also indications to the contrary, as in tank and radar development. After 1943, there was definitely nothing left of "qualitative superiority", in spite of National Socialist slogans which culminated in the myth of "wonder weapons".

Qualitative superiority implied the use of general purpose machine tools which made production flexible and allowed rapid innovations. A precondition for producing superior weapons would have been intensive research and especially development work. As to these, there were, however, serious deficiencies. Owing to the stipulations of the Versailles treaty, research and development in military technology were forbidden in Germany, although this prohibition was often evaded in the 1920s.[66] In the late thirties and early forties aircraft, tanks and warships were produced in great haste. A lack of qualified engineers and research and development personnel prevented an "armament in depth" with an emphasis on innovative potential. People like Goering never seem to have realised the importance of research and development. Aircraft designers reminded him not "of men to be taken seriously, but of jugglers and magicians, they seemed to him like a circus."[67] From the beginning in 1933 onwards, the German aircraft industry had been subsidised by the state. The firms were not subject to pressures from the market and there were few incentives for rationalisation. Waste during the production process, especially the squandering of aluminium, was notorious.[68]

Often the lack of raw materials made substitutions necessary. Apart from the well-known cases of synthetic fuel, rubber[69] and textiles there were other projects, some of them rather bizarre, like gold prospecting in the Rhine. Alas, yields were not even sufficient to pay for the fuel used for drilling.[70] There were also methods for developing fat and leather substitutes; again, as in the First World War, *Ersatz* was the word of the day. Tin free cans and coal dust engines were developed; the latter failed conspicuously.[71] Mineral oil production in Germany was increased at considerable cost but with little success.[72] The substitution of copper by aluminium was partly successful, however. Copper consumption was reduced from 448,000 tons in 1938 to 221,000 tons in 1943. Something similar goes for tin and nickel.[73]

The three most persistent bottlenecks in German armament production were an insufficient output of high-grade steel, inadequate supplies of component parts and a shortage of skilled labour. Components were produced by a large number of small scale artisans who hardly used any mass production methods.[74] From the autumn of 1941 onwards German industry tried to convert armament production to mass production. With the well sounding slogan "not quality *or* mass production, but quality *and* mass production" a "German style" of armament production was to be created.[75] At least as far as quantity is concerned the new production drive was successful.

In armament production there were three phases of rapid increase from February 1942 to July 1942, from October 1942 to May 1943 and from March 1944 to July 1944. Between these three periods of growth there are two phases of stagnation, from July to October 1942 and from May 1943 to February 1944. The period from July 1944 to the end of the war is marked by a gradual and - later - rapid decrease of armament production.

Normally, it took from three to nine months before an organisational innovation had any effect on actual output. Therefore the first increase in production from the beginning of 1942 to July 1942 cannot be linked with Speer's appointment as Minister of Armament and Munitions, but was the result of Todt's organisational changes. The second increase reflects successes in rationalisation and an enlarged labour force which grew by 10 per cent between May 1942 and May 1943. The main reasons for the increase from May 1943 to February 1944 are a decisive political turn towards armament production while curtailing the production of consumer goods and an increased mobilisation and exploitation of labour in Germany and in the "greater economic area".[76]

There are several instances of spectacular production increases, especially in aircraft production. The introduction of special flow-production machinery at the BMW plant in Augsburg in 1944, for example, cut production costs and raw materials use by half and reduced worktime per engine from 3,150 hours to 1,250. Similar reports came from Messerschmitt where, after the introduction of flow-production methods, construction time on the Me 109 was cut by 53 per cent during 1942 and a further 15 per cent in 1943. Although less aluminium was supplied in 1942 than in 1941, about 50 per cent more aircraft were produced.[77]

Figure 7.4: Index of total armament production 1942-1945 [a]

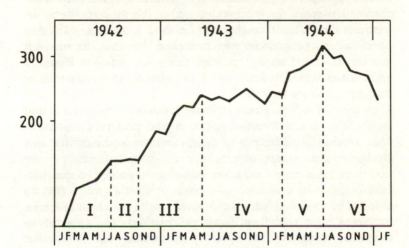

Note: [a] Semi-logarithmic scale

Source: Hans-Joachim Weyres-von Levetzow, *Die deutsche Ruestungswirtschaft von 1942 bis zum Ende des Krieges* (Diss. rer.pol., Munich, 1975), pp.200-1.

These success stories have, however, to be seen in the context of a production process, the reorganisation of which was beset with difficulties. These were particularly due to the shortages of factory space, lack of special machinery, frequent modifications of air-craft and shortage of qualified labour. Moreover, at the beginning of 1943, there was only one shift daily with ten hours work.

A case which illustrates the haphazardness of Hitler's and the Air Ministry's production policy particularly well is Henschel's attempt to build the Ju 188 bomber. In 1943 Henschel was as-signed the task of building this bomber by using the "hole system" developed by Dornier. This involved the mass pre-punching of holes to do away with the need for extensive jigs and dies. The system was very effective in large production runs provided no changes were made in the aircraft's design. Henschel tooled up for producing the Ju 188 by the "hole system". When ready for production the Air Ministry told the firm that it would not be producing the Ju 188 after all. The new objective was to produce the Me 410 - a larger version of the Me 210 fighter bomber. After eight months, when about 80 per cent of the tools needed had been completed, the programme was cancelled. Henschel was ordered to prepare for the production of the Ju 388, which the company did. When Henschel had finished about half of the preparations the programme was cancelled, because the war was nearing its end. Due to this administrative confusion Henschel had wasted between three and four million man-hours without producing a single aircraft.[78]

In spite of a higher output, mass production progressed only slowly. The armed forces despised it and preferred craftsmen, who could respond flexibly to design changes and modifications. Designers and military authorities both associated mass production with large-scale capitalism and shoddy goods. Special purpose machine-tools necessary for mass production were often resisted. The workshop with the *Meister* (master-craftsman) system preferred using traditional handwork methods and opposed attempts to undermine its skills by introducing new production methods using semi-skilled labour. Even by 1945 it proved impossible to apply time-and-motion studies in German factories.[79]

Although it is difficult to assess the development of productivity during the Second World War, there was most probably an increase in productivity from 1942 to 1944. In spite of opposition to rationalisation and mass production the number of workers employed in the armament industry increased by 9.8 per cent from May 1942 to May 1943 whereas output rose by 70 per cent.[80]

Shortly before the end of the war the contradiction between quality and quantity in armament production became visible to everybody. The "secret weapons" or "wonder weapons", the V1 and the V2, were to be the new and last means of demonstrating the qualitative superiority of German armaments.[81] However, these two weapons were particularly unfit to achieve this aim. They did not come "too late", as many contemporaries thought, but "too early" in the sense that their stage of development was far from complete. Because of their poor accuracy of aim they could be used only against area targets, not against strategically important targets. They therefore brought death and destruction to numerous civilian people. In their use to boost the Germans' morale, their overall political significance was mainly one of political stabilisation in Germany. While the V1 and V2 dropped about 5,900 tons of explosives on British soil, the British bombers dropped bombs weighing 437,570 tons on Germany during the Second World War.

Notes

1. Hans-Erich Volkmann, "Die NS-Wirtschaft in Vorbereitung des Krieges", in Militaergeschichtliches Forschungsamt (ed.), *Ursachen und Voraussetzungen der deutschen Kriegspolitik. Das Deutsche Reich und der Zweite Weltkrieg* (Deutsche Verlags-Anstalt, Stuttgart, 1979), vol. 1, p.366.
2. Timothy W. Mason, "Innere Krise und Angriffskrieg 1938/1939", in Friedrich Forstmeier and Hans-Erich Volkmann (eds), *Wirtschaft und Ruestung am Vorabend des Zweiten Weltkrieges* (Droste, Duesseldorf, 1975), pp.158-88. See also by the same author "Some origins of the Second World War", *Past and Present*, no. 29 (1964), pp.67-87 and *Arbeiterklasse und Volksgemeinschaft. Dokumente und Materialien zur deutschen Arbeiterpolitik 1936-1939* (Westdeutscher Verlag, Opladen, 1975).
3. Ian Kershaw, *The Nazi dictatorship. Problems and perspectives of interpretation* (Edward Arnold, London, 1985), p.55.
4. Michael Geyer, *Deutsche Ruestungspolitik 1860-1980* (Suhrkamp, Frankfurt am Main, 1984), p.153. See also Alan S. Milward, *War, economy and society 1939-1945* (University of California Press, Berkeley, Los Angeles, 1979), p.14 and Ludolf Herbst, "Die Krise des nationalsozialistischen Regimes am Vorabend des Zweiten Weltkrieges und die forcierte Aufruestung", *Vierteljahrshefte fuer Zeitgeschichte*, vol. 25 (1978), p.361. See also Richard J. Overy, "Germany, «domestic crisis» and war in 1939", *Past and Present*, Nr. 116 (1987), pp.138-68.
5. Georg Thomas, *Geschichte der deutschen Wehr- und Ruestungswirtschaft (1918-1943/45)*, ed. by Wolfgang Birkenfeld (Boldt, Boppard, 1966).
6. Alan S. Milward, "Der Einfluss oekonomischer und nicht-oekonomischer Faktoren auf die Strategie des Blitzkrieges", in Friedrich Forstmeier and Hans-Erich Volkmann (eds), *Wirtschaft und Ruestung am Vorabend des Zweiten Weltkrieges* (Droste, Duesseldorf, 1975), pp.189-201 and, by the same author, *The German economy at war* (Athlone Press, London, 1965), p.6. Also Ludolf Herbst, *Der totale Krieg und die Ordnung der Wirtschaft. Die Kriegswirtschaft im Spannungsfeld von Politik, Ideologie und Propaganda 1939-1945* (Deutsche Verlags-Anstalt, Stuttgart, 1982), p.98.
7. Richard J. Overy, *Goering, the "Iron Man"* (Routledge and Kegan Paul, London, 1984), p.103. Also, by the same author, ""Blitzkriegswirtschaft"? Finanzpolitik, Lebensstandard und Arbeitseinsatz in Deutschland 1939-1942", *Vierteljahrshefte fuer Zeitgeschichte*, vol. 36 (1988), pp.379-435 and "Mobilization for Total War in Germany", *English Historical Review*, vol. 103 (1988), pp.613-39. See also Rolf Dieter Mueller, "Die Mobilisierung der deutschen Wirtschaft für Hitlers Kriegfuehrung" in Militaergeschichtliches Forschungsamt (ed.), *Organisation und Mobilisierung des deutschen Machtbereichs. Das deutsche Reich und der Zweite Weltkrieg* (Deutsche Verlags-Anstalt, Stuttgart, 1988), vol. 5/1, pp.349-50.
8. Richard J. Overy, "Hitler's war and the German economy: A reinterpretation", *Economic History Review, Second Series*, vol. 35 (1982), p.282.
9. Overy, "Hitler's war and the German economy: A reinterpretation", p.283.
10. On the literature see especially Hans-Erich Volkmann, "Das Verhaeltnis von Grosswirtschaft und NS-Regime im Zweiten Weltkrieg", in Waclaw Dlugoborski (ed.), *Zweiter Weltkrieg und sozialer Wandel* (Vandenhoeck and Ruprecht, Goettingen, 1981), pp.87-116.
11. See for example Dietrich Eichholtz, *Geschichte der deutschen Kriegswirtschaft 1939-1945* (2 vols, Akademie-Verlag, Berlin (GDR), 1969, 1985).
12. Overy, *Goering*, p.124, and, for the following, pp.133-6. See also John R. Gillingham, *Industry and politics in the Third Reich* (Franz Steiner Verlag Wiesbaden, Stuttgart, 1985); Helmut Fiereder, *Reichswerke "Hermann Goering" in Oesterreich (1938-1945)* (Geyer, Wien, Salzburg, 1983); Stefan Karner, *Die Steier-*

mark im Dritten Reich 1938-1945. Aspekte ihrer politischen, wirtschaftlich-sozialen und kulturellen Entwicklung (Leykam, Graz, Wien, 1986) and, by the same author, *Kaerntens Wirtschaft 1938-1945. Unter besonderer Beruecksichtigung der Ruestungsindustrie* (Magistrat der Stadt Klagenfurt, Klagenfurt, 1976). Also Norbert Schausberger, "Die Bedeutung Oesterreichs fuer die deutsche Ruestung waehrend des Zweiten Weltkrieges", *Militaergeschichtliche Mitteilungen*, vol. 1972/1, pp.57-84 and Gerhard Th. Mollin, *Montankonzerne und "Drittes Reich". Der Gegensatz zwischen Monopolindustrie und Befehlswirtschaft in der deutschen Ruestung und Expansion 1936-1944* (Vandenhoeck and Ruprecht, Goettingen, 1988).

13. Volkmann,"Das Verhaeltnis von Grosswirtschaft und NS-Regime" in Dlugoborski (ed.), *Zweiter Weltkrieg und sozialer Wandel*, p.93.

14. Charles P. Kindleberger, *A financial history of Western Europe* (Allen & Unwin, London, 1984), p.405 and Karl-Heinrich Hansmeyer and Rolf Caesar, "Kriegswirtschaft und Inflation (1936-1948)" in Deutsche Bundesbank (ed.), *Waehrung und Wirtschaft in Deutschland 1876-1975* (Knapp, Frankfurt am Main, 1976, p.403. See also Fritz Federau, *Der zweite Weltkrieg: Seine Finanzierung in Deutschland* (Wunderlich, Tuebingen, 1962).

15. Dietmar Petzina, *Die deutsche Wirtschaft in der Zwischenkriegszeit* (Steiner, Wiesbaden, 1977), p.155.

16. Willi A. Boelcke, "Kriegsfinanzierung im internationalen Vergleich" in Friedrich Forstmeier and Hans-Erich Volkmann (eds), *Kriegswirtschaft und Ruestung 1939-1945* (Droste, Duesseldorf, 1977), pp.52-3.

17. Hansmeyer and Caesar, "Kriegswirtschaft und Inflation" in Deutsche Bundesbank (ed.), *Waehrung und Wirtschaft in Deutschland 1876-1975*, p.399.

18. Boelcke, "Kriegsfinanzierung" in Forstmeier and Volkmann (eds), *Kriegswirtschaft und Ruestung 1939-1945*, pp.50-1.

19. Kindleberger, *Financial history*, p.405.

20. Hansmeyer and Caesar, "Kriegswirtschaft und Inflation" in Deutsche Bundesbank (ed.), *Waehrung und Wirtschaft in Deutschland 1876-1975*, p.403 and Karl Hardach, *The political economy of Germany in the twentieth century* (University of California Press, Berkeley, Los Angeles, London, 1980), p.85.

21. Hans-Erich Volkmann, "NS-Aussenhandel im «geschlossenen» Kriegswirtschaftsraum (1939-1941)" in Friedrich Forstmeier and Hans-Erich Volkmann (eds), *Kriegswirtschaft und Ruestung 1939-1945* (Droste, Duesseldorf, 1977), p.93.

22. Volkmann, "NS-Aussenhandel" in Forstmeier and Volkmann (eds), Kriegswirtschaft und Ruestung 1939-1945, pp.110, 116.

23. Herbst, *Der totale Krieg*, pp.130-1.

24. Milward, *War, economy and society*, p.139.

25. Hans-Joachim Braun,"Technology transfer under conditions of war: German aero-technology in Japan during the Second World War", *History of Technology*, vol. 11 (1986), p.5.

26. Rolf-Dieter Mueller, "Von der Wirtschaftsallianz zum kolonialen Ausbeutungskrieg", in Militaergeschichtliches Forschungsamt (ed.), *Der Angriff auf die Sowjetunion. Das Deutsche Reich und der Zweite Weltkrieg* (Deutsche Verlags-Anstalt, Stuttgart, 1983), vol. 4, pp.98-189; also, by the same author, "Industrielle Interessenpolitik im Rahmen des Generalplans Ost", *Militaergeschichtliche Mitteilungen* 1981/1, pp.101-41.

27. Bernd Martin, "Friedensplanungen der multinationalen Grossindustrie (1932 bis 1940) als politische Strategie", *Geschichte und Gesellschaft*, vol. 2 (1976), p.157.

28. Milward, *War, economy and society*, pp.144-63.

29. Matthias Riedel, "Bergbau- und Eisenhuettenindustrie in der Ukraine unter deutscher Besatzung (1941-1944)", *Vierteljahrshefte fuer Zeit-*

geschichte, vol. 21 (1973), pp.245-84. See also Christoph Buchheim, "Die besetzten Laender im Dienste der deutschen Kriegswirtschaft waehrend des Zweiten Weltkrieges", *Vierteljahrshefte fuer Zeitgeschichte*, vol. 34 (1986), pp.117-45.

30. Gillingham, *Industry and politics*, pp.147-8.

31. Dietmar Petzina, "Die Mobilisierung deutscher Arbeitskraefte vor und waehrend des Zweiten Weltkrieges", *Vierteljahrshefte fuer Zeitgeschichte*, vol. 18 (1970), pp.451-2.

32. Ulrich Herbert, *Fremdarbeiter. Politik und Praxis des "Auslaender-Einsatzes" in der Kriegswirtschaft des Dritten Reiches* (Dietz, Berlin, Bonn, 1985), pp.67-95. See also: Eva Seeber, *Zwangsarbeiter in der faschistischen Kriegswirtschaft* (Deutscher Verlag der Wissenschaften, Berlin (GDR), 1964).

33. Edward L. Homze, *Foreign Labour in Nazi Germany* (Princeton University Press, Princeton, N.J., 1967), p.235.

34. Hans Pfahlmann, *Fremdarbeiter und Kriegsgefangene in der deutschen Kriegswirtschaft 1939-1945* (Verlag Wehr und Wissen, Darmstadt, 1968), pp.232-3.

35. Dietrich Eichholtz, Geschichte der deutschen Kriegswirtschaft 1939-1945 (2 vols, Akademie-Verlag, Berlin (GDR), 1969, 1985), vol. 2, pp.290-2.

36. Milward, *War, economy and society*, pp.221-6.

37. Christian Streit, *Keine Kameraden. Die Wehrmacht und die sowjetischen Kriegsgefangenen 1941-1945* (Deutsche Verlags-Anstalt, Stuttgart, 1978).

38. Herbst, *Fremdarbeiter*, p.335.

39. Anton J. Grossmann, "Fremd- und Zwangsarbeiter in Bayern 1939-1945", *Vierteljahrshefte fuer Zeitgeschichte*, vol. 34 (1986), pp.495-8.

40. Enno Georg, *Die wirtschaftlichen Unternehmungen der SS* (Deutsche Verlags-Anstalt, Stuttgart, 1963), pp.42-69.

41. Milward, *German economy*, pp.145-6.

42. Karl-Heinz Ludwig, *Technik und Ingenieure im Dritten Reich* (Droste, Duesseldorf, 1974), p.483.

43. Doerte Winkler, *Frauenarbeit im "Dritten Reich"* (Hoffmann and Campe, Hamburg, 1977); Marie-Luise Recker, *Nationalsozialistische Sozialpolitik im Zweiten Weltkrieg* (Oldenbourg, Munich, 1985), pp.184-5; Ursula von Gersdorff, *Frauen im Kriegsdienst, 1914-1945* (Deutsche Verlags-Anstalt, Stuttgart, 1965).

44. Rolf Wagenfuehr, *Die deutsche Industrie im Kriege 1939-1945*, 2nd edn (Duncker and Humblot, Berlin, 1963), pp.139-40.

45. Milward, *War, economy and society*, pp.236-9. See also Wolfgang Franz Werner, *"Bleib uebrig". Deutsche Arbeiter in der nationalsozialistischen Kriegswirtschaft* (Schwann, Duesseldorf, 1983).

46. Eichholtz, *Deutsche Kriegswirtschaft*, vol. 2, pp.258-67.

47. John E. Farquharson, *The Plough and the swastika. The NSDAP and agriculture in Germany 1928-45* (SAGE Publications, London, Beverly Hills, 1976), pp.161-81. Also: Max Rolfes, "Landwirtschaft 1914-1970" in Hermann Aubin and Wolfgang Zorn (eds), *Handbuch der deutschen Wirtschafts- und Sozialgeschichte*, 2 vols. (Klett, Stuttgart, 1976), vol. 2, pp.775-6 and Arthur Hanau and Roderich Plate, *Die deutsche landwirtschaftliche Preis- und Marktpolitik im Zweiten Weltkrieg* (G. Fischer, Stuttgart, 1975).

48. Joachim Lehmann, "Die deutsche Landwirtschaft im Kriege" in Eichholtz, *Deutsche Kriegswirtschaft*, vol. 2, p.602; Joachim Lehmann, "Agrarpolitik und Landwirtschaft in Deutschland 1939 bis 1945" in Bernd Martin and Alan S. Milward (eds), Agriculture and food supply in the Second World War (Scripta Mercaturae, Ostfildern, 1985), pp.29-49.

49. Friedrich-Wilhelm Henning, *Landwirtschaft und laendliche Gesellschaft im Kriege* (2 vols, Schoeningh, Paderborn, 1978), vol. 2, pp.224-8.

50. Milward, *War, economy and society*, pp.261-9. See also by the

same author *The Fascist economy in Norway* (Oxford University Press, Oxford, 1972).

51. For this and the following see Burton H. Klein, *Germany's economic preparations for war* (Harvard University Press, Cambridge, Mass., 1959), pp.148-50.

52. Franz W. Seidler, *Die Organisation Todt. Bauen fuer Staat und Wehrmacht 1938-1945*, (Bernard and Graefe, Koblenz, 1987). On Todt also by the same author *Fritz Todt. Baumeister des Dritten Reiches* (Herbig, Munich, Berlin, 1986).

53. Berenice A. Carroll, *Design for total war. Arms and economics in the Third Reich* (Mouton, The Hague, 1968), pp.217-31 for this and the following.

54. Milward, *German economy*, p.65.

55. Carroll, *Design*, pp.232-8.

56. Albert Speer, *Erinnerungen* (Propylaeen, Berlin, 1969), p.223. Critical on Speer among others: Matthias Schmidt, *Albert Speer: Das Ende eines Mythos. Speers wahre Rolle im Dritten Reich* (Scherz, Berne, Munich, 1982).

57. For this and the following Edward R. Zilbert, *Albert Speer and the Nazi Ministry of Arms. Economic institutions and industrial production in the German war economy* (Fairleigh Dickinson University Press, Rutherford, London, 1981), pp.91-111.

58. Milward, *War, economy and society*, pp.116-25, also for the following. See also Willi A. Boelcke, *Deutschlands Ruestung im Zweiten Weltkrieg. Hitlers Konferenzen mit Speer 1942-1945* (Akademischer Verlag Athenaion, Frankfurt am Main, 1969).

59. Milward, *German economy*, p.85.

60. For this and the following K. Hardach, *Political economy*, pp.83-6.

61. Gregor Janssen, *Das Ministerium Speer. Deutschlands Ruestung im Krieg* (Ullstein, Berlin, 1968), p.249.

62. Speer, *Erinnerungen*, pp.238-9.

63. Willi A. Boelcke, "Hitlers Befehle zur Zerstoerung oder Laehmung des deutschen Industriepotentials 1944/45", *Tradition*, vol. 13 (1968), pp.301-16.

64. Friedrich-Wilhelm Henning, *Das industrialisierte Deutschland 1914 bis 1972* (Schoeningh, Paderborn, 1974), p.184.

65. Milward, *War, economy and society*, pp.57-8.

66. Ernst-Willi Hansen, *Reichswehr und Industrie. Ruestungswirtschaftliche Zusammenarbeit und wirtschaftliche Mobilmachungsvorbereitungen 1923-1932* (Boldt, Boppard, 1978).

67. Milward, *War, economy and society*, p.181.

68. Richard J. Overy, *The air war* (Europa Publications, London, 1980), p.166.

69. Gottfried Plumpe, "Die Kautschuksynthese in Deutschland 1906-1944/45", *Geschichte und Gesellschaft*, vol. 9 (1983), pp.564-97; Frank Atherton Howard, *Buna rubber. The birth of an industry, (D. van Nostrand Company*, New York, 1947).

70. Willi A. Boelcke, *Die deutsche Wirtschaft 1930-1945. Interna des Reichswirtschaftsministeriums* (Droste, Duesseldorf, 1983), p.166.

71. Hans-Joachim Braun, "Ein gescheiterter Innovationsversuch: Der Kohlenstaubmotor 1916-1940", *Kultur und Technik*, vol. 6 (1982), pp.154-61.

72. Raymond G. Stokes, "The oil industry in Nazi Germany", *Business History Review*, vol. 59 (1985), pp.254-77.

73. Eichholtz, *Deutsche Kriegswirtschaft*, vol. 2, p.318.

74. Milward, *German economy*, p.110.

75. Herbst, *Der totale Krieg*, p.323.

76. Hans-Joachim Weyres-von Levetzow, *Die deutsche Ruestungswirtschaft von 1942 bis zum Ende des Krieges* (Diss. rer.pol., Munich, 1975), p.201.

77. Overy, *Air war*, pp.187-90.

78. Zilbert, *Albert Speer*, p.226.

79. Overy, *Air war*, pp.160-84. On tank production see Hartmut H. Knittel, *Panzerfertigung im Zweiten Weltkrieg. Industrieproduktion fuer die deutsche Wehrmacht* (Maximilian-Verlagsgruppe, Herford, 1988).

80. Weyres-von Levetzow, *Deutsche Ruestungswirtschaft*, p.46.

81. Rudolf Lusar, *Die deutschen Waffen und Geheimwaffen des Zweiten Weltkrieges und ihre Weiterentwicklung*, 6th edn (Lehmanns, Munich, 1971); David Irving, *The mare's nest. The war against Hitler's secret vengeance weapons* (Panther Books, London, 1985).

82. Heinz-Dieter Hoelsken, *Die V-Waffen. Entstehung - Propaganda - Kriegseinsatz* (Deutsche Verlags-Anstalt, Stuttgart, 1984), pp.205-11.

Chapter Eight

THE POST-WAR ECONOMY, 1945-1948

The post-war situation

By the end of the war economic life in Germany seemed to have
come to a complete halt. For Germany, the outcome of the Second World War was devastating: about eight million Germans
killed or presumed dead, of whom three million were civilians.
More than four million Germans were injured and there were still
millions of ex-soldiers in prisoners of war camps. Large parts of
the country were little more than heaps of rubble. Therefore, the
housing situation was catastrophic: out of a total of 17.1 million
about 3.4 million houses or flats had been destroyed and a further
30 per cent severely damaged. Refugees and expellees from the
eastern parts of the former German *Reich* had difficulty finding
housing.[1] Apart from that the German transport system had been
largely destroyed in the last months of the war. Consequently the
German economy disintegrated into a number of regional sub-
economies. A severe energy crisis, owing mainly to a shortage of
coal, worsened the situation.

Besides, German territorial losses were severe and amounted to
roughly 25 per cent of the former Third Reich area. The Sude-
tenland was returned to Czechoslovakia whereas France not only
took back Alsace-Lorraine but also gained effective sovereignty
over the Saar; Poland received land up to the Rivers Oder and
Neisse (this included the rich coal, zinc and lead deposits of Upper Silesia); the Soviet Union took Koenigsberg and the northern
half of East Prussia; Austria regained her former independence.
German nationals living in the eastern parts of the former Ger-

Table 8.1: *Gross fixed industrial assets in the territory which is now the Federal Republic of Germany 1939-1948* [a]

Year	Initial level	Capacity creating[b] investments	War damage	Dismantle- ment	Final level
1939	54.28	+ 3.17	-	-	57.45
1940	57.45	+ 3.44	-	-	60.89
1941	60.89	+ 3.97	-	-	64.86
1942	64.86	+ 4.31	-	-	69.17
1943	69.17	+ 3.43	- 1.40	-	71.20
1944	71.20	+ 1.25	- 7.15	-	65.30
1945	65.30	- 0.49	- 5.24	- 0.95	58.62
1946	58.62	- 0.43	-	- 1.14	57.05
1947	57.05	- 0.19	-	- 0.50	56.36
1948[c]	56.36	- 0.24	-	- 0.21	55.91

Notes: [a] new values in DM thousand million at 1950 prices
[b] gross investment in plant, less scrapping
[c] first half-year only

Source: Rolf Krengel, "Some reasons for the rapid economic growth of the German Federal Republic", *Banca Nazionale del Lavoro Quarterly Review*, vol. 16 (1963), p.123.

man *Reich* were expelled. Although West Germany could make use of over 60 per cent of the industrial capacity of the former

Reich, it had lost access to the rich agricultural land in the east. In 1949 the Soviet zone of occupation became the German Democratic Republic and the areas occupied by Britain, the United States and France became the Federal Republic of Germany.[2]

At the end of the war the extent of devastation in Germany was large indeed, especially as regards residential areas. It turned out, however, that the damage done to industry was not as extensive as it had first seemed in spite of heavy losses and the fact that machines were generally worn out by continuous use during the war and that spare parts were difficult to obtain. Although it is difficult to make reliable calculations, fixed industrial assets in the area which is now the Federal Republic of Germany were, at the end of the war, probably larger than they had been in 1939. Investments in German industry during the war very likely exceeded the war damage. The heavy losses during the last war years, the current value of which amounted to about DM 13.8 thousand million or 28 per cent of the capacity of early 1936, and the losses from dismantlements after the war brought the rate of growth down to only one per cent a year. Calculations by the *Deutsches Institut fuer Wirtschaftsforschung* give the above figures.

Although the current gross asset value at the end of 1943 was only surpassed in early 1953, industrial development in Germany was noticeably retarded by the war. On the other hand, plants damaged during the war were often replaced by modern buildings and equipment. In the period from 1936 to the first half of 1948 gross investments more than doubled (normal) retirement. In May 1945 the German economy certainly did not start from scratch.[3]

At the end of the war the index numbers of both age-structure and the relation of net-to-gross value of fixed assets were high which also goes for 1948, a year of allegedly high disinvestment and dismantlement.

The table below shows that fixed assets at the end of the war were not in such a poor state as to cause complete economic stagnation. The same is true of the - well-trained - labour force which was rapidly increased by refugees coming over from East Germany.[4] For the West German economy these refugees were not an unmixed blessing, however, especially as regards the difficult food situation.[5]

After the virtual economic standstill in May 1945 the British and American zones of occupation experienced a revival of industrial activity until the end of 1946. Then, however, during the cold winter of 1946/7, the poor state of the German transport system

Table 8.2: Age structure of fixed assets in industry [a]

Age (years)	1935	1945	1948
0-5	9	34	16
5-10	20	21	34
10-15	71	6	12
over 15		39	38

Note: [a] in per cent

Source: Rolf Krengel, *Anlagevermoegen, Produktion und Beschaeftigung im Gebiet der Bundesrepublik von 1924 bis 1956* (Duncker and Humblot, Berlin, 1958), pp.52-3.

Figure 8.1: Indices of industrial production in the Bizone [a] and the French zone of occupation [b] 1946-1949

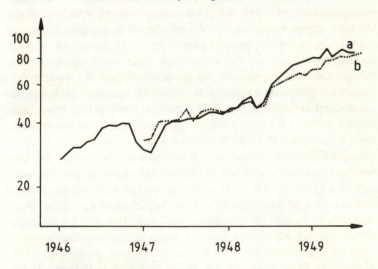

Source: Albert Ritschl, "Die Waehrungsreform von 1948 und der Wiederaufstieg der westdeutschen Industrie. Zu den Thesen von Mathias Manz und Werner Abelshauser über die Produktionswirkungen der Waehrungsreform", *Vierteljahrshefte fuer Zeitgeschichte*, vol. 33 (1985), p.153.

caused grave problems. Although many repairs had been done by that time on railway tracks, roads and bridges, transport facilities were still inadequate. As a consequence, an energy crisis developed with large supplies of coal, which could not be carried to the places where they were needed, piling up near the Ruhr pits. Apart from transport and energy, iron and steel production and the difficult food situation were other bottlenecks for economic revival.[6]

By the autumn of 1947, these bottlenecks were partly overcome. Repairs of the transport network improved the situation; incentives offered by the Allied and German authorities - better wage rates and special food rations - increased coal production and attracted more miners to work in the pits. In the "Bizone", the former British and American zones of occupation, moderate economic growth set in before both the Marshall Plan and currency reform could have an effect on economic growth in Germany.[7] In anticipation of ERP funds the West German economy was already growing in the autumn and winter of 1947.[8] After the currency reform of 20/21 June 1948 the economic upswing was significant.

In late summer 1944 U.S. Secretary of the Treasury Henry Morgenthau Jr. proposed a policy of complete deindustrialisation and reagrianisation of Germany. This implied the destruction of the German engineering, electrical and chemical industries and the conversion of the German economy to a pre-industrial, agricultural economy. At the Potsdam conference in July/August 1945 the question of the political and economic future of Germany was discussed. Although a realisation of the Morgenthau plan was not considered as being in the Allies' interest and had for some time ceased to be a feasible political option, a rigorous cut of Germany's economic strength was planned so that it would be impossible for Germany to wage war in the future. Therefore a German armament industry and "excess industrial capacity" was interdicted. Her economy was to concentrate on the internal market and was not to play a large role on the world market, a plan which would have benefited countries like Great Britain. All countries affected by the war were to receive reparations from Germany.[9]

On 28 March 1946 the Allied Control Council issued the "Level-of-Industry Plan" in which details of dismantling German industrial plants were laid down. Germany's industrial production was to be reduced to between 50 and 55 per cent of the 1938 level, a figure which amounted to the level of 1932, the trough of the

Great Depression. Apart from the armament industry, numerous others, like heavy machinery, ball bearings and aluminium, were interdicted, as well as the production of aircraft, ocean-going ships, synthetic rubber and gasoline, magnesium or beryllium. Coal mining in the Ruhr, however, expanded, because it supplied the Allies with coal well below the world market price. Ocean-going ships and aircraft owned by Germans had to be handed over to the Allies; German foreign assets, which in 1945 amounted to about RM ten thousand million, were confiscated as were German foreign patents, licenses and trademarks.[10] In addition, occupation costs had to be paid by Germany, which, as far as West Germany was concerned, amounted to 20.7 thousand million in the period 1945-9.

From the beginning there had been criticism in the United States against the Allied policy of dismantlement. This criticism increased when the antagonism between the United States and the Soviet Union became more severe. Apart from this it became increasingly obvious that dismantlement was an extremely inefficient way of transferring reparations. As a consequence, the "Second Level-of-Industry Plan" of 26 August 1947 which applied only to the Bizone - an amalgamation of the American and British zones from 1 January 1947 - permitted German industrial production to reach 90 to 95 per cent of the 1936 level. Still, dismantlement continued to a lesser degree and was only stopped in April 1951. The Western Allies calculated the reparations they had received at DM 1.5 thousand million whereas German officials computed DM 5 thousand million. The latter figure is probably much closer to the mark. In the Soviet zone of occupation the value of dismantlement was much higher and amounted to about DM 50 thousand million for the period 1945-53.[11]

The Allied policy of reparations caused obvious disadvantages to the German economy, especially as regards the dismantlement of new or recently built plants or machinery. Still, even after dismantlement, German productive capacity was probably higher than it had been in 1936 because of modernisation and extension during the war. Dismantlement probably did not cut more than 5 per cent of German pre-war industrial capital stock. Dismantled plants were often replaced by modern ones which put German industry in a favourable competitive position. The benefits for the recipient countries, however, were not as large as they had hoped because of difficulties with assembly, transport or other problems.[12]

Allied policy

To weaken the German economy by reparations and disintegration was not the way many American politicians thought suitable
to serve American interests in Europe. In a speech in Stuttgart on
6 September 1946 the American Secretary of State James F.
Byrnes pointed out that Germany's economic problems could not
be solved by the destruction but only by the reconstruction of
German industry. This implied a close cooperation between the
Allies in the western zones of occupation and - to a limited extent
- German self-government. Britain basically agreed with this policy, although the British views sometimes differed from the
American on matters of democratic socialisation and economic
order.[13] In the beginning, France refrained from a close cooperation with the American and British zones of occupation because
of her territorial claims on Germany. France aimed at weakening
Germany to such a degree that her old enemy would never again
be able to become a security risk for her and for Europe as a
whole. Also, to regain its status as a world power, France wanted
to have free access to some of Germany's economic resources.[14]
The Soviet Union regarded the intended cooperation between the
Western Allies as a violation of the Potsdam agreement. Apart
from this, the Soviet ideas regarding the economic and political
order of her zone of occupation were incompatible with the views
of the Western powers.[15]

From July 1946 onwards there had been negotiations between
the Anglo-American allies to unite their two zones enabling them
to deal more efficiently with the problems of refugees or the distribution of industrial resources. After the foundation of the
"United Economic Region" (*Vereinigtes Wirtschaftsgebiet*, "Bizone") on 1 January 1947 they established on 11 July 1947 a German "Economic Council" (*Wirtschaftsrat*), which, under the super-
vision of the allied "Bipartite Economic Control Group" (BICO)
had administrative functions. Already in January 1947 the BICO
had proposed that a "guide plan" on increasing production and
foreign trade in the Bizone should be set up; in February of the
same year the economic council presented a guide plan with de-
tailed proposals for increasing coal production. On 10 June 1947
the Bizone administration was established on a parliamentary basis with an economic council founded shortly afterwards and an
executive committee. These institutions were important steps to-

wards the foundation of the Federal Republic of Germany in 1949.[16]

In the meantime the French government had decided to cooperate closely with the Bizone for the main reason of making available American food deliveries to the French zone of occupation. In exchange the French zone had to admit more refugees into its territory than it had been willing to accept before. In the spring of 1949 the three western zones of occupation united into the "Trizone", a forerunner of the Federal Republic of Germany.

In order to make it impossible for Germany to wage war in the future and - also - to create the prerequisites for a democratic structure of economy and society in Germany, the Allies had set up guidelines at Potsdam according to which excessive concentration of economic power in Germany was to be abolished. "Excessive concentration" meant all cartels and cartel-like arrangements as well as corporations with more than 10,000 employees or, in the French zone of occupation, with a capital stock exceeding DM 50 million. A deconcentration branch of the Allied military government had to identify such companies and go ahead with measures of deconcentration.

Deconcentration took place mainly in the chemical industry (*IG Farben*)[17], in the iron and steel (*Montan*) industry and in banking. *IG Farben* was split up into three companies, *BASF* (*Badische Anilin- und Sodafabrik*), Bayer and Hoechst, corporations which still had considerable economic power. In the iron and steel industry the twelve largest companies which, before deconcentration, had had an output of about 90 per cent of the steel produced in Germany and more than 50 per cent of the coal, were divided into 28 companies with no links whatsoever between them. *Vereinigte Stahlwerke*, founded in 1926, was split up into 13 companies independent of each other. From the economic point of view this policy of rigorous deconcentration made hardly any sense. In banking, deconcentration of the "big three" (*Deutsche Bank, Dresdner Bank, Commerzbank*) failed completely and "reconstruction" soon brought back the status quo.[18] In spite of the questionable economic rationale there is a direct link between Allied deconcentration policy and the Federal German anti-cartel policy, which, from 1957 onwards, was directed against companies which by their size and economic power reduced competition and aimed at controlling the market.

In an attempt to ease the difficult economic situation in 1946, especially as regards food supply in Germany, the American government and private organisations carried through various aid programmes. Of special importance were UNRRA ("United States Reconstruction and Rehabilitation Administration"), an aid organisation which especially assisted displaced persons; CARE ("Cooperative for American Remittances to Europe") which from 1946 onwards sent parcels of victuals to a starving European population and GARIOA ("Government and relief in occupied areas").[19] GARIOA aid was financed by funds from the US War Department for the administration of the occupied areas the aim of which was to "prevent disease and unrest".

GARIOA deliveries to Germany, which consisted mainly of foodstuffs but also included fertilizers, seeds, gasoline and pharmaceuticals, amounted to roughly $ 1.62 thousand million during the period July 19.5 to March 1950[20] and thus exceeded deliveries of the Marshall Plan which between its inauguration in 1948 and 31 December 1952 amounted only to $ 1.537 thousand million. Between 1945 and 1948 65 to 70 per cent of the yearly Trizone imports were financed by foreign aid, especially by GARIOA. In the British zone of occupation the UK contributions to pay for imported goods served a purpose similar to GARIOA, albeit to a smaller degree.

Marshall Plan and currency reform

Allied aid programmes surely helped to alleviate the situation, but there were still severe supply problems in Germany because of bad harvests in 1946 and 1947 and insufficient industrial production. At the same time political tensions were growing mainly due to the Americans being suspicious of Soviet aims of extending their sphere of influence. In order to stabilise the shaky economic and political situation in Western Europe and particularly in West Germany the US Secretary of State George Marshall in his Harvard speech of 5 June 1947 announced the "European Recovery Program" (ERP) or "Marshall Plan" as it was also called.[21] This plan intended to lead Western Europe out of its difficult economic situation and also to create a liberal economic system. While receiving American aid, the western nations were obliged to cooperate economically and politically. ERP conditions were such that the Soviet zone of occupation and Eastern Europe did not participate in the programme. On 16 April 1948 the "Organisation for European Economic Cooperation" (OEEC) was founded as an administrative organisation which had to ensure that American aid would have the desired economic and political effects.[22] Until the foundation of the Federal Republic of Germany in 1949 the military governors represented the western zones of Germany. Although West Germany suffered more wartime destruction than other western countries, its share of aid under the Marshall Plan was smaller than that of Britain or France.

Marshall Plan aid was given in two ways, namely goods and services especially from the United States and the dollar area to countries in Western Europe, which received them on credit, and secondly "counterpart funds". According to the ERP treaty of July 1948 the German recipients had to pay for ERP imports in German currency, which was collected in a counterpart account, the ERP Special Fund (ERP-*Sondervermoegen*) with the *Bank Deutscher Laender*.[23] From this account, credit was made available for investment purposes in West Germany and West Berlin. The recipients had to pay interest and amortization payments into this account with the consequence that the fund became a revolving capital fund which the Federal Republic of Germany still uses today.

Public utilities and the transport sector benefited most from Marshall Plan aid (about 50 per cent of the fund), but the iron and steel industry received a considerable share, too. Since the 1950s the fund has been used especially for investments in West Berlin, for the support of economically weak areas within the FRG, particularly at the GDR border, for the financing of exports to those countries which could not (yet) pay for them - the fund thus became a means of development policy - and for environmental protection.[24]

As the counterpart funds were made available only for part-financing, investments based on Marshall Plan aid had cumulative effects which were generally much higher than the ERP credit itself. During the year 1949 ERP credits financed 6.4 per cent of the gross domestic fixed investment of trade and industry in the FRG and a maximum of 8.6 per cent in 1950.[25] Technical assistance programmes under the ERP also played an important role. These consisted mainly of information visits of German economists, businessmen and engineers to the United States to study the latest developments in management and production technology; American engineers and businessmen also assisted German firms as consultants.[26]

West Germany's economic and political revival is hardly imaginable without Marshall Plan aid. It is true that deliveries of goods under the ERP were not as ample as many Germans had hoped and that they often arrived late.[27] There had been moderate economic growth in West Germany before Marshall Plan aid was put into operation, but the issue as to whether this growth was in any way self-sustaining and whether American aid was a primer of West German economic recovery, is still a matter of debate.[28] What seems to be certain, however, is that ERP aid strengthened the rather fragile economic growth in West Germany. In the textile industry American raw cotton deliveries contributed significantly to West German textile production and Marshall Plan counterpart funds accelerated the hitherto insufficient capacities of electricity generating plants thus contributing to the growth of West German industrial production.[29]

As far as concepts of economic order are concerned the Marshall Plan did everything but square with the "social market economy" philosophy. Businessmen found it hard to understand why a liberal capitalist system had to be complemented by public programmes directing capital investments.[30] On the other hand, it was mainly due to the Marshall Plan that the West German economy could be reintegrated into the international economy.

Currency reform in West Germany was planned in conjunction with the Marshall Plan and had similar effects. Supply problems with food and raw materials had required a continuation of the wartime system of rationing and of price and wage controls which caused the increase of black markets and barter trade. Moreover, high demand and few goods heightened inflationary tendencies with which the Allied system of administrative allocation and control could hardly cope.[31] For both economic and political reasons a contraction of the money supply and a reorganisation of public and private debts were needed.

After various futile attempts by German administrative bodies the three economists Gerhard Colm, Raymond W. Goldsmith and Joseph Dodge presented a plan on 20 May 1946, the "Colm-Dodge-Goldsmith Plan", which they had worked out on order of the American military government. This plan provided the basis for the currency reform of 20/21 June 1948.[32] The main features of this reform were the following: the *Deutsche Mark* (*DM*) replaced the *Reichsmark* (*RM*) as the new monetary unit. The exchange ratio was graded according to the nature of the debt: wages, salaries and rents were transposed at the ratio of 1:1,

mortgages and other private debts at the rate of 1:10.[33] Holders
of bank deposits and cash had to be satisfied with an exchange
ratio of DM 6.5 : RM 100. Altogether 93.5 per cent of the former
stock of *Reichsmark* was withdrawn from circulation. The West
German population received a sum of DM 40 per head which
each citizen could exchange at the rate of DM 1 : RM 10; two
months later this sum was increased to DM 60. In order to enable
businessmen to make payments, firms were allowed to exchange
another DM 60 per employee at the rate of 1:10. States (*Laender*)
and municipalities received one-sixth of their earnings during the
period 1 October 1947 to 31 March 1948; the postal services and
railways only received one-twelfth.

With the currency reform all Reich claims and liabilities (more
than RM 400 thousand million) became ineffective. Apart from
the claims from some banks against the *Laender*, currency reform
was a good deal for the public sector which, by this means, got rid
of all its debts at one blow.[34] Holders of both money savings and
public debt, however, came off badly in this transformation process, whereas private capital accumulation was promoted. Similar
to the period after the Weimar inflation, owners of real assets and
private means of production did not do badly at all. There are direct links between currency reform and Erhard's "social market
economy". It was left to the German authorities to "equalise burdens" later.[35]

The short-term effects of the currency reform were astonishing for everybody.[36] Immediately after the reform large numbers
of commodities which had been unavailable for a long time appeared in the shop windows, an indication of the seriousness of
the black market after the war. Before the currency reform not
only shopkeepers but manufacturers, too, had hoarded masses of
goods. Although it is obviously difficult to assess the extent of
hoarding it can be assumed that about 50 per cent of production
during 1947 and the first half of 1948 went into hoards or was
used for barter purposes. Furthermore, probably a portion of
these hoarded goods did not appear in the official production
statistics. From the second to the third quarter of 1948 these
statistics show a rise of about 30 per cent, whereas the growth rate
of the year before had only been 5 per cent. This may, however,
also have been partly due to rapid stock reduction shortly before
and immediately after the currency reform.[37] Although actual
industrial output before the currency reform was probably higher
than given in the statistics - how much higher is difficult to say - it

is also likely that the official production figures for the period after the reform are too low because of an inadequate weighing of the statistical indices.[38]

As with the Marshall Plan, the economic effects of the currency reform are difficult to assess. Although output increased by 50 per cent during the second half of 1948 the economic situation was by no means stable. Price controls were - apart from essential food-stuffs - abolished in July 1948, which led to a temporary upsurge of inflation owing to high demand and insuffient output. Gene-rally, it seems safe to say, however, that together with Marshall Plan aid, the removal of the "veil of money" which the currency reform brought about created more stable conditions for future economic growth.[39]

Foreign trade

Until 1948 the Western zones of occupation had hardly any for-eign trade in the proper sense of the word. In January 1947 the JEIA ("Joint Export-Import Agency") was founded in the Bizone, which took charge of all imports and exports and remained re-sponsible for bizonal foreign trade until October 1949. Because of its bureaucratic behavior this agency did more to impede than to advance foreign trade.[40] For the French zone of occupation an agency similar to the JEIA was established, the *OFICOMEX* (*Office du Commerce Extérieur*). With the foundation of the Tri-zone on 8 April 1949 *OFICOMEX* became part of the JEIA.

Before the war German exports had consisted mainly of finished goods. Under Allied occupation, the picture changed completely and shifted towards the export of raw materials, mainly timber, coal and scrap. The German exporters did not, however, receive world market prices for their goods but prices which had been fixed by the Allies who were also the recipients of the goods. These prices amounted to only a third of world market prices. It would not be unfair to call these exports "veiled reparations".[41]

As far as imports are concerned there were two categories. Un-der category A came all goods which satisfied the basic needs of the West German population, mainly food, but also seeds, ferti-lizers, gasoline and pharmaceuticals. The import of these goods was financed by GARIOA funds, later also by Marshall Plan aid, whereas imports under category B - raw materials for industrial production - had to be paid for in dollars from export earnings of the United Economic Area. In view of the fact that, for reasons given above, export earnings were rather low, the Western Allies' "New Industrial Plan" as well as Marshall Plan aid were badly needed.[42]

Foreign aid as a percentage of imports had an almost completely reverse development to the ratio of exports to imports. Apart from low yields from exports, occupation costs were high, especially in the French zone of occupation.

Table 8.3: West German balance of payments 1945-1952 [a]

Year	Exports	Foreign aid	Imports	Current account
1945	53	64	96	+ 21
1946	206	468	689	- 15
1947	318	600	843	+ 75
1948	641	1025	1558	+ 78
1949	1123	956	2237	- 158
1950	1981	480	2704	- 243
1951	3471	427	3506	+ 392
1952	4026	45	3858	+ 213

Note: [a] in million dollars

Source: Friedrich-Wilhelm Henning, "Wege und Wirkungen des Marshall-Plans in Deutschland", *Scripta Mercaturae*, vol. 15 (1981), p.103.

After the foundation of the Bizone at the beginning of 1947 the JEIA started negotiations with various countries with the objective of arranging bilateral trade agreements. The trade agreements with Greece (21 January 1948), Benelux (11 June 1948) and Switzerland (27 August 1949) were concluded together with the gradual removal of West German foreign trade barriers.[43] In conjunction with Marshall Plan aid the American government pursued an active policy of reintegrating West Germany into the world trade system, a system which the USA tried to shape according to their interests.

During the year 1948 the major part of West German exports shifted from raw materials to finished products. Until 1 October 1951, when the Federal Republic of Germany became a member with equal rights, the Western occupying powers represented West Germany and the newly founded Federal Republic of Germany in GATT.[44]

Notes

1. Rainer Schulze, Doris von der Brelie-Lewin, Helga Grebing (eds), *Fluechtlinge und Vertriebene in der westdeutschen Nachkriegsgeschichte* (August Lax, Hildesheim, 1987); Volker R. Berghahn, *Modern Germany. Society, economy and politics in the twentieth century* (Cambridge University Press, Cambridge, 1982), p.177.

2. Eric Owen Smith, *The West German economy* (Croom Helm, London, 1983), p.6; R.E.H. Mellor, *The two Germanies. A modern geography* (Harper and Row, London, New York, 1978), pp.131-4.

3. Rolf Krengel, "Some reasons for the rapid economic growth of the German Federal Republic", *Banca Nazionale del Lavoro Quarterly Review*, vol. 16 (1963), pp.121-7.

4. Werner Abelshauser, "West German economic recovery 1945-1951: A reassessment", *Three Banks Review*, No. 135 (1982), p.37. See also by the same author *Wirtschaft in Westdeutschland 1945-1948. Rekonstruktion und Wachstumsbedingungen in der amerikanischen und britischen Zone* (Deutsche Verlagsanstalt, Stuttgart, 1975), pp.100-7 and *Wirtschaftsgeschichte der Bundesrepublik Deutschland 1945-1980* (Suhrkamp, Frankfurt am Main, 1983), pp.22-4. Abelshauser's publications on the German postwar economy have recently been subject to strong criticism.

5. Bernd Klemm and Guenter J. Trittel, "Vor dem «Wirtschaftswunder»: Durchbruch zum Wachstum oder Laehmungskrise? Eine Auseinandersetzung mit W. Abelshausers Interpretation der Wirtschaftsentwicklung 1945-1948", *Vierteljahrshefte fuer Zeitgeschichte*, vol. 35 (1987), p.592; Gerold Ambrosius, "Fluechtlinge und Vertriebene in der westdeutschen Wirtschaftsgeschichte - Methodische Ueberlegungen und forschungsrelevante Probleme", in Rainer Schulze, Doris von der Brelie-Lewin and Helga Grebing (eds), *Fluechtlinge und Vertriebene in der westdeutschen Nachkriegsgeschichte. Bilanzierung der Forschung und Perspektiven fuer die kuenftige Forschungsarbeit* (August Lax, Hildesheim, 1987), pp.216-28; Falk Wiesemann, "Fluechtlingspolitik und Fluechtlingsintegration in Westdeutschland", *Aus Politik und Zeitgeschichte*, vol. 35.1 (1985), pp.35-44.

6. Abelshauser, "West German economic recovery 1945-1951: A reassessment", p.39; Klemm and Trittel, "Vor dem «Wirtschaftswunder»: Durchbruch zum Wachstum oder Laehmungskrise?", pp.603-9 and Christoph Weisz, "Versuch zur Standortbestimmung der Landwirtschaft", in Ludolf Herbst (ed.), *Westdeutschland 1945-1955* (Oldenbourg, Munich, 1986), pp.117-26. On the food supply situation see also Karl Heinz Rothenberger, *Die Hungerjahre nach dem Zweiten Weltkrieg. Ernaehrung und Landwirtschaft in Rheinland-Pfalz 1945-1950* (Harald Boldt, Boppard, 1980) and Gabriele Stueber, *Der Kampf gegen den Hun-*

ger 1945-1950. Die Ernaehrungslage in der britischen Zone Deutschlands, insbesondere in Schleswig-Holstein und Hamburg (Wachholtz, Neumuenster, 1984). On technical reconstruction in several German firms see the articles in *Technikgeschichte* vol. 53 (1986), pp.277-320.

7. This is stressed by Charles P. Kindleberger, *Europe's postwar growth: The role of labour supply* (Harvard University Press, Cambridge, Mass. 1967), p.30, who drew attention to the elastic supply of labour in West Germany as a key element of growth and refuted Henry C. Wallich's argument of the decisive role of the Marshall Plan for economic growth in Germany. (Henry C. Wallich, *Mainsprings of German revival* < Yale University Press, New Haven, 1955 >). Werner Abelshauser took up and extended Kindleberger's view (Werner Abelshauser, "Wiederaufbau vor dem Marshall-Plan. Westeuropas Wachstumschancen und Wirtschaftsordnungspolitik in der zweiten Haelfte der vierziger Jahre", *Vierteljahrshefte fuer Zeitgeschichte*, vol. 29 (1981), pp.545-78). See also Michael J. Hogan, *The Marshall Plan. America, Britain and the reconstruction of Western Europe, 1947-1952* (Cambridge University Press, New York, 1987).

8. John H. Backer, *Priming the German economy. American occupation policies 1945-1948* (Duke University Press, Durham, N.C., 1971), p.179.

9. Harald Winkel, *Die Wirtschaft im geteilten Deutschland 1945-1970* (Steiner, Wiesbaden, 1974), p.41.

10. Karl Hardach, *The political economy of Germany in the twentieth century* (University of California Press, Berkeley, Los Angeles, London, 1980), pp.92-3.

11. Owen Smith, *West German economy*, p.14.

12. Winkel, *Wirtschaft*, p.48.

13. As to the question of economic order the British government went a long way towards socialisation of key industries in the British zone; the American government pursued a policy which did not rule out democratically based socialisation in her zone. On the topic of socialisation of the Ruhr the American government left it to the Germans to decide. (Werner Link, "Der Marshall Plan und Deutschland", *Aus Politik und Zeitgeschichte*, vol. B50 < 1980 > , p.11). See also, among others, Doerte Winkler, "Die amerikanische Sozialisierungspolitik in Deutschland 1945-1948", in Heinrich A. Winkler (ed.), *Politische Weichenstellungen im Nachkriegsdeutschland 1945-1953* (Vandenhoeck and Ruprecht, Goettingen, 1979), pp.88-110; Rolf Steininger, "Die Rhein-Ruhr-Frage im Kontext britischer Deutschlandpolitik 1945/6", in Heinrich A. Winkler (ed.), *Politische Weichenstellungen*, pp.111-66. See also the essays in Dietmar Petzina and Walter Euchner (eds), *Wirtschaftspolitik im britischen Besatzungsgebiet 1945-1949* (Schwann, Duesseldorf, 1984).

14. Gerhard Kiersch, "Die franzoesische Deutschlandpolitik 1945-1949", in Claus Scharf and Hans-Juergen Schroeder (eds), *Politische und oekonomische Stabilisierung Westdeutschlands 1945-1949. Fuenf Beitraege zur Deutschlandpolitik der westlichen Alliierten* (Steiner, Wiesbaden, 1977), p.65. On the economic development of the French zone see Mathias Manz, *Stagnation und Aufschwung in der franzoesischen Besatzungszone von 1945 bis 1948* (Scripta Mercaturae, Ostfildern, 1985).

15. For this and the following see Winkel, *Wirtschaft*, pp.16-25.

16. Winkel, *Wirtschaft*, pp.17-8. See also Wolfgang Benz, *Von der Besatzungsherrschaft zur Bundesrepublik. Stationen einer Staatsgruendung 1946-1949* (Fischer-Taschenbuch-Verlag, Frankfurt am Main, 1984). Although in 1947 German administrative bodies and business associations had some influence on economic policy, the military governments had the final say as far as principles of economic order were concerned. (Gerold Ambrosius, *Die Durchsetzung der Sozialen Marktwirtschaft in Westdeutschland 1945-1949* < Deutsche Verlags-Anstalt, Stuttgart, 1977>, p.126). See also by the same author, "Marktwirtschaft oder Planwirtschaft? Planwirtschaftliche Ansaetze der bizonalen deutschen Selbstver-

waltung 1946-1949", *Vierteljahrschrift fuer Sozial- und Wirtschaftsgeschichte*, vol. 66 (1979), pp.74-108.

17. Raymond G. Stokes, *Divide and prosper. The heirs of I.G. Farben under Allied authority, 1945-1951* (University of California Press, Berkeley, Los Angeles, London, 1988).

18. Owen Smith, *West German economy*, p.16.

19. Winkel, *Wirtschaft*, pp.36-7.

20. Manfred Knapp, "Reconstruction and West-Integration: The impact of the Marshall Plan on Germany", *Zeitschrift fuer die gesamte Staatswissenschaft*, vol. 137 (1981), pp.423-4 for this and the following. See by the same author, "Deutschland und der Marshallplan: Zum Verhaeltnis zwischen politischer und oekonomischer Stabilisierung in der amerikanischen Deutschlandpolitik nach 1945", in Claus Scharf and Hans-Juergen Schroeder (eds), *Politische und oekonomische Stabilisierung Westdeutschlands 1945-1949. Fuenf Beitraege zur Deutschlandpolitik der westlichen Alliierten* (Steiner, Wiesbaden, 1977), pp.19-43.

21. John Gimbel, *The Origins of the Marshall Plan* (Stanford University Press, Stanford, 1976) maintains that ERP was not part of a long-term American economic and political strategy. See, however, Manfred Knapp, "Das Deutschlandproblem und die Urspruenge des europaeischen Wiederaufbauprogramms. Eine Auseinandersetzung mit John Gimbels Untersuchung «The Origins of the Marshall Plan»", *Politische Vierteljahresschrift*, vol. 19 (1979), pp.48-65.

22. Alan S. Milward, *The reconstruction of Western Europe 1945-51* (Methuen, London, 1984), pp.168-95; Hans Moeller, "The reconstruction of the international economic order after the Second World War and the integration of the Federal Republic of Germany into the world economy", *Zeitschrift fuer die gesamte Staatswissenschaft*, vol. 137 (1981), pp.344-66.

23. Abelshauser, "West German economic recovery 1945-1951: a reassessment", p.44.

24. Friedrich-Wilhelm Henning, "Wege und Wirkungen des Marshall-Planes in Deutschland", *Scripta Mercaturae*, vol. 15 (1981), p.98.

25. Knapp, "Reconstruction and West-integration: The impact of the Marshall Plan on Germany", p.425.

26. Link, "Der Marshall-Plan und Deutschland", pp.14-6.

27. Abelshauser, "West German economic recovery 1945-1951: A reassessment", pp.45-7.

28. See the publications by Abelshauser on the one hand and Klemm and Trittel on the other.

29. Knut Borchardt and Christoph Buchheim, "Die Wirkung der Marshallplan-Hilfe in Schluesselbranchen der deutschen Wirtschaft", *Vierteljahrshefte fuer Zeitgeschichte*, vol. 35 (1987), pp.317-47. See on this Werner Abelshauser, "Hilfe und Selbsthilfe. Zur Funktion des Marshallplans beim westdeutschen Wiederaufbau", *Vierteljahrshefte fuer Zeitgeschichte*, vol.37 (1989), pp.85-113. See also on the Marshallplan: Ute Daniel, *Dollardiplomatie in Europa. Marshallplan, Kalter Krieg und US-Aussenwirtschaftspolitik 1945-52* (Droste, Duesseldorf, 1982) ; Stanley Hoffman and Charles Maier (eds), *The Marshall Plan: A retrospective* (Westview, Boulder Co., London, 1984), and Gerd Hardach, "The Marshall Plan in Germany", *Journal of European economic history*, vol. 16 (1987), pp.433-85.

30. Reinhard Blum, *Soziale Marktwirtschaft. Wirtschaftspolitik zwischen Neoliberalismus und Ordoliberalismus* (Mohr, Tuebingen, 1969), p.207.

31. Klaus Hinrich Hennings, "West Germany", in Andrea Boltho (ed.), *The European economy. Growth and crisis* (Oxford University Press, Oxford, 1982), p.478.

32. Owen Smith, *West German economy*, p.10.

33. On this and the following see K. Hardach, *Political economy*, pp.107-8.

34. Otto G. Mayer, "Deutschland heute: Die Wirtschaft der Bundesrepublik Deutschland", in Norbert Walter (ed.), *Deutschland. Portraet einer Nation*, vol. 3, *Wirtschaft* (Bertelsmann, Guetersloh, 1985), p.236.
35. Alfred Grosser, *Germany in our time* (Pelican Books, Harmondsworth, 1974), pp.97-8; Owen Smith, *West German economy*, p.11.
36. For this and the following see Abelshauser, *Wirtschaftsgeschichte*, pp.51-2 and Abelshauser, "West German economic recovery 1945-1951: A reassessment", pp.41-2.
37. Albrecht Ritschl, "Die Waehrungsreform von 1948 und der Wiederaufstieg der westdeutschen Industrie. Zu den Thesen von Mathias Manz und Werner Abelshauser ueber die Produktionswirkungen der Waehrungsreform", *Vierteljahrshefte fuer Zeitgeschichte*, vol. 33 (1985), p.160.
38. Rainer Klump, *Wirtschaftsgeschichte der Bundesrepublik Deutschland. Zur Kritik neuerer wirtschaftshistorischer Interpretationen aus ordnungspolitischer Sicht* (Steiner Verlag Wiesbaden, Stuttgart, 1985), p.56. The debate on this issue continues and has, because of the nature of the topic under consideration and the problematic statistical sources, a highly speculative element to it. See Ritschl, "Die Waehrungsreform von 1948 und der Wiederaufstieg der westdeutschen Industrie"; Werner Abelshauser, "Schopenhauers Gesetz und die Waehrungsreform. Drei Anmerkungen zu einem methodischen Problem", *Vierteljahrshefte fuer Zeitgeschichte*, vol. 33 (1985), pp.214-8; Christoph Buchheim, "Der Ausgangspunkt des westdeutschen Wirtschaftswunders. Zur erneuten Diskussion ueber die Wirkungen von Waehrungs- und Bewirtschaftungsreform 1948", *Ifo Studien*, vol. 34 (1988), pp.69-77. Also Eckhard Wandel, *Die Entstehung der Bank deutscher Laender und die Waehrungsreform von 1948* (Knapp, Frankfurt am Main, 1980); Heinz Sauermann, "On the economic and financial rehabilitation of Western Germany", *Zeitschrift fuer die gesamte Staatswissenschaft*, vol. 135 (1979), pp.301-19; Hans Moeller, "Die westdeutsche Waehrungsreform von 1948", in Deutsche Bundesbank (ed.), *Waehrung und Wirtschaft in Deutschland 1876-1975* (Fritz Knapp, Frankfurt am Main, pp.433-83.
39. Christoph Buchheim, "Die Waehrungsreform 1948 in Westdeutschland", *Vierteljahrshefte fuer Zeitgeschichte*, vol. 36 (1988), pp.189-231.
40. Friedrich Jerchow, *Deutschland in der Weltwirtschaft 1944-1947. Alliierte Deutschland- und Reparationspolitik und die Anfaenge der westdeutschen Aussenwirtschaft* (Droste, Duesseldorf, 1978), pp.479-80.
41. Abelshauser, *Wirtschaftsgeschichte*, p.31.
42. For this and the following see Manfred Knapp, "Einleitung: Aussenpolitik und Aussenwirtschaftsbeziehungen in der Entstehungsphase des westdeutschen Nachkriegsstaates" in Manfred Knapp (ed.), *Von der Bizonengruendung zur oekonomisch-politischen Westintegration. Studien zum Verhaeltnis zwischen Aussenpolitik und Aussenwirtschaft in der Entstehungsphase der Bundesrepublik Deutschland (1947-1952)* (Haagen und Herchen, Frankfurt am Main, 1984), pp.55-70.
43. Walter Motz, *Die Regelung des Aussenhandels in Deutschland von 1945-1949* (Ph. Diss. Basel, Loerrach, Stetten, 1954), pp.52-69.
44. Hans Moeller, "The reconstruction of the international economic order after the Second World War and the Integration of the Federal Republic of Germany into the world economy", *Zeitschrift fuer die gesamte Staatswissenschaft*, vol. 137 (1981), pp.360-1; Friedrich Jerchow, "Aussenhandel im Widerstreit. Die Bundesrepublik auf dem Wege in das GATT 1949-1951" in Heinrich August Winkler (ed.), *Politische Weichenstellungen im Nachkriegsdeutschland 1945-1953* (Vandenhoeck and Ruprecht, Goettingen, 1979), p.256. Until 1 October 1951 the FRG felt discriminated against because she had to grant the other GATT members preference even in those cases in which members did not do the same towards her.

PART II: THE FEDERAL REPUBLIC OF GERMANY 1949-1985

Chapter Nine

ECONOMIC GROWTH AND FLUCTUATIONS

Models of economic growth

During the 1950s, in the period of the *Wirtschaftswunder* ("economic miracle") economic growth rates in the Federal Republic of Germany were spectacular, but they declined from the 1950s onwards.[1] There are various models which try to explain the astonishing economic growth in the 1950s and its gradual decline. The most popular of them are the "structural change model", the "long wave model" and the "reconstruction model". Whereas the structural change model stresses the new factors which influenced the economic development of the Federal Republic of Germany from the 1950s onwards the two other models emphasise aspects of continuity from the 1870s.[2]

In the "structural change model" the high economic growth rates during the first years of the Federal Republic of Germany are explained by the special conditions of the post-war period, especially by the economic concept of neo-liberalism and the institutional context of the social market economy. According to this view, economic order provided excellent conditions for economic growth. Theory and reality of the "social market economy" fundamentally changed the economic process and made it more efficient. The adherents of the structural change model hold the opinion that it was the market which brought about an optimal allocation of economic resources and that the government assisted this process in interfering as little as possible with the economy. This model has various deficiencies, because it is very difficult to reconcile growing government expenditure and growing government intervention with it.[3]

The "long wave model", which is linked with names like Nikolai Kondratieff,[4] Joseph Schumpeter[5] and Leon Dupriez,[6] regards the development of the capitalist economies from the early nineteenth century onwards as a succession of growth cycles with a duration of 40 to 50 years. According to Schumpeter, clusters of technical innovations are responsible for the beginning of a new wave. In this context the German *Wirtschaftswunder* can be explained as an upswing of a new Kondratieff cycle caused by a cluster of basic technological innovations during the 1930s and 1940s, favourable demand expectations during the reconstruction after the Second World War and the liberalisation of world trade. According to this view, the gradual cessation of technical innovations during the 1960s introduced a cyclical downswing which reached its nadir in the 1970s. Like the "structural change model" the "long wave model" is highly problematic, too, because it is extremely difficult to really prove the existence of long waves of economic development; they bear some resemblance to the Loch Ness monster. It seems that statistical methods are sometimes applied in a way to produce these waves.[7]

The third model was developed by the Hungarian economist Ferenc Jánossy.[8] When applied to German economic development after the Second World War it can be called the "model of economic reconstruction". According to Jánossy it is possible to detect a long term path of "normal" economic growth in German economic development which started in 1870/1. The two World Wars and the "Great Depression" interrupted this trend, but they were to an extent counteracted by economic spurts which enabled the economy to reach the "normal growth path" again. In this sense, the German "economic miracle" of the 1950s is such a temporary spurt which also had to be extremely rapid because the interruption of growth which preceded it had been so severe.

Jánossy's model is based on three key assumptions, namely that it is possible to distinguish "normal growth" from interruptions of growth and that, after an interruption, the economy returns to its former growth path. This is an extremely problematic assumption with a deterministic ring to it. Furthermore he holds the opinion that the normal growth trend is mainly determined by the number and the skill of the workforce, but, because of a lack of capital at the end of an economic crisis, this growth potential cannot be exploited satisfactorily. At the same time, however, there is a high productivity of capital: relatively high growth rates can be achieved by comparatively low levels of investment. During the period

Figure 9.1: Gross national product 1950-1985 [a]

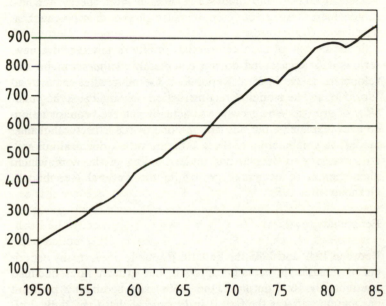

Note: [a] in DM thousand million, 1970 prices, until 1959 without West Berlin and Saarland

Source: Statistisches Bundesamt

of reconstruction the productivity of capital declines until the long-term path of normal economic growth has been reached again.

There are a number of controversial assumptions in Jánossy's model. Moreover, as far as the Federal Republic of Germany is concerned, economic growth in the 1950s far exceeded the process of adjustment to the secular trend. The idea of a long term "normal" growth path is difficult to accept and has a somewhat arbitrary element to it. Not only the mere existence of productive factors but particularly their efficient combination makes economic growth possible. Several factors affected West German economic development after the Second World War which went far beyond "reconstruction", for example the international liberalisation of trade, the Federal Republic's integration into the international trade system and especially into the Western European economy, the immigration of millions of workers from East Germany, many of whom were highly skilled, and an economic order and economic policy which were conducive to growth. Technical change and innovations like nuclear energy and the rapidly increasing use of computers also played an important role from the 1960s onwards.[9]

It shows that all the three models briefly reviewed above have serious deficiencies and do not completely fit the economic development of the Federal Republic of Germany after the Second World War. The model of reconstruction only indicates the *possibility* of growth. Why growth was actually achieved cannot be adequately explained, but this can be done by the "structural change model". A combination of these two can, with a due grain of salt, go some way to deepen our understanding of the complicated phenomenon of economic growth in the Federal Republic of Germany after 1950.[10]

Economic growth

Between 1949 and 1985 the Federal Republic of Germany experienced remarkable economic growth, but growth rates declined continuously. Real output in the 1950s grew by about 8 per cent per annum and was the fastest in Europe at that time.[11] By 1960 unemployment was reduced to less than one per cent, inflation was low, the current account of the balance of payments showed a continuous surplus from 1951 onwards and the Federal Republic's share in world exports of manufactures nearly trebled.

Although growth rates in the 1960s declined, they were still remarkable.[12] As in the 1950s, export-led growth dominated, but the export surplus generated "imported" inflation. The government concentrated on maintaining internal rather than external stability, although both were closely related to each other.

The slower growth in the 1960s was mainly caused by a lower elasticity of the labour supply. With full employment the economy ran up against a supply ceiling.[13] Because of a changing age structure of the population, longer periods spent on education and training and an earlier retirement age, the participation rate declined. Also, the building of the Berlin Wall in August 1961 stopped immigration from East Germany which had played an important role in providing often highly qualified labour for the FRG economy. To make up for a growing labour deficiency, industry in the Federal Republic started recruiting workers from South and South Eastern Europe, Italy, Spain, Greece, Yugoslavia and Turkey. These *Gastarbeiter*, about 250,000 in 1960 and 1.8 million in 1970, were normally not very skilled and generally required more training than those Germans from the East, who had come to work in the FRG in the 1950s. Also, problems of integrating people with a completely different social and cultural background arose, especially Turkish *Gastarbeiter*. In the sixties occupational mobility and labour productivity which had both been high in the 1950s, declined markedly.

Industry reacted to this by introducing capital-intensive methods of production which increased output significantly. A substantial share of goods produced in the FRG was exported, facilitated by an undervalued *Deutsche Mark*. During the 1960s inflation started to increase which, in view of the sad experiences many Germans had with inflation in the 1920s, caused some apprehension. Under the regime of fixed exchange rates and an undervalued *Deutsche Mark* it would have been difficult to avoid inflation, because the Federal German balance of payments surpluses generated a constant increase in the money supply.

In the 1970s growth and conditions for growth deteriorated even further. Inflation and unemployment increased, income grew at a reduced rate. Whereas in the early 1970s a shortage of labour - especially qualified labour - had been an obstacle to growth which was partly remedied by the substitution of labour by capital, the situation changed with the beginning of the recession of 1974/5 and the first oil price shock of October 1973: unemployment rose while vacancies fell. The average 1975 unemployment level of just over one million was about twice as high as it had been in 1967.[14]

After the cyclical downturn in the mid-1970s growth in the second half of the decade was lower than in the first. The economy was beset with several problems which explain the comparatively low rate of investment after the first oil price shock: more difficult foreign trade conditions because of a floating exchange rate against the dollar, growing inflation, higher energy costs (although exports to OPEC countries increased because of higher purchasing power there) and a decline in population growth which implied a falling growth rate of demand. There were also tendencies of market saturation of consumer goods such as washing machines and freezers (although the market for new products, like hi-fi or video equipment, grew and the consumption ratio in the 1970s remained relatively constant) and concern about high public expenditure which might impair private investment and reduce demand because of a high unemployment rate. During the 1970s the terms of trade deteriorated and imports of manufactured goods rose which pointed to lower competitiveness at home.

In the early 1980s real GNP growth slowed down considerably reflecting the deflationary demand impact of the dramatic oil price rise after the end of 1978 and a restrictive economic and financial policy.[15] The fall in the external value of the *Deutsche Mark*, partly brought about by market reaction to the external situation and by differentials between German and United States' interest rates, exacerbated the effects of rising oil and other import prices. Since early 1983 the Federal German economy has experienced a recovery, sparked off by domestic demand but afterwards sustained by foreign demand, which pushed up the current external surplus to over 2 per cent of GNP in 1985, and low raw material (especially mineral oil) prices. Owing to the fact that this period was also one of adjustment and disinflation, economic recovery was weak compared with past experiences.

Fluctuations

During the period 1950-1982 there were eight cycles with a ninth starting in early 1983.[16] These cycles had a duration of between two and five years with most of them lasting about four years.

Figure 9.2: Real growth rates of GNP 1951-1985 [a]

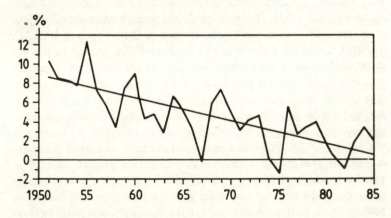

Note: [a] 1970 prices, until 1959 without West Berlin and Saarland
Source: Statistisches Bundesamt

Only five of them, namely the first three, the fifth and the seventh, were "growth cycles" in the sense that they had positive growth rates even in a recession (1953, 1958, 1963, 1971, 1977). This is not completely true of the year 1971, however, in which no proper turn of the business cycle took place, and particularly not of 1975 and 1981/2. From the mid-1960s onwards the "growth cycles" have been replaced by "proper" business cycles.

The above figure shows that the business cycles from 1950 to 1985 have different intensities. Examining the development of the yearly rates of fluctuations the following pattern emerges: a relatively strong upswing is followed by a relatively weak downswing, this is followed by a relatively weak upswing which, in turn, is followed by a relatively strong downswing. However, several downswings (1954, 1971) are hardly below the trendline or do not even touch it (1977), whereas other downswings fall considerably below the trend. It shows that the division of the period 1950-1982 into eight separate cycles is therefore not without problems. In view of the varying intensity of the fluctuations it is also possible to distinguish four long business cycles (1950-8; 1959-67; 1968-75; 1976-82). There are, really, two kinds of business cycles which overlap each other: the short-term "Kitchin cycles" which last about 40 months and are mainly inventory investment cycles and the medium-term "Juglar cycles" (7-9 years) which are usually brought about by fluctuations of investment and have a greater impact on the development of the economy than the Kitchin cycles.[17]

As was pointed out above the trend shows declining growth rates. This trend is in line with growth concepts which suggest that in economies with an imbalance of productive factors a high productivity of capital encourages investment which results in a marked increase in GNP. This expansion of capital will, however, soon lead to a lower productivity of capital with lower investment and growth rates as a consequence. Finally the capital stock reaches a level from which an increase in technological know-how and population determine future economic growth.[18]

Looking at the different business cycles in more detail it shows that the first cycle had a duration of four years and lasted from 1950 to 1954. The currency reform of 1948 had been the main cause for a short, hectic upswing, but as early as the beginning of 1949 a downswing started with growing unemployment which reached 1.3 million in July 1949 after it had amounted to only 450,000 in July 1948.[19] The upswing of 1950 was due to government economic policy measures, especially to an employment and a housing programme, to growing exports and especially to the outbreak of the Korean War in June 1950. With unused capacity which could satisfy export demand the Federal Republic experienced one of many export-generated booms which, however, broke at the turn of 1950-1, when bottlenecks in coal-mining, iron and steel production and electricity generation stifled industrial production.

The next boom was sparked off by the tax reform of 1954, the further liberalisation of external trade and increased demand in the United States. It reached its peak in 1955, when full employment was attained in the FRG for the first time. The boom was broken mainly by the impact of restrictive monetary policies. During the first two cycles the average yearly price increase amounted to only 2 per cent.

The third cycle from 1958/9 to 1963 with its peak in 1960 was mainly generated by strong foreign - particularly US - demand and by internal construction activity. The revaluation of the *Deutsche Mark* in March 1961 and the curtailment of public building orders had contractive effects. In the 1958/9 to 1963 cycle as well as in other cycles the upswing generally came from export demand, because a comparatively low rate of inflation in the FRG, high productivity growth and lagging wage increases generated competitive prices of export goods.

The fourth cycle began at the end of 1963, again because of growing export demand. It reached its peak in 1964 and then declined into the severe recession of 1966/7. Although the cycle had surpassed its peak in 1965, demand was still strong and inflation rose, partly owing to high public expenditure. To curb inflation and stabilise the economy fiscal policy in 1965 decided on cuts in public expenditure. These, however, became effective only in 1966, coinciding with a fall in private investment which declined because of deteriorating profit expectations owing to relatively high wage costs. After the recession had set in unused productive capacities prevented industry from further investment. Helped by an anticyclical fiscal and monetary policy from the beginning of 1967 onwards a new boom developed in the second half of 1967, with a rise in internal demand especially in the investment goods sector and rapidly increasing demand from 1968 onwards which, however, also generated inflation.

The 1970s began with a downswing of this cycle but even then inflation remained high. A new export-led upswing developed in

1972 which peaked in early 1973 when the Ministry of Finance and the *Bundesbank* agreed that fiscal and monetary policy action was required to prevent an overheating of the economy. After the transition to "managed floating" in the spring of 1973 monetary policy was progressively tightened and in May 1973 the Federal government adopted a tough anti-inflationary programme. Consequently internal demand and output fell and unemployment rose.[20]

The outbreak of the oil price crisis in October 1973 worsened the situation dramatically. The trebling of crude oil prices had a (price) inflationary and (demand) deflationary impact on the economy. After the 1974 wage bargaining round in which inflationary expectations played a large role, average contractual wages reached 14 per cent including fringe benefits. This, together with a continuing tight monetary policy, caused a severe profit squeeze to which industry responded by cutting both investment and employment. A slowdown in world trade worsened the situation.[21]

A relaxation of restrictive fiscal and monetary policies and a rise in foreign demand generated an upswing in the second half of 1975 which was, however, not followed by a significant increase in investment demand and faltered towards the end of 1977.[22] Compared with the development after the recession of 1963, growth and investment after 1967 and 1975 were rather weak. Also contrary to the mid 1960s unemployment remained high and so did the public debt. During the upswing following the 1975 crisis two important factors deteriorated markedly, namely the current account deficit and the public debt which increased significantly.[23]

The upswing from 1975 onwards was followed by a "mini" decline until mid-1978 and by a "mini" upswing which ended in 1980; both were characterized by a relatively low capacity utilisation and sluggish investment. In contrast to earlier post-war recessions which lasted only a year on average, the following downswing was unusually long, lasting almost three years. This downturn was also the first after the war with a fall of both private and public consumption. After the oil price shock of 1979/80 exports dropped markedly in the initial phase of the 1980-2 recession, but foreign demand increased in the second year of the downswing, helped by the depreciation of the exchange rate.[24]

Mainly because of weak foreign demand the last upswing has been much slower than the previous ones. In 1968 GNP rose by

6.1 per cent compared with 1967, in 1976 by 5.6 per cent, but in 1983 only by 1.3 per cent. During the upswing exports caught up vigorously in 1984, but fiscal policy remained restrictive compared with the years following the previous two upswings. It was mainly the pick-up in private consumption which led the economy out of recession early in 1983.[25] Owing to sluggish exports and sharply increased imports the upswing began to run out of steam from the middle of 1986 onwards with production stagnating in late 1986 and even declining early in 1987.[26] Recently, however, the performance of the Federal German economy has improved markedly.

Notes

1. As will be shown later there was nothing miraculous about the "miracle".

2. For this and the following see especially Knut Borchardt, "Die Bundesrepublik in den saekularen Trends der wirtschaftlichen Entwicklung", in Werner Conze and M. Rainer Lepsius (eds), *Sozialgeschichte der Bundesrepublik Deutschland* (Klett Cotta, Stuttgart, 1983), pp.20-45.

3. Werner Abelshauser, *Wirtschaftsgeschichte der Bundesrepublik Deutschland 1945-1980* (Suhrkamp, Frankfurt am Main, 1983), p.87.

4. Nikolai D. Kondratieff, "Die langen Wellen der Konjunktur", *Archiv fuer Sozialwissenschaft und Sozialpolitik*, vol. 56 (1926), pp.573-609; Hans Bieshar and Alfred Kleinknecht, "Kondratieff long waves in aggregate output?, *Konjunkturpolitik*, vol. 30 (1984), pp.279-303; Rainer Metz, "Zur empirischen Evidenz 'langer Wellen'", *Kyklos*, vol. 37 (1984), pp.266-90.

5. Joseph Schumpeter, *Business cycles* (2 vols, McGraw-Hill, New York, 1939).

6. Leon H. Dupriez, *Des mouvements économiques généraux* (B. Nauwelaerts, Louvain, 1966).

7. Hansjoerg Siegenthaler, "Vertrauen, Erwartungen und Kapitalbildung im Rhythmus von Strukturperioden wirtschaftlicher Entwicklung: Ein Beitrag zur theoriegeleiteten Konjunkturgeschichte" in Gottfried Bombach and others (eds), *Perspektiven der Konjunkturforschung* (Mohr, Tuebingen, 1984), p.123; Abelshauser, *Wirtschaftsgeschichte*, pp.89-90. See, however, Hans Joachim Gerster, *Lange Wellen wirtschaftlicher Entwicklung. Empirische Analyse langfristiger Zyklen für die USA, Grossbritannien und weitere vierzehn Industrielaender von 1800 bis 1980* (Peter Lang, Frankfurt am Main, Berne, 1988).

8. Ferenc Jánossy, *The end of the economic miracle* (White Plains, New York, 1971).

9. Dietmar Petzina, *Die deutsche Wirtschaft in der Zwischenkriegszeit* (Steiner, Wiesbaden, 1977), p.20. Other examples in which the Federal German economy from the 1950s onwards differed markedly from the period before are given in Borchardt, "Die Bundesrepublik in den saekularen Trends der wirtschaftlichen Entwicklung", p.38.

10. Borchardt, "Die Bundesrepublik", pp.27-8.

11. For this and the following see Klaus Hinrich Hennings, "West Germany" in Andrea Boltho (ed.), *The European economy. Growth and crisis* (Oxford University Press, Oxford, 1982), pp.479-94; Bernd Rohwer, *Konjunktur und Wachstum. Theorie und Empirie der Produktionsentwicklung in der Bundesrepublik Deutschland seit 1950* (Duncker and Humblot, Berlin, 1988).

12. Harald Winkel, *Die Wirtschaft im geteilten Deutschland 1945-1970* (Steiner, Wiesbaden, 1974), pp.78-85.

13. Rainer Vollmer, "The structure of West German foreign trade", *Zeitschrift fuer die gesamte Staatswissenschaft*, vol. 35 (1981), p.577; Eric Owen Smith, *The West German economy* (Croom Helm, London, 1983), p.34.

14. OECD, *Economic surveys, Germany* (OECD, Paris, 1967), p.7.

15. OECD, *Economic surveys, Germany* (OECD, Paris, 1981), p.5.

16. For this and the following see Werner Glastetter, Ruediger Paulert, Ulrich Spoerel, *Die wirtschaftliche Entwicklung in der Bundesrepublik Deutschland 1950-1980. Befunde, Aspekte, Hintergruende* (Campus, Frankfurt am Main, New York, 1983), pp.47-69. See also Adolf Wagner, *Die Wachstumszyklen der Bundesrepublik Deutschland. Eine komparativ-dynamische Komponentenanalyse fuer die Jahre 1951-1970* (Mohr, Tuebingen, 1972), pp.1-7 and Alfred E. Ott and Adolf Wagner, "Materialien zu den Wachstumszyklen in der Bundesrepublik Deutschland" in Alfred E. Ott (ed.), *Wachstumszyklen. Ueber die neue Form der Konjunkturschwankungen. Theoretische und empirische Belege* (Duncker and Humblot, Berlin, 1973), pp.157-81; Winfried Vogt, *Wachstumszyklen der westdeutschen Wirtschaft 1950-1965 und ihre theoretische Erklaerung* (Mohr, Tuebingen, 1968); Philip A. Klein, "Postwar growth cycles in the German economy" in Wilhelm H. Schroeder and Reinhard Spree (eds), *Historische Konjunkturforschung* (Klett, Stuttgart, 1980), pp.115-40; Gernot Mueller, *Der Aktienmarkt im Wachstumszyklus. Eine theoretische und empirische Analyse* (Campus, Frankfurt am Main, New York, 1980), pp.127-53.

17. Elmar Altvater, Juergen Hoffmann and Willi Semmler, *Vom Wirtschaftswunder zur Wirtschaftskrise. Oekonomie und Politik in der Bundesrepublik* (Olle and Wolter, Berlin, 1980), p.209 distinguish investment cycles of 7-9 years duration which are interrupted by an intermediary crisis.

18. Karl Hardach, *The political economy of Germany in the twentieth century* (University of California Press, Berkeley, Los Angeles, London, 1980), p.179. See also the above remarks on Jánossy.

19. For this and the following see Winkel, *Wirtschaft*, pp.85-9.

20. Hennings, "West Germany", p.493.

21. OECD, *Economic surveys, Germany* (OECD, Paris, 1975), p.5.

22. Hennings, "West Germany", p.493.

23. Glastetter, Paulert, Spoerel, *Wirtschaftliche Entwicklung*, pp.38-9. See also Gerhard Willke, *Globalsteuerung und gespaltene Konjunktur. Stabilisierungspolitik bei sektoral differenziertem Zyklus* (Sijthoff, Leyden, London, Boston, 1978), pp.73-96.

24. Hans-Guenther Suesser, "Lehren aus den Konjunkturzyklen der Gegenwart", *Wirtschaftsdienst*, vol. 65 (1985), p.393; OECD, *Economic surveys, Germany* (OECD, Paris, 1985), p.43.

25. Peter Witterauf, "Die konjunkturelle Erholung 1983/84: Ein Vergleich mit den Konjunkturaufschwuengen 1968/69 und 1976/77", *List-Forum*, vol. 13 (1985/6), pp.137, 141.

26. OECD, *Economic surveys, Germany* (OECD, Paris, 1987), p.9.

Chapter Ten

ECONOMIC DOCTRINE AND POLICY

The concept of the Social Market Economy

In the period of reconstruction, ideas on the economic order of a future West German state differed widely. In 1947 there was a widespread consensus that relying on self-regulatory market forces and the self-responsibility of the individual would not provide a remedy for the current economic and social problems. The consequence of unpleasant experiences with "black markets" and the dependence of many citizens on public assistance led many politicians to the conviction that a speedy economic reconstruction and an even distribution of proceeds and burdens could only be achieved by government control of the economy.[1] Not only the Social Democrats but also the Christian Democratic Party in its Ahlen Programme of February 1947 opted for a nationalisation of "enterprises of monopoly character" like the coal and iron industries. At that time many CDU members were convinced that private capitalism had failed and that the nationalisation of key economic sectors would be more conducive to general welfare. In Hesse the state assembly adopted a constitution containing a nationalisation clause.[2]

After prolonged discussions in the party and under the influence of growing East-West tensions which, among others, found expression in the Soviet Berlin blockade and the American *Luftbruecke*, the Christian Democrats decided on a liberal economic system worked out by the neoliberal members of the "Freiburg School", especially Walter Eucken and Franz Boehm. These Neoliberals or *Ordoliberalen* did not advocate an economic *lais-*

sez-faire system. Having experienced the effects of the Great Depression, the inability of liberal parties to solve the social question, the growing concentration of business power among a few corporations, fascism and totalitarianism, their trust in a self-regulatory economic order was badly shaken. On the other hand, the centrally planned and centrally controlled economy did not promise a viable alternative either, because it was incompatible with their political convictions, especially their idea of a constitutional state.[3] The Neoliberals regarded the maintenance and enforcement of the rules of a competitive economic order as their prime objective.[4] Economic stability was to be achieved by a strict control of the money supply. Income inequalities were to be mitigated by a progressive tax system which aimed at relatively low marginal tax rates in order not to undermine risk taking.[5]

Neoliberal ideas exercised a strong influence on the concept of the social market economy which was mainly developed by Alfred Mueller-Armack and then put into practice by Ludwig Erhard, director of the bizonal economic administration 1948/9, Minister of Economic Affairs from 1949 to 1963 and Chancellor of the Federal Republic of Germany from 1963 to 1966. Not only critics of the concept regarded the link between "social" and "market" as contradictory but there was widespread doubt that social progress could be achieved by a market system.[6] Its adherents described the "social market economy" as a permanent search for an economic and social framework designed to encourage both the efficient production of the means of material welfare and personal freedom in a socially balanced order.[7] Whereas the Neoliberals regarded monetary policy as sufficient to smooth business cycles, Mueller-Armack advocated additional fiscal policy measures.[8] Based on neoliberal thinking the "social market economy" tried to work out a "third path" between liberalism on the one hand and socialism on the other, an economic synthesis with the competitive order at the centre. According to the adherents of the social market economy concept, economic growth in a market economy was the best social policy.[9] The social security system was to be shaped according to the principle of "subsidiarity" which meant that the state would only assist those citizens who could not help themselves.[10] This applied to the old and disabled and those who had lost their property during the war and were therefore entitled to receive their share of the "equalisation of burdens levy". Apart from that Mueller-Armack maintained that the social market economy should also provide social security by a certain

177

amount of income redistribution. Government was, however, not to interfere directly with the market process and redistribution was to be carried out by direct transfers. The "social" component in the social market economy did not entail a Scandinavian-type "welfare state" which, according to Erhard, was unsocial, because it incapacitated its citizens. No government, he maintained, could give its citizens more than it had taken away from them beforehand, less the cost of a constantly growing bureaucracy.[11] Mueller-Armack demanded that a second phase of the social market economy was to be inaugurated from 1960 onwards with an extension of the social framework.[12] At the same time Ludwig Erhard proposed the institution of a new social and economic guiding principle, the *formierte Gesellschaft*, with a "new solidarity" between all social groups.[13]

Although not all the aims of the social market economy concept were put into practice the concept later exercised a profound influence on economic policy making.[14] Already in the 1950s, however, there were critics who raised the question as to how the concept would work in a period of declining growth rates. The difficulty of checking powerful organised interests was soon recognized as was the problem of "market failures" in a market economy.[15]

Economic policy 1948-1966

In the beginning Erhard found it difficult to put the concept of the social market economy into practice. Many German politicians and especially members of the Allied High Commission had difficulty believing that the great economic and social problems of the time, especially unemployment, could be solved by neoliberal economic policy. In August 1949 the Allied Bizonal control office demanded measures suitable to reduce unemployment and assist reconstruction. When the growth of industrial production came to a halt at the end of 1949 and the unemployment figure reached two million in February 1950 it insisted on launching a government employment programme. Ludwig Erhard, Minister of Economic Affairs, reluctantly consented to two employment programmes which were, however, rather small.[16]

After the outbreak of the Korean War in June 1950 Federal German economic conditions improved markedly,[17] because the productive capacities of countries like the United States were to a large extent used for armament production which enabled German exporters to sell their products. This was helped by the fact that the *Deutsche Mark* was undervalued against most other currencies. Price stability in Germany was largely due to wage restraint exercised by the trade unions which, with high unemployment, were in a difficult bargaining position.

Although conditions for economic growth were favourable, it would be wrong to neglect the contribution of economic policy and the concept of the social market economy in bringing about a remarkable period of economic growth which is often called the *Wirtschaftswunder* (economic miracle).[18] This contribution consisted mainly of tax exemptions and privileges to business and industrial firms most of which were designed to stimulate capital formation by encouraging savings and ploughed-back profits. There were also export incentives, tax incentives to the shipbuilding industry and housing subsidies. The tax exemptions granted between 1949 and 1957 for the purpose of capital formation have been estimated at DM 28 thousand million.[19]

A much published example of this policy was the investment aid act of January 1952 *(Gesetz ueber die Investitionshilfe der gewerblichen Wirtschaft, Investitionshilfegesetz)* in which bottleneck-industries such as coal mining, iron and steel, electricity and the Federal railways received the proceeds of a levy of DM one thousand million placed on other - mainly the consumer goods - industries which had particularly benefited from economic development after 1948.[20] The first move towards this law came from the top associations of German industry and from the trade unions.[21] It would not be wrong to call this kind of economic and financial policy a supply-side policy.

Between 1952 and 1956 the Federal Finance Minister Fritz Schaeffer managed to keep the Federal budget in surplus. This surplus, which was frozen at the Central Bank, became known as the "Julius Tower" *(Juliusturm)*, a reference to the fortress tower where the Prussian kings had kept their war treasure, and was mainly designed to be spent on setting up the Federal Armed Forces. Without actually intending it Schaeffer with his budget surplus exercised an anticyclical effect on the economy, damping down the boom of 1955-6,[22] which had mainly been caused by high investment owing to strong export demand. In order to assist this policy the German Central Bank *(Bank Deutscher Laender)*, which had been founded by the Allied authorities in March 1948 and was largely independent of the Federal Government established one and a half years later,[23] raised its discount rate and

179

special deposits ratio.

However, before the General Elections of September 1957, the Federal government's expenditure policy jeopardized monetary stability. In order to assure its re-election the government was exceedingly generous with costly spending operations such as an improved old-age pension scheme and the extension of agricultural subsidies known as the "Green Plan". Schaeffer had his *Juli-usturm* pillaged by his cabinet colleagues.[24]

Still, with high growth rates prevailing economic policy did not encounter any major problem. Tax receipts grew and the outlay for the armed forces was smaller than had been expected. It soon became clear, however, that the increasing expenditure on social and agricultural policy could only be financed by continuously high economic growth rates.

A well-functioning competitive order was the cornerstone of the social market economy concept. Already in 1952 the draft of an anti-trust law had been introduced, but strong industrial opposition delayed the enactment of anti-trust legislation until 1957, when the "law against restraints of competition" (*Gesetz gegen Wettbewerbsbeschraenkungen*) was enacted which prohibited cartels and other competition-limiting agreements (with some exceptions) and gave authority to act against abuse of market power and mergers creating or strengthening market dominance. While the first and the last provision have worked out reasonably well, the second has not been very effective, because the statute permitted so many exceptions that it proved unable to stop the continuing trend towards increasing oligopolistic and quasi-monopolistic structures.[25]

In spite of the anti-trust law industrial concentration in the FRG increased markedly during the 1950s and 1960s, especially in shipbuilding, mining and the electrical, chemical and automobile industries. There were also "regulated sectors" like agriculture, housing, transportation, banking and insurance which were exempted from the cartel law and were not - or only to a small degree - subject to market pressures.[26] In its *Mittelstandspolitik* (third estate policy) the government attempted to protect competition in spite of expanding market domination by large corporations. This policy aimed at protecting the economic position of the *Mittelstand* - considered to be a vital pillar of society in the FRG[27] - by trying to assure the survival of small and medium-size enterprises. Cheap public credits and tax privileges were extended to finance the establishment of new small and medium-sized firms. In order to improve the financial position of the lower income groups a limited number of shares of some Federal German denationalised corporations were made available at a "social discount" like the *Volkswagenwerk* shares in 1961.[28]

Economic policy in the 1950s was anything but dogmatically liberal. Although *Ordnungspolitik* aimed at granting as much market freedom as possible the extent of that freedom was not so much determined by economic rationality as by political calculations. Realising this might be the case, neoliberal economists and politicians had advocated the institution of a Central Bank, the *Bundesbank*, with a large measure of independence from short-term political interests. Although government members were entitled to attend the sessions of the *Bundesbank*'s council - the *Bundesbank* had succeeded the *Bank Deutscher Laender* in 1957 and became the FRG's Central Bank - they had no right of vote and could only demand that a Central Bank council decision was delayed for a maximum of two weeks. Also the government would only expect the *Bundesbank* to support governmental economic policy providing the Central Bank's prime objective, monetary stability, was not endangered.

During the 1960s the economic situation deteriorated. Labour became scarce and more expensive which led corporations to substitute labour by capital. Productivity of capital and economic growth rates declined. The hallmark of the German economy in the 1950s, high growth rates combined with monetary stability, no longer existed. After 1958, external problems aggravated the situation. Because of the dollar's weakness and vulnerability the *Deutsche Mark* became the target of international speculation. Inflowing dollars thwarted the *Bundesbank*'s attempts to maintain internal monetary stability. To check the speculative inflow of dollars the *Bundesbank* lowered its discount rate from 5 to 3.5 per cent in November 1960, in the middle of the boom. It urged the Federal government to revalue the *Deutsche Mark* - a measure long overdue - which was finally carried out in March 1961, when the *Deutsche Mark* was revalued by 5 per cent.

During the years 1961 and 1962 the rate of inflation in the FRG was at 4 per cent and in 1963, during a declining business cycle, it still amounted to 3 per cent. Foreign currency continued to flow into the Federal Republic. In this situation there was a growing conviction that the inadequate instruments of monetary policy had to be complemented by a systematic government business cycle policy.[29] To assist the government's economic and financial policy-making the "Council of Economic Experts" (*Sachverstaen-digenrat zur Begutachtung der gesamtwirtschaftlichen Entwicklung*) was founded in 1963. In its first annual report in 1964 the council proposed the introduction of flexible exchange rates to stop imported inflation. Although the government declined, mainly in consideration of the interests of the export industry, it voiced the opinion that some anticyclical intervention into the economy was necessary.[30]

All these intentions were, however, soon forgotten. In 1964, the year before the 1965 elections,[31] the business cycle, which had started in 1963, had reached its peak. In this situation, an anticyclical fiscal policy would have been appropriate. Instead of curtailing state expenditure, outlays were increased by several costly economic and social programmes.[32] Contrary to 1956/7, when the Adenauer government had got away with distributing electoral blessings in a lavish manner, this was now problematic with the economy in a much weaker position than in the 1950s. At the end of 1965 foreign and internal demand shrank. Federal expenditure started exceeding budgetary stipulations and increased faster than national income.

In 1965 and 1966 the *Bundesbank* carried on its policy of fighting inflation; in May 1965 the discount rate reached 5 per cent, the highest so far. As tax receipts were much lower than had been expected, the government on 20 December 1965 passed a bill to stabilise the budget (*Haushaltssicherungsgesetz*) by which some expenditure programmes were suspended. Because of financial difficulties and high interest rates the states and municipalities pursued a procyclical policy by cutting their investment, thus aggravating the cyclical downswing. To remedy the difficult budgetary situation, Chancellor Erhard proposed increasing taxes which the FDP, the Christian Democrats' coalition partner, declined. For this and other reasons the coalition broke apart.[33]

Generally it can be said that until the mid-1960s the government was reluctant to interfere with the economy - apart from matters of competition policy - and had much confidence in the self-regulatory powers of the market. The period from the mid-1960s to the early 1980s, a period of increased social service expenditure, high taxes and adverse budgets, was characterised by attempts at pursuing a systematic anticyclical policy which in the 1970s and early 80s was complemented by a policy to improve the structure of the economy (*Strukturpolitik*).[34]

From macroeconomic state intervention to the *Wende* 1967-1982/5

The first objective of the new "Grand Coalition" government led by Erhard's successor Kurt Georg Kiesinger, which included both Christian and Social Democrats and took office on 1 December 1966, was to overcome the recession. In the first half of 1967 the new government tried to stimulate investment by special depreciations, provided additional investment in the railways and postal services and increased unemployment benefits in order to support consumer demand. In the spring of 1967 the *Bundesbank* lowered its discount rate in successive steps from 5 to 3 per cent. As a basis for Federal economic and financial policy-making and in order to provide the government with various instruments of planning and stabilisation the "Act to promote economic stability and growth" (*Gesetz zur Foerderung der Stabilitaet des Wachstums der Wirtschaft, Stabilitaetsgesetz*) was passed on 8 June 1967.[35]

Medium term anticyclical planning and the use of Keynesian policy instruments were at the centre of Professor Karl Schiller's, the new minister of economic affairs, "new economics". To the economic goal of price stability other policy objectives were added, namely full employment, external equilibrium and an adequate economic growth rate, all adding up to the "magic square" of economic policy.

The Act of 1 December 1967 stipulated that the Federal government engage in medium term (five year) fiscal planning and that Federal, *Laender* and municipal governments' budgeting should be closely linked together. The Federal government had to submit an annual economic report to the *Bundestag* outlining its economic goals for the coming year and - every second year - give an account of the subsidies and grants it had financed. A council for anticyclical policy (*Konjunkturrat*) was established consisting of representatives of the Federal, state and municipal governments and of the *Bundesbank*.[36] Another newly founded institution, the *Konzertierte Aktion* ("concerted action") consisting of government, management and trade union representatives as well as members of the *Bundesbank* and the Council of Economic Experts tried to "prearrange" a stability-oriented income policy in which the development of productivity was regarded as a yardstick for wage settlements.[37]

Karl Schiller aimed at macroeconomic state intervention (*Globalsteuerung*) into the economic process. Strongly influenced by John Maynard Keynes he advocated both the continuation of a market economy and state intervention according to the principle "as much competition as possible, as much planning as necessary". Only "macro-decisions", for example state intervention in order to influence aggregates like investment, income or consumption, were to be made by economic and financial policy, whereas "micro-decisions", for example the determination of prices, were to be left to the market and microeconomic competition. Schiller regarded his concept, which could also be called "demand management",[38] as "enlightened social market economy". He did not believe in "complete competition" à la Walter Eucken which, according to him, could hardly be achieved in practice and if feasible, then only in the form of a "sleepyhead competition", because many small suppliers would not be in the position to compete efficiently. What Schiller aimed at was "workable competiton" which meant that a limitation of competition was permissible if the overall economic aims could be achieved.[39] It is therefore not surprising that the concentration ratio of Federal German industry increased significantly after the mid-1960s.

In achieving the aims of the "magic square" fiscal policy played the largest role in overcoming a depression, whereas *Bundesbank* monetary policy was considered most suitable for curbing a boom. The efficiency of these instruments could, however, be impaired by external factors so that external economic measures like devaluation, revaluations or foreign-exchange controls could become necessary.[40]

Schiller's reflationary policy in the years 1967 and 1968 proved to be successful. By the end of 1967 economic indicators showed an upward trend and at the end of October 1968 not only had full employment been achieved, but also the "dream combination" of an adequate economic growth and stable prices. In 1968 GNP rose by 7.5 per cent while the inflation rate was down to 1.5 per cent.[41]

This impressive achievement did not last for long. Already at that time there were critical voices which feared that macroeconomic state intervention could not achieve its objectives. It took considerable time, for example, before the desired effects of fiscal measures occurred. By that time the economic situation had sometimes changed so that the effects of fiscal policy became counterproductive.[42] Also, macroeconomic state intervention could only have worked satisfactorily if economic forecasting had been in the position to provide fairly reliable information on future economic development, which it was not able to do and probably never will be. Karl Schiller's objective of economic "fine tuning" was, under these conditions, certainly overambitious. As far as "concerted action" is concerned, it seemed that this institution was superfluous in a recession while it did not reach its desired aims in a boom period.[43] Some critics moreover feared that *Globalsteuerung* would sooner or later lead to *Totalsteuerung* (total intervention). Still, in spite of all these reservations and failures *Globalsteuerung* went a long way in breaking the inflationary mentality which had developed over the years.[44]

After the quick overcoming of the 1966/7 recession there was a widespread belief that by means of the "new economic policy" the future business cycle would be "engineered" according to the government's desire. With the boom of the late 1960s inflation increased. According to the concept of global state intervention, overall economic demand should now have been reduced and the price rise dampened. This was tried by curtailing state expenditure and by the *Bundesbank* increasing its discount rate. However, the *Bundesbank*'s monetary instrument did not work adequately because of foreign exchange inflows owing to a Federal German foreign trade surplus. After prolonged speculation about a possible - and necessary - revaluation the *Deutsche Mark* was finally revalued in September 1969.[45] In March of that year the discount rate had already reached a post-war record of 7 per cent. Although this measure had a depressing effect on domestic demand the *Bundesbank*'s policy of keeping interest rates high caused further foreign exchange inflows. The German Central Bank was in a dilemma: in order to fight inflation the interest rate had to be kept high. This, however, attracted foreign exchange inflows which ran counter to the objectives of a tight monetary policy and stimulated inflation.

Financial policy, too, continued its attempts to dampen the boom. On 6/7 July 1970 the first "stabilisation programme" took effect with a 10 per cent repayable surcharge on corporate and personal income taxes and the temporary suspension of degressive depreciation allowances on investment goods.[46]

In 1971 the business cycle weakened, but inflation continued to increase even during the cyclical downturn. Trying to cope with the problem of "stagflation"[47] global state intervention was in a new dilemma: in order to curb inflation overall economic demand would have required some dampening, in order to increase employment it would, however, have been necessary to take completely different measures. In this situation the *Bundesbank* corroborated its policy of price stability which - at least in the short run - was not conducive to higher employment.[48]

In this difficult economic and financial situation problems within the government, which from 1969 onwards had consisted of Social Democrats and Free Democrats - the social-liberal coalition - mounted. In June 1972 the cabinet, following the advice of *Bundesbank* president Karl Klasen, imposed tight exchange controls by requiring foreigners to seek the Central Bank's approval for their purchase of domestic bonds. Federal Economics and Finance Minister Schiller regarded this measure as an unwarrantable constraint on the free market economy and expected it to lead to more controls. He also disagreed with his cabinet colleagues on various other budgetary questions and resigned from the government in July 1972. He was later replaced by Helmut Schmidt.[49]

After the intermediate cyclical upswing in 1972 the main business cycle indicators in 1973 pointed to an incoming recession. In view of continuing inflation both the Federal government with its second "stabilisation programme" of May 1973 and the *Bundesbank* continued their restrictive policies. After the introduction of flexible exchange rates of the *Deutsche Mark* against the dollar - floating - in March 1973 the *Bundesbank* was in a better position to control the internal money supply and more effectively pursue a policy of monetary stabilisation. But in spite of all these efforts the rate of inflation could not be lowered. The restrictive fiscal and monetary policy measures curbed production and employment even further thus contributing to an aggravation of the cyclical downswing.[50]

Although the various causes of the 1974/5 economic crisis are difficult to disentangle, procyclical public expenditure, high wage settlements first in the public sector, then in the private sector, a restrictive monetary policy and the government's hesitation to revalue the *Deutsche Mark* because of export interests, stand out.[51] Inflation put future growth at risk and private capital was increasingly invested in real estate which was considered inflation proof. Profits declined because of high wage settlements and incidental wage costs which induced many industrialists to invest only for increased efficiency. In October 1973 and the following months not only did mineral oil prices rise dramatically, but also many other raw material prices which aggravated the difficult situation. As industry had to cope with high energy and raw material prices in conjunction with receding foreign demand, higher interest rates and high wage settlements, investment was cut even further.[52]

With unemployment rising rapidly during 1974 the government announced three anticyclical programmes comprising a total of DM 3.6 thousand million or 0.4 per cent of GNP. The last of these programmes included a 7.5 per cent investment grant which did not have the desired effect because many corporations, in view of unused capacity, used this grant not for an extension of productive capacity but for investment to increase efficiency which led to further unemployment. On 1 January 1975 a comprehensive fiscal reform package comprising tax reductions and increases of family allowances took effect; in August 1975 an additional support programme was announced to compensate for cyclical demand weaknesses in the construction sector.[53]

These costly state expenditure programmes strained the public purse and led to attempts at consolidating public finance.[54] By the *Gesetz zur Verbesserung der Haushaltsstruktur* (*Haushaltsstrukturgesetz*) of 10 September 1975 future state expenditure was cut substantially. This meant a temporary renunciation of the principles of anticyclical fiscal policy. However, for much of the period 1977 to 1979, fiscal and monetary policy was stimulatory and aimed at reducing the persistently high level of unemployment without exacerbating inflationary pressures. This policy was moderately successful: the public sector deficit fell successively from 6 per cent of GNP in 1975 to 3 per cent in 1979,[55] the number of employees was increased by about one million from 1976 to 1980, although there were still over 900,000 unemployed in 1980[56] while the rate of inflation was reduced successively to 2.7 per cent in 1978.

After 1976 the Federal government in its stabilisation and employment policy relied more on supply-side than on demand measures. Unemployment was considered to be the outcome of insufficient private investment, not the result of insufficient consumer demand. According to this reasoning supply-side conditions had to be improved by lowering taxes, interest rates, social service expenditure and wage costs. The assumption was that under these conditions the industrialists' propensity to invest would be stimulated. These investments would then increase employees' incomes and purchasing power which would not have an inflationary effect as productive capacities were extended accordingly.[57]

In the contemporary debate on economic policy this line of reasoning, which the majority of the "Council of Economic Experts" put forward was by no means undisputed. The trade unions and many Social Democrat politicians maintained that wage increases and lower taxes would strengthen effective demand and overcome unemployment[58] and they repeatedly advocated governmental pump-priming programmes.

Increasing unemployment and stagnating production in the summer of 1980 indicated a business cycle downswing which was mainly caused by the second oil price shock of 1979/80. Also a stronger dollar made raw material imports, which were often paid for in dollars, more costly. At the beginning of 1981 the *Bundesbank* tightened its restrictive stance mainly because of interest rate differentials between the FRG and the United States. Owing to a large public debt in the United States interest rates were high with the likelihood of large capital outflows from the Federal Republic which would have increased the latter's current account deficit.

The Federal government pursued a policy of budget consolidation. It declined to inaugurate new public employment programmes because, according to the government's view, unemployment was not so much due to business fluctuations but to structural problems of the Federal German economy.[59] From 1974 onwards, monetary policy had tried to refrain from anticyclical demand-management. In that year the *Bundesbank* began to announce periodically an annual target growth for the Central Bank money stock (CBM).[60] The main objective was to generate monetary conditions conducive to economic growth without creating a potential for a resurgence of inflation. The new policy approach of setting an 8 per cent target for the growth of the Central Bank money stock during 1975 was inspired by the assumption that optimal long-term stabilisation could best be achieved by ensuring steady growth of monetary aggregates. However, CBM growth overshot its targets from 1975 to 1978 and increasing overshooting was the reason why a target range replaced the fixed-point target.[61]

While monetary policy was restrictive in 1979 and 1980 following the oil price rise and pressures on the exchange rate the *Bundesbank* in 1982, with the current balance swinging back into surplus but the economy still in recession, allowed CBM growth to drift towards the upper limit of the target range which caused interest rates to fall.

Because of the precarious state of public finance during the recession of the early 1980s - the government had failed to reduce the public debt during the cyclical upswing of 1977-9 - the SPD-FDP coalition government agreed in September 1981 on a financial consolidation programme - "Operation 82" - which applied to both the public expenditure and the revenue side: cuts in family allowances, tighter conditions for entitlement to employment benefits and employment subsidies, abolition of tax exemptions, in-

Figure 10.1: Central bank monetary targets and growth 1975-1986

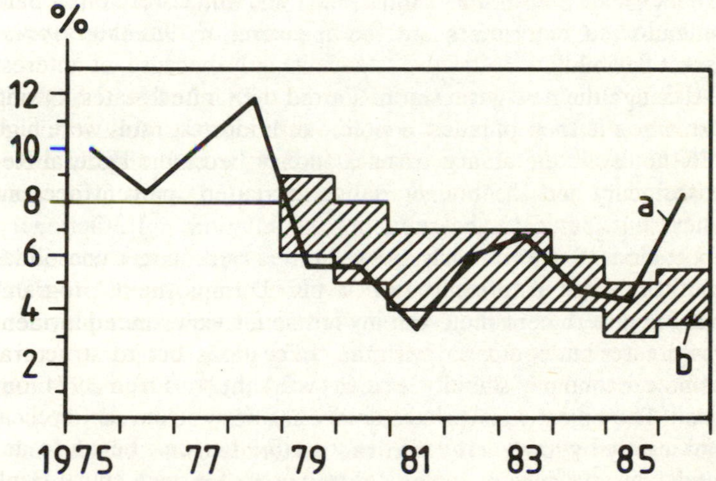

Notes: [a] CBM growth; [b] CBM target
Source: Deutsche Bundesbank, *Monatsberichte*

creases in some indirect taxes and social service contributions.[62] In view of the sharp rise in unemployment, however, the government introduced an employment creation package in February 1982 which was primarily geared to stimulate investment. In this increasingly difficult economic and financial situation negotiations about balancing the budget led to the break-up of the social-liberal coalition in September 1982.[63]

In late 1982 internal and external conditions for economic policy improved. Interest rates began to decline worldwide, the Federal Republic's foreign trade surplus was considerable and wage settlements were modest. In its economic policy the new CDU-FDP coalition government, which had taken office in October 1982, was medium-term oriented and focused on improving supply-side conditions and strengthening market forces, thus, according to their representatives, trying to bring about a fundamental political "turn" (*Wende*) away from former social-liberal policy. It aimed at a reduction of public sector borrowing and at a cutback in the size of the public sector in order to make resources available for the private sector and thereby encourage growth. To achieve its aim the government embarked on the privatisation of public holdings and services, cuts in the social service sector, dismantlement of bureaucratic impediments, promotion of risk capital formation, support for technological innovations and the foundation of small and medium-sized enterprises and on measures to increase labour market flexibility.

Although the new government started with a further rise of net borrowings it then pursued a policy of budget consolidation. In 1986, however, the stance of fiscal policy became slightly more expansionary and the budget deficit increased again. Monetary policy contributed to the reduction of inflation and inflationary expectations. Since the early 1980s interest rates have come down significantly to historically low levels. During the CDU-FDP coalition government the economy has so far experienced modest growth rates but compared with the policy goals set by the "Act to promote economic stability and growth" the results have been mixed. The objective of price stability has been achieved - helped significantly by low energy and raw material costs - but the substantial current account surplus does not square with the goal of external equilibrium. Above all the high employment objective has not been achieved.[64] Also subsidisation which had grown rapidly during the 1970s and had stabilised at the beginning of the 1980s has started rising again more recently.[65] Within industry structurally weak branches such as coal mining and shipbuilding have received increasing support. Furthermore subsidisation has been extended to both "sunrise industries" e.g. aircraft and aero-space firms and to branches characterised by chronic overcapacity such as steel.[66]

Notes

1. Reinhard Blum, "Marktwirtschaft, soziale" in *Handwoerterbuch der Wirtschaftswissenschaften* (G. Fischer, Mohr, Vandenhoeck and Ruprecht, Stuttgart, Tuebingen, Goettingen, 1980), vol. 5, p.154; Christian Watrin, "The principles of the Social Market Economy - its origins and history", *Zeitschrift fuer die gesamte Staatswissenschaft*, vol. 135 (1979), p.414; Otto Schlecht, "Die Genesis des Konzeptes der Sozialen Marktwirtschaft" in Otmar Issing (ed.), *Zukunftsprobleme der Sozialen Marktwirtschaft. Verhandlungen auf der Jahrestagung des*

Vereins fuer Socialpolitik - Gesellschaft fuer Wirtschafts- und Sozialwissenschaften - in Nuernberg 1980 (Duncker and Humblot, Berlin, 1981), pp.9-31.

2. Karl Hardach, *The political economy of Germany in the twentieth century* (University of California Press, Berkeley, Los Angeles, London, 1980), p.142; Alfred Mueller-Armack, "Die Anfaenge der Sozialen Marktwirtschaft - Zugleich eine Dokumentation ihrer Entwicklung in den Jahren 1945, 1946, 1947, 1948" in Richard Loewenthal and Hans-Peter Schwarz (eds), *Die zweite Republik. 25 Jahre Bundesrepublik Deutschland - eine Bilanz* (Seewald, Stuttgart-Degerloch, 1974), p.126; Gerold Ambrosius, *Die Durchsetzung der Sozialen Marktwirtschaft in Westdeutschland 1945-1949* (Deutsche Verlags-Anstalt, Stuttgart, 1977); Gerold Ambrosius, "Marktwirtschaft oder Planwirtschaft? Planwirtschaftliche Ansaetze der bizonalen Selbstverwaltung 1946-1949", *Vierteljahrschrift fuer Sozial- und Wirtschaftsgeschichte*, vol. 66 (1979), pp.74-110.

3. Helmut Leipold, "Gesellschaftstheoretische Fundierung der Wirtschaftssysteme" in Hannelore Hamel (ed.), *Bundesrepublik Deutschland - DDR. Die Wirtschaftssysteme. Soziale Marktwirtschaft und sozialistische Planwirtschaft im Systemvergleich*, 4th edn (Beck, Munich, 1983), p.32.

4. Joachim Starbatty, "Ordoliberalismus" in Otmar Issing (ed.), *Geschichte der Nationaloekonomie* (Vahlen, Munich, 1984), pp.187-203.

5. Eric Owen Smith, *The West German economy* (Croom Helm, London, 1983), p.20.

6. Joachim Starbatty, "Die Soziale Marktwirtschaft aus historisch-theoretischer Sicht" in Hans Pohl (ed.), *Entstehung und Entwicklung der Sozialen Marktwirtschaft* (Steiner, Stuttgart, 1986), pp.7-9; Alfred Mueller-Armack, "Soziale Marktwirtschaft" in *Handwoerterbuch der Sozialwissenschaften* (G. Fischer, Stuttgart, 1956), vol. 9, p.390; Hans G. Schachtschabel, *Wirtschaftspolitische Konzeptionen* (Kohlhammer, Stuttgart, Mainz, 1967), pp.88-97.

7. Watrin, "The principles of the Social Market Economy - its origins and history", p.419; Andreas Mueller-Armack, "Das Konzept der Sozialen Marktwirtschaft - Grundlagen, Entwicklung, Aktualitaet", in Dieter Grosser, Thomas Lange, Andreas Mueller-Armack and Beate Neuss (eds) *Soziale Marktwirtschaft. Geschichte - Konzept - Leistung* (Kohlhammer, Stuttgart, Berlin, 1988), pp.1-34.

8. Rainer Klump, *Wirtschaftsgeschichte der Bundesrepublik Deutschland. Zur Kritik neuerer wirtschaftshistorischer Interpretationen aus ordnungspolitischer Sicht* (Steiner, Stuttgart, 1985), p.65.

9. Blum, "Marktwirtschaft, soziale", p.155; Reinhard Blum, *Soziale Marktwirtschaft. Wirtschaftspolitik zwischen Neoliberalismus und Ordoliberalismus* (Mohr, Tuebingen, 1969).

10. Leipold, "Gesellschaftstheoretische Fundierung der Wirtschaftssysteme", p.36.

11. Ludwig Erhard, *Deutsche Wirtschaftspolitik. Der Weg der Sozialen Marktwirtschaft* (Econ, Duesseldorf, Vienna, 1962), p.393.

12. Alfred Mueller-Armack, *Wirtschaftsordnung und Wirtschaftspolitik* (Rombach, Freiburg i.B., 1966).

13. Erhard, *Deutsche Wirtschaftspolitik*, p.491; Christoph Heusgen, *Ludwig Erhards Lehre von der Sozialen Marktwirtschaft. Urspruenge, Kerngehalt, Wandlungen* (Haupt, Berne, Stuttgart, 1981),pp.225-33.

14. Terence W. Hutchison, "Notes on the effects of economic ideas on policy: the example of the German social market economy", *Zeitschrift fuer die gesamte Staatswissenschaft*, vol. 135 (1979), pp.426-41.

15. Knut Borchardt, "Die Konzeption der Sozialen Marktwirtschaft in heutiger Sicht" in Otmar Issing (ed.), *Zukunftsprobleme der Sozialen Marktwirtschaft. Verhandlungen auf der Jahrestagung des Vereins fuer Socialpolitik - Gesellschaft fuer Wirtschafts- und Sozialwissenschaften - in Nuernberg 1980* (Duncker and Humblot, Berlin, 1981), pp.43, 46.

16. Werner Abelshauser, *Wirtschaftsgeschichte der Bundesrepublik*

Deutschland 1945-1980 (Suhrkamp, Frankfurt am Main, 1983), pp.65-6.

17. For this and the following see Dieter Grosser, "Das Verhaeltnis von Staat und Wirtschaft in der Bundesrepublik Deutschland" in Dieter Grosser (ed.), *Der Staat in der Wirtschaft der Bundesrepublik* (Leske and Budrich, Opladen, 1985), pp.38-59.

18. Ludwig Erhard did not approve of this term and quite rightly maintained that there are few miracles in economics and politics.

19. Karl W. Roskamp, "Competition and growth - the lesson of West Germany: Comment", *American Economic Review*, vol. 50 (1960), pp.1015-18; Henry C. Wallich, *The mainsprings of the German revival* (Yale University Press, New Haven, 1955), pp.161-2. See also Joachim Scheide, "Die deutsche Konjunkturpolitik in den fünfziger Jahren - Beginn einer Globalsteuerung?", *Konjunkturpolitik*, vol. 33 (1987), pp.243-67.

20. Heiner R. Adamsen, *Investitionshilfe fuer die Ruhr. Wiederaufbau, Verbaende und Soziale Marktwirtschaft 1948-1952* (Hammer, Wuppertal, 1981), pp.154-235; Andrew Shonfield, *Modern Capitalism. The changing balance of public and private power* (Oxford University Press, London 1965), p.25.

21. Werner Abelshauser, "The first post-liberal nation: stages in the development of modern corporatism in Germany", *European History Quarterly*, vol. 14 (1984), p.306.

22. Owen Smith, *West German economy*, p.73.

23. Hans-Hermann Francke and Michael Hudson, *Banking and finance in West Germany* (Croom Helm, London, 1984), pp.27-8.

24. Shonfield, *Modern capitalism*, p.285.

25. Sima Lieberman, *The growth of European mixed economies 1945-1970*, (Schenkman, Cambridge, Mass., 1977), p.199; OECD, *Economic surveys, Germany* (OECD, Paris, 1987), p.58.

26. Hardach, *Political economy*, pp.147-51.

27. Heinrich August Winkler, "Stabilisierung durch Schrumpfung: Der gewerbliche Mittelstand in der Bundesrepublik" in Werner Conze and M. Rainer Lepsius (eds), *Sozialgeschichte der Bundesrepublik Deutschland, Beitraege zum Kontinuitaetsproblem* (Klett-Cotta, Stuttgart, 1983), pp.201-2.

28. Lieberman, *European mixed economies*, p.200.

29. Grosser, "Das Verhaeltnis von Staat und Wirtschaft in der Bundesrepublik", pp.44-5.

30. Shonfield, *Modern Capitalism*, p.287; Owen Smith, *West German economy*, p.73.

31. Reinhard Lenk, "Politische Konjunkturzyklen" in Gottfried Bombach, Bernhard Gahlen, Alfred E. Ott (eds) *Moeglichkeiten und Grenzen der Staatstaetigkeit* (Mohr, Tuebingen, 1982), p.337.

32. Herbert Giersch, "Episoden und Lehren der Globalsteuerung", in Heiko Koerner, Peter Meyer-Dohm, Egon Tuchtfeldt and Christian Uhlig (eds), *Wirtschaftspolitik - Wissenschaft und politische Aufgabe. Festschrift zum 65. Geburtstag von Karl Schiller* (Haupt, Berne, Stuttgart, 1976), p.278.

33. Klaus Hildebrandt, *Von Erhard zur Grossen Koalition 1963-1969 (= Geschichte der Bundesrepublik Deutschland, vol. 4)* (Deutsche Verlags-Anstalt, Stuttgart, 1984), pp.218-40. On how far the *Bundesbank* was responsible for the crisis of 1966/7 see Gudrun Narr-Lindner, *Grenzen monetaerer Steuerung. Die Restriktionspolitik der Bundesbank 1964-1974* (Campus, Frankfurt am Main, New York, 1984), pp.180-94.

34. Grosser, "Das Verhaeltnis von Staat und Wirtschaft in der Bundesrepublik", p.47.

35. Egbert Osterwald, *Die Entstehung des Stabilitaetsgesetzes. Eine Studie ueber Entscheidungsprozesse des politischen Systems* (Campus, Frankfurt am Main, New York, 1982).

36. Lieberman, *European mixed economies*, p.209.

37. Heinz-Dieter Hardes, *Einkommenspolitik in der BRD. Stabilitaet und Gruppeninteressen: Der Fall Konzertierte Aktion* (Herder and Herder, Frankfurt am Main, New York, 1974).

38. Giersch, "Episoden und Lehren der Globalsteuerung", p.277-8. Also Walter Adolf Joehr, "Karl Schiller - ein Mann der Synthese" in Heiko Koerner and others (eds), *Wirtschaftspolitik - Wissenschaft und politische Aufgabe* (Haupt, Berne, Stuttgart, 1976), pp.17-44 and Karl Schiller, *Der Oekonom und die Gesellschaft. Das freiheitliche und das soziale Element in der modernen Wirtschaftspolitik* (Gustav Fischer, Stuttgart, 1964).

39. Hans-Rudolf Peters, "Anmerkungen zu Karl Schillers wirtschaftspolitischer Konzeption der globalgesteuerten Marktwirtschaft", in Heiko Koerner and others (eds), *Wirtschaftspolitik - Wissenschaft und politische Aufgabe* (Haupt, Berne, Stuttgart, 1976), p.159; Marianne Welteke, *Theorie und Praxis der Sozialen Marktwirtschaft. Einfuehrung in die politische Oekonomie der BRD* (Campus, Frankfurt am Main, New York, 1976), pp.132-4.

40. Bernhard Keller, *Wirtschaftstheorie und Wirtschaftspolitik in der Bundesrepublik Deutschland,* 2nd edn (Diesterweg, Frankfurt am Main, Berlin, Munich, 1984), pp.62-95 for this and the following.

41. Peters, "Anmerkungen", p.157.

42. Giersch, "Episoden", p.284.

43. Peters, "Anmerkungen", pp.165-8.

44. Otto Schlecht, "Hat die Globalsteuerung versagt?" in Heiko Koerner and others (eds), *Wirtschaftspolitik - Wissenschaft und politische Aufgabe* (Haupt, Berne, Stuttgart, 1976), p.305.

45. Otmar Emminger, "Deutsche Geld- und Waehrungspolitik im Spannungsfeld zwischen innerem und aeusserem Gleichgewicht" in Deutsche Bundesbank (ed.), *Waehrung und Wirtschaft in Deutschland 1876-1975* (Knapp, Frankfurt am Main, 1976), p.517-20.

46. Sachverstaendigenrat zur Begutachtung der gesamtwirtschaftlichen Entwicklung, *Konjunktur im Umbruch - Risiken und Chancen. Jahresgutachten 1970/71* (Kohlhammer, Stuttgart, Mainz, 1970), p.34.

47. See on stagflation Gottfried Haberler, "Stagflation: an analysis of its causes and cures" in Bela Balassa and Richard Nelson (eds), *Economic progress, private values and public policy. Essays in honour of William Fellner* (North Holland Publ., Amsterdam, New York, Oxford, 1977), pp.311-29. Also: Christoph von Roehl, *Grosse Depression und Stagflation. Eine kritische Analyse der deutschen Wirtschaftspolitik 1927/33 und 1970/86* (Vandenhoeck and Ruprecht, Goettingen, 1988).

48. Joachim Starbatty, *Erfolgskontrolle der Globalsteuerung. Konjunkturpolitik unter dem Einfluss der politischen Willensbildung* (Knapp, Frankfurt am Main, 1976), pp.202-17.

49. Owen Smith, *West German economy*, p.78.

50. Gernot Mueller, "Die Rolle der staatlichen Konjunkturpolitik bei Entstehung und Verlauf der Krise seit 1973", *WSI-Mitteilungen*, 1980, pp.174-86. On monetary and financial policy also Hans-Hermann Francke, "Konsistenzprobleme der Geld- und Finanzpolitik in den siebziger Jahren" in Werner Ehrlicher and Diethard B. Simmert (eds), *Geld- und Waehrungspolitik in der Bundesrepublik Deutschland* (Duncker and Humblot, Berlin, 1982), pp.231-43.

51. Harald Scherf, *Enttaeuschte Hoffnungen - vergebene Chancen. Die Wirtschaftspolitik der Sozial-Liberalen Koalition 1969-1982* (Vandenhoeck and Ruprecht, Goettingen, 1986), pp.36-7.

52. Grosser, "Das Verhaeltnis von Staat und Wirtschaft in der Bundesrepublik", p.51.

53. OECD, *Economic surveys, Germany* (OECD, Paris, 1976), p.20.

54. By the *Gesetz zur Verbesserung der Haushaltsstruktur* of 10 September 1975 (*Haushaltsstrukturgesetz)* future state expenditure was cut to a substan-

tial degree.

55. OECD, *Economic surveys, Germany* (OECD, Paris, 1980), p.28.

56. Scherf, *Enttaeuschte Hoffnungen,* p.51.

57. Grosser, "Das Verhaeltnis von Staat und Wirtschaft in der Bundesrepublik", pp.54-5.

58. Critical on this are Peter von der Lippe and Horst-Dieter Westerhoff, "Die sozialliberale Reformpolitik: ein wirtschaftspolitischer Irrweg", *Ordo,* vol. 36 (1985), pp.25-6.

59. Keller, *Wirtschaftstheorie und Wirtschaftspolitik,* pp.88-9.

60. The *Bundesbank's* target variable - the "adjusted" Central Bank money stock - is defined as currency in circulation plus banks' minimum reserves on domestic bank liabilities at constant reserves ratios of January 1974. See OECD, *Economic surveys, Germany* (OECD, Paris, 1980), p.28.

61. Manfred Willms, "Zehn Jahre Geldmengensteuerung", *Wirtschaftsdienst, vol. 63 (1983),* pp.597-8. OECD, *Economic surveys, Germany* (OECD, Paris, 1984), p.30.

62. Werner Ehrlicher, "Wandlungen in den Konzepten der Geld-, Finanz- und Lohnpolitik 1948-1986" in Wolfgang Filc, Lothar Huebl and Ruediger Pohl (eds), *Herausforderungen der Wirtschaftspolitik. Festschrift zum 60. Geburtstag von Klaus Koehler* (Duncker and Humblot, Berlin, 1988), pp.315-36. OECD, *Economic surveys, Germany* (OECD, Paris, 1982), p.29; *Economic surveys, Germany* (OECD, Paris, 1984), p.30.

63. Scherf, *Enttaeuschte Hoffnungen,* pp.56-61.

64. OECD, *Economic surveys, Germany* (OECD, Paris, 1985), pp.8-9; 1986, p.62; 1987, p.17; 1986, p.81.

65. Sachverstaendigenrat zur Begutachtung der gesamtwirtschaftlichen Entwicklung, *Weiter auf Wachstumskurs. Jahresgutachten 1986/87* (Kohlhammer, Stuttgart, Mainz, 1986), p.89.

66. OECD, *Economic surveys, Germany* (OECD, Paris, 1987), p.56.

Chapter Eleven

PUBLIC FINANCE

Government revenue and expenditure

During the last hundred years the state's share in GNP has risen rapidly. Whereas it accounted for only 11 per cent in 1881 it rose

Figure 11.1: Government receipts and expenditure 1950-1985 ^{c}

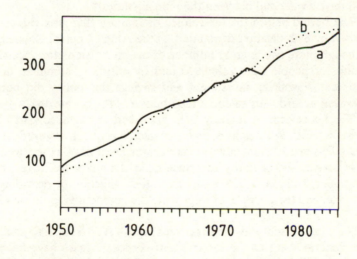

Notes: ^{a} revenue; ^{b} expenditure;
         ^{c} 1970 prices, until 1959 excluding Saarland or West-Berlin
Source: Statistisches Bundesamt

195

to more than 15 per cent in 1913, more than 25 per cent in 1928, 31 per cent in 1960, 37 per cent in 1969 and roughly 49 per cent in 1982.[1]

According to the basic law (*Grundgesetz*) the distribution of tax receipts is regulated between the three governmental units (Federal government, states and local authorities) in a way that the Federal government receives, among others, the consumption tax (without the beer tax), customs duties, state monopolies like the duty on matches (until 1983) and the turnover tax. The *Laender* receive the tax on property, the automobile tax and the beer tax, whereas the receipts of the occupation tax and the land tax go to the municipalities. The income and corporate taxes are distributed between the Federal government and the *Laender*. With the financial reform of 1969 the pay-as-you-earn income tax and the turnover tax were added to this as "communal taxes" (*Gemeinschaftssteuern*).

In demanding similar living conditions (*Einheitlichkeit der Lebensverhaeltnisse*) in the *Laender* the basic law also stipulated provisions for tax sharing between the Federal German states (*Laenderfinanzausgleich*) with the consequence that the wealthier states had to transfer part of their revenue to the less affluent. There has also been tax sharing between the Federal government and the *Laender* and between the municipalities.[2]

The period before the tax reform of January 1955 was characterised by high taxation demanded by the Allied Control Council, although there was a great number of tax concessions for special groups of people (like refugees) and by efforts to stimulate investment. Favouring investment and savings this policy did not, however, accord with an equal distribution of the tax burden.

The tax reform of January 1955 abolished or curtailed part of these benefits. Although income tax rates have been lowered repeatedly since 1955 mainly to make up for fiscal drag, other taxes have been raised or newly introduced, like the motor traffic tax or the mineral oil tax, which, apart from their function of providing revenue, had the purpose of improving the competitive position of the Federal Railways.[3]

Until the present day the turnover tax or VAT (from 1968) and the Federal share of the income and corporate taxes have been the main pillars of taxation. Compared with these, the other taxes have declined in significance, like the tobacco tax or other consumption taxes (coffee, tea) or the customs duties which, in their significance for the Federal budget, have declined mainly because of the FRG's membership in the Common Market.[4]

While the share of the Federal government's current revenue in GNP rose considerably in the 1960s and early 1970s it has, since then, risen more slowly and roughly stabilised in recent years. Although VAT rates have been raised repeatedly (from 10 per

Table 11.1: Federal government revenue 1950-1985 [a]

	Total	Taxes				Customs
		Turnover	Direct[b]	Min. oil	Tobacco	
1950	12.4	4.9	---	0.1	2.1	0.7
		(39.5%)	---	(0.8%)	(16.9%)	(5.6%)
1955	26.1	11.1	4.1	1.1	2.6	1.8
		(42.5%)	(15.7%)	(4.2%)	(10.0%)	(6.9%)
1961	44.7	17.9	10.4	3.3	3.9	3.1
		(40.0%)	(23.3%)	(7.4%)	(8.7%)	(6.9%)
1965	59.0	24.3	16.0	7.4	4.7	2.9
		(41.2%)	(27.1%)	(12.5%)	(8.0%)	(4.9%)
1970	87.3	26.8	27.3	11.5	6.5	2.8
		(30.7%)	(31.3%)	(13.2%)	(7.4%)	(3.2%)
1975	123.0	34.2	48.8	17.1	8.9	0.08[c]
		(27.8%)	(39.7%)	(13.9%)	(7.2%)	(0.1%)
1980	189.5	56.9	75.8	21.4	11.3	0.08[c]
		(30.0%)	(40.0%)	(11.3%)	(6.0%)	(0.04%)
1985	235.9	62.1	93.9	24.5	14.5	0.06[c]
		(26.3%)	(39.8%)	(10.4%)	(6.2%)	(0.03%)

Notes: [a] in DM thousand million

[b] Federal government's share of income and corporate taxes

[c] excluding share of Common Market (EEC)

Source: Statistisches Bundesamt, *Statistische Jahrbuecher.*

cent in 1968 to 14 per cent in 1983) the relative contribution of in-direct taxes to revenue has diminished. Social security contributions have risen fastest - between 1970 and 1981 the share of social security contributions to GNP rose from 11 per cent to 14 per cent, because of demographic developments, more generous benefits and weaker economic growth after the first oil shock. Although the share of total direct taxes changed little their structure changed significantly. Wage receipts increased much faster than other direct taxes, mainly because of the rising share of wage incomes in total income, the progressive income tax schedule and the growing number of taxpayers in the steepest part of the schedule.[5]

Tax evasion and the shadow economy have created particular problems. By international standards the difference between take-home pay and labour costs for the employers is large and the high tax burden has contributed to shadow economy activities. Although the extent of those activities is difficult to assess their share in GNP was probably only 1 to 2 per cent in the early 1960s but might have reached more than 10 per cent in the early 1980s.[6]

According to the Federal German basic law the Federal government, the *Laender* and the local authorities have different tasks to fulfil. In the early 1980s the main areas of Federal government expenditure were social security and defense. The *Laender* spent most on education and the municipalities on the health service. From the 1950s onwards there has been a tendency for the Federal government to intervene in the financial affairs of the *Laender*, assisting in costly higher educational reform programmes, the improvement of the regional economic structure and the agricultural sector.[7]

After the initial high outlays on the Federal armed forces the share of defense expenditure fell significantly. Since 1953 expenditures on social security (excluding outlays of social security agencies) and housing have been falling relative to other outlays, because government expenditure on these items in the years immediately after the Second World War had been particularly high.[8] While the share of outlays on public security has risen only slowly that on research and education (especially higher education) more than doubled in the period 1950 to 1985 owing to an educational policy which aimed at substantially increasing undergraduate figures. Between 1965 and 1975 student numbers in higher education grew by about 10 per cent per annum. Owing to demographic pressures - the structure of the Federal German population has been steadily ageing - and costly health policy outlays have risen.

Table 11.2: *Expenditure of the Federal government, the regional and the local authorities by functions, 1950-1985* [a]

	1950	1956	1961	1965	1970	1975	1980	1985
total	28.1	59.9	95.3	140.6	196.3	344.4	486.8	574.9
defense	4.7	7.3	13.2	18.9	19.8	33.6	41.8	51.7
(%)	16.7	12.2	13.4	13.4	10.1	9.8	8.6	9.0
law and order	1.1	2.5	3.7	5.3	7.9	17.9	25.4	30.4
(%)	3.9	4.2	3.9	3.8	4.0	5.2	5.2	5.3
research, education, higher education	2.1	5.2	9.6	15.9	27.6	61.5	85.1	94.9
(%)	7.5	8.7	10.0	11.3	14.1	17.9	17.5	16.5
social security	7.6	15.6	22.2	31.3	40.4	81.4	100.1	116.1
(%)	27.1	26.0	23.3	22.3	20.6	23.6	20.6	20.2
health service and recreation	1.0	2.2	3.8	6.3	10.2	16.1	15.1	26.9
(%)	3.6	3.8	4.0	4.5	5.2	4.7	3.1	4.7
housing, regional planning	3.5	5.8	7.6	10.3	10.7	12.0	21.5	20.0
(%)	12.5	9.7	8.0	7.3	5.5	3.5	4.4	3.5
state assistance to the economy	1.9	4.3	6.3	10.2	14.4	16.1	13.0	17.9
(%)	6.8	7.2	6.6	7.3	7.3	4.7	2.8	3.1
transport and communication	1.3	3.7	6.9	11.3	17.6	32.9	40.5	37.5
(%)	4.6	6.2	7.2	8.0	9.0	9.6	8.3	6.5
others	4.9	13.3	22.0	30.3	48.1	72.9	144.3	179.5
(%)	17.4	22.2	23.1	21.5	24.5	21.2	30.0	31.2

Note: [a] in DM thousand million, until 1959 without Saarland

Source: Statistisches Bundesamt and own computations

In 1980 payments and transfers for social security comprised 17 per cent of total household incomes and one-third of total Federal government outlays. Social security expenditure has been influenced by a changing population, by accelerating inflation during the 1970s and especially by the strong secular growth of real benefits provided to individuals.[9]

During the 1970s the share of investment outlays in total government expenditure fell. Government consumption rose more than 25 times in the period 1950 to 1985 and the number of people employed in the public sector grew by about 250 per cent.[10]

In connection with high public spending and a rapidly increasing public debt during the 1970s outlays for debt service grew rapidly. Whereas until 1966 the share of interest payments in public expenditure amounted to less than 3 per cent and was still below 4 per cent in 1974 it rose to 8 per cent in 1982. Between 1970 and 1983 payments for debt service rose almost eightfold from DM 6.55 thousand million to DM 50.69 thousand million.[11] Government subsidies were another matter of concern which, in spite of the declared intentions of government members to cut them drastically, rose from DM 490 million in 1950 to DM 11,780 million in 1970 and DM 36,920 million in 1985.

Public debt

From 1950 to 1985 the debts of the Federal government and the regional and local authorities rose from DM 20,634 million to DM 760,192 million. Whereas the share of the public debt in GNP was below 20 per cent during the first half of the 1970s it rose to over 31 per cent in 1980 and over 41 per cent in 1985.

Until the 1960s the major part of the public debt did not arise from government borrowing, but consisted of "old debts" taken over from the "Third Reich" and from foreign debts which were added after the agreement on repaying German pre-war debts at the London conference of 27 February 1953.[12] During the 1950s and the first half of the 1960s the government did not contract any significant debts. Owing to the first recession of the post-war period (1967), which the Federal government tried to overcome by two investment programmes, the public debt rose significantly, but by 1969 the government's net borrowing was again reduced substantially. The deep recession of 1974/5 and anticyclical fiscal measures caused another steep rise of the public debt: from 1974 to 1975 public borrowing rose two and a half times. During the period 1975-7 the Federal, regional and local authorities incurred more internal debts than they had done during the whole preceding 25 years.

Figure 11.2: Public debt 1950-1985 ^c

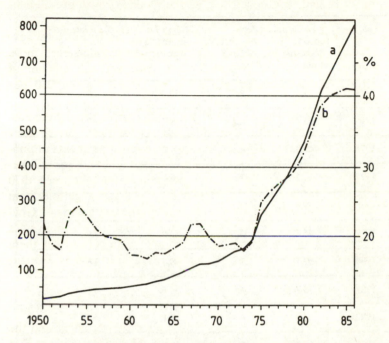

Notes: ^a amount (left scale); ^b share of GNP (right scale)
 ^c current prices in DM thousand million, before 1959 excluding Saarland
Source: Deutsche Bundesbank, *Monatsberichte.*

Although the government's anticyclical policy during the recession was in line with Keynesian fiscal policy prescriptions, its behaviour during the time after the crisis was not: in the period from 1977 to 1982 continuously high deficits were incurred in good and bad years alike. The government, partly under foreign pressure to act as an "engine of growth", did not even avail itself of the favourable economic conditions of the late 1970s to slow down new borrowing. Mainly as a consequence of the second oil shock and higher unemployment public expenditure in 1980 rose by 8 per cent.[13]

Throughout the 1970s the Federal government's share of the public debt increased from a little more than one-third to about one-half, while the local authorities' share declined from one-third to one-fifth. From 1983 to 1985 considerable progress was made in the consolidation of the public debt by pursuing a policy

Table 11.3: New public debt and interest rates 1974-1985

Year	New public debt in DM thousand million	in per cent of GNP	Capital market interest rates in per cent	Real interest rates in per cent
1974	27.3	2.8	10.6	3.5
1975	63.8	6.2	8.7	2.7
1976	48.0	4.3	8.0	4.3
1977	31.2	2.6	6.4	2.6
1978	39.6	3.1	6.1	1.9
1979	46.6	3.3	7.6	3.6
1980	57.1	3.8	8.6	3.8
1981	75.7	4.9	10.6	6.6
1982	69.9	4.4	9.1	4.7
1983	55.0	3.3	8.0	4.8
1984	46.2	2.6	7.8	5.8
1985	36.5	2.3	6.9	4.7

Sources: Rudolf Hickel and Jan Priewe, "Die Finanzpolitik seit 1974 auf dem Pruefstand. Argumente fuer ein umweltorientiertes Langzeit-Beschaefti-gungsprogramm", *Aus Politik und Zeitgeschichte*, vol. 36 (1986), p.8; *Monatsberichte der Deutschen Bundesbank.*

of retrenchment which had already been started in the midst of the 1981/2 recession, before the CDU-FDP government took office.[14]

There has been a growing debate on aspects of the "crowding out problem", namely on the issue as to what extent the large credit demand of the public sector increased interest rates and thereby prevented businessmen from investing in industry.[15] The dramatically increased public debt of 1975 could not have had this effect, because in that year interest rates fell and continued to fall until 1978. In 1979 the picture changed, however: from 1979 to

1981 a growing public debt coincided with a worldwide trend of rising interest rates. It is therefore possible - but cannot be proved - that during those three years business demand for credit was crowded out. On the other hand, it can be shown that both in 1973/4 and 1980/1 rising interest rates preceded a fall in business investment *and* growing public deficits. If there was a crowding out, then it was probably a crowding out caused by monetary rather than fiscal policy. In view of unfavourable business expectations and high interest rates businessmen preferred monetary wealth formation to the formation of tangibles.[16]

Financial and social policy

In the early years of the Federal Republic of Germany financial policy provided important incentives for investment without which the "economic miracle" would hardly have been possible.[17] In view of the high taxes of the early 1950s industry had practically no other choice but to invest as much as possible in order to avoid surrendering most of their profits to the inland revenue. The policy objective of high growth and high employment was achieved by changing the allocation of resources, curbing consumption and strengthening investment. The promotion of housing construction was another objective high on the agenda of fiscal policy.[18]

In that period social policy was mainly assigned the task of assisting war victims, widows, orphans, bombed-out persons, expellees and refugees ("Federal Provisions Act" of 1950).[19] The "equalisation of burdens act" of 1952 compensated institutions and persons who had lost their property during the war or their savings by the default of the NS government's debts.[20] In addition, the Federal government provided assistance for housing construction by subsidising mortgages and granting tax concessions (housing construction act of 1951) and by providing subsidies for building society savings. During the 1950s more than 5 million housing units were completed, 63 per cent of them with public money.

Already in 1953 the Federal government declared its objective to extend the social security system. During the 1950s only a small part of this "social reform" was put into effect, such as the payment of family allowances (*Kindergeldgesetz* of 1954) and the agricultural acts of 1955 which aimed at improving the position of farmers by raising their incomes to those in industry. The index-linked "dynamic pension" of 1957 provided for a periodic adjust-

ment of old-age and invalidity pensions in line with the development of employees' incomes.[21] In 1959 and 1961 attempts at a
wider distribution of wealth were started.

After impressive growth rates had been achieved in the 1950s
the stabilisation of this process played a major role in the financial
policy of the 1960s, especially during the recession of 1966/7. Stabilisation policy did not start then, however, because even in the
1950s the Federal government and the *Laender* had occasionally
used the policy tool of an anticyclical fiscal policy in the construction sector.[22] In the late 1960s Schiller's *Globalsteuerung* ran
into problems, partly because of insufficient coordination between
Federal government, regional and local authorities.

During the 1960s and especially after the social-liberal coalition's taking office in 1969, there were attempts at "strengthening
the social net". At the end of the 1960s continuing wage payment
for up to six weeks in case of illness was stipulated. The "employment promotion act" of 1969, which granted allowances for participation in vocational training, further training and re-training,
put new emphasis on an active labour market and on employment
policy, mainly with the objective of improving the mobility of the
labour force. Needy university students were supported by cost of
living payments (*Bundesausbildungsfoerderungsgesetz* of 1971).[23]

After the dramatic increase in outlays in 1974 which resulted in
large deficits, fiscal policy between mid-1975 and mid-1982 vacil-
lated between expansion and consolidation, although an expansive
stance with rising public deficits was predominant.[24] In March
1977 the government decided upon an "investment programme for
the future" (*Zukunftsinvestitionsprogramm, ZIP*) which provided
DM 16 thousand million for the improvement of the transport
system, an efficient and ecological energy supply, provisions for
water supply, the protection of the environment and vocational
training. After an expansive phase between 1978 and 1981 a
restrictive period followed from 1982 onwards owing to large government debt and high interest payments. This policy had already
been inaugurated in September 1981 by the social-liberal coalition
government with cuts in the social security system.[25]

Whereas total social security expenditure from the social insurance funds had increased at an average rate of 11 per cent per
annum between 1965 and 1969, the average rate of increase had
reached 16.5 per cent in the period 1970-5. There was a "cost explosion" in the health service: total health expenditure almost
trebled during the 1970s. As a result of unemployment benefits in-

creases during the recession of 1974-5 the Federal Labour Office's total expenditure rose from DM 4 thousand million in 1970 to 22 thousand million in 1980.[26] Because of growing unemployment and reduced wage growth the Federal German social system ran into difficulties.[27] As a consequence, services were reduced or became more costly for the insured as in the health service, in old age or invalidity pensions and in the eligibility requirements for unemployment payments.[28] In view of the still growing outlays for the social security system this policy of cutting back social security benefits was continued after the *Wende* of September 1982.

Notes

1. Otto Weitzel, Die Entwicklung der Staatsausgaben in Deutschland (Diss. rer.pol., Erlangen/Nuremberg, 1967),Table 7; Roland Vaubel, "Die deutschen Staatsausgaben: Wende oder Anstieg ohne Ende?", *Ordo*, vol. 35 (1984), p.4; Dieter Vesper, "Entwicklung und Struktur des Staatsverbrauchs 1961 bis 1974", *Vierteljahrshefte zur Wirtschaftsforschung* (DIW), 1977, pp.33-54.
2. Wolfgang Wetter, "Die wirtschaftliche Bedeutung des Staates" in Norbert Walter (ed.), *Deutschland. Portraet einer Nation, vol. 3. Wirtschaft* (Bertelsmann, Guetersloh, 1985), pp.326-7.
3. Wilhelmine Dreissig, "Die Entwicklung der oeffentlichen Finanzwirtschaft seit dem Jahre 1950" in Deutsche Bundesbank (ed.), *Waehrung und Wirtschaft in Deutschland 1876-1975* (Knapp, Frankfurt am Main, 1976), pp.712-7; Guenter Hedtkamp, "Die Entwicklung der oeffentlichen Einnahmen in der Bundesrepublik", in Heinz Koenig (ed.), *Wandlungen der Wirtschaftsstruktur in der Bundesrepublik Deutschland. Schriften des Vereins fuer Socialpolitik*, new series, vol. 26, 1962, pp.151-97.
4. Harald Winkel, *Die Wirtschaft im geteilten Deutschland* (Steiner, Wiesbaden, 1974),p.122.
5. OECD, *Economic surveys, Germany* (OECD, Paris, 1985), p.27; Otto-Erich Geskes, "Die Entwicklung der Steuerquote und der Steuerstruktur nach 1970", *Wirtschaftsdienst*, vol. 63 (1983), pp.603-9.
6. Gebhard Kirchgaessner, "Verfahren zur Messung des in der Schattenwirtschaft erarbeiteten Sozialprodukts", *Allgemeines Statistisches Archiv*, vol. 68 (1984), pp.378-405; by the same author, "Size and development of the West German shadow economy" in *Zeitschrift fuer die gesamte Staatswissenschaft*, vol. 139 (1983), pp.197-215; OECD, *Economic surveys, Germany* (OECD, Paris, 1985), p.28. See also Wolfgang Gerstenberger, "Wachstumsfelder am Rande der offiziellen Wirtschaft", *Ifo-Schnelldienst* vol. 39 (22 Sept. 1986), pp.11-20; Wolf Schaefer (ed.), *Schattenoekonomie. Theoretische Grundlagen und wirtschaftspolitische Konsequenzen* (Vandenhoeck and Ruprecht, Goettingen, 1984); Bruno S. Frey, Hannelore Weck, Werner W. Pommerehne, "Has the shadow economy grown in Germany? An explanatory study", *Weltwirtschaftliches Archiv*, vol. 118 (1982), pp.499-524; Roland Doehrn, "Wie groß ist die Schattenwirtschaft - Versuche einer sektoralen Erklaerung", *RWI-Mitteilungen. Zeitschrift fuer Wirtschaftsforschung*, vol. 37/8 (1986/7), pp.365-85.
7. Wetter, "Die wirtschaftliche Bedeutung des Staates", pp.323-5.
8. Klaus Hinrich Hennings, "West Germany" in Andrea Boltho (ed.), *The*

European economy. Growth and crisis (Oxford University Press, Oxford 1982), p.235.

9. OECD, *Economic surveys, Germany* (OECD, Paris, 1982), pp.37-9; Sachverstaendigenrat zur Begutachtung der gesamtwirtschaftlichen Entwicklung, *Investieren fuer mehr Beschaeftigung. Jahresgutachten 1981/2* (Kohlhammer, Stuttgart, Mainz, 1981), pp.114-6.

10. Dreissig, "Die Entwicklung der oeffentlichen Finanzwirtschaft seit dem Jahre 1950", p.693; Horst Claus Recktenwald, "Die Entwicklung der oeffentlichen Ausgaben in der Bundesrepublik", in Heinz Koenig (ed.), *Wandlungen der Wirtschaftsstruktur in der Bundesrepublik Deutschland. Schriften des Vereins fuer Socialpolitik*, new series, vol. 26, Berlin 1962, pp.199-248.

11. Gerhard Fels, "Die Konsequenzen der Staatsverschuldung", in Horst Siebert (ed.), *Perspektiven der deutschen Wirtschaftspolitik* (Kohlhammer, Stuttgart and Mainz, 1983), p.87. See also Thilo Sarrazin, "Die Finanzpolitik des Bundes 1970 bis 1982. Eine kritische Wuerdigung", *Finanzarchiv*, vol. 41 (1983), p.374.

12. For this and the following see Norbert Kloten and K.H. Ketterer, "Fiscal policy in West Germany: anticyclical versus expenditure reducing policies" in Stephen F. Frowen (ed.), *Controlling industrial economies. Essays in honour of Christopher Thomas Saunders* (Macmillan, London, 1983), pp.291-307.

13. Sarrazin, "Die Finanzpolitik des Bundes 1970-1982. Eine kritische Wuerdigung", p.374.

14. OECD, *Economic surveys, Germany* (OECD, Paris, 1981), p.38; (OECD, Paris, 1986), p.11.

15. Gerhard Maier, "Hat die Staatsverschuldung die Rezession mit verursacht?", *Wirtschaftsdienst*, vol. 63 (1983), pp.255-60; Uwe Westphal, "Empirische Aspekte des Crowding out" in Werner Ehrlicher (ed.), *Geldpolitik, Zins und Staatsverschuldung* (Duncker and Humblot, Berlin, 1981), pp.209-26; Hans Peter Froehlich, "Do public budget deficits crowd out private capital expenditures?", *Intereconomics*, vol. 20 (1985), pp.136-40; Wolfgang Gerstenberger, "Wachstumsfelder am Rande der offiziellen Wirtschaft".

16. Rudolf Hickel and Jan Priewe, "Die Finanzpolitik seit 1974 auf dem Pruefstand. Argumente fuer ein umweltorientiertes Langzeit-Beschaeftigungsprogramm", *Aus Politik und Zeitgeschichte*, vol. 36 (1986), pp.8-9; Werner Glastetter, Ruediger Paulert, Ulrich Spoerel, *Die wirtschaftliche Entwicklung in der Bundesrepublik Deutschland 1950-1980. Befunde, Aspekte, Hintergruende* (Campus, Frankfurt am Main, New York, 1983), pp.449-52; Sarrazin, "Die Finanzpolitik des Bundes 1970-1982. Eine kritische Wuerdigung", pp.382-5; Ruediger Pohl, "Die Geldpolitik der Deutschen Bundesbank im Lichte steigender Arbeitslosigkeit", *WSI-Mitteilungen*, vol. 35 (1982), pp.15-22.

17. See also my remarks on financial policy in the preceding chapter.

18. Wilhelm Noelling, "Finanzpolitik und Wirtschaftswachstum in der Bundesrepublik Deutschland", *Hamburger Jahrbuch fuer Wirtschafts- und Gesellschaftspolitik*, vol. 26 (1981), pp.108-12; Konrad Littmann, "Wirtschaftswachstum, Konjunktur und oeffentliche Finanzen", in Hans Herbert von Arnim and Konrad Littmann (eds), *Finanzpolitik im Umbruch: Zur Konsolidierung oeffentlicher Haushalte* (Duncker and Humblot, Berlin, 1984), pp.31-50.

19. Heinz Lampert, "The development and the present situation of social policy in West Germany", *Zeitschrift fuer die gesamte Staatswissenschaft*, vol. 138 (1982), pp.351-66 for this and the following. Also Gerhard Kleinhenz and Heinz Lampert, "Zwei Jahrzehnte Sozialpolitik in der BRD. Eine kritische Analyse", *Ordo*, vol. 22 (1971), pp.103-58.

20. Eric Owen Smith, *The West German economy* (Croom Helm, London, 1983), p.92.

21. Hans G. Hockerts, *Sozialpolitische Entscheidungen im Nachkriegsdeutschland. Alliierte und deutsche Sozialversicherungspolitik 1945-1957* (Klett-Cotta, Stuttgart, 1980); Volker Hentschel, *Geschichte der deutschen Sozi-*

alpolitik 1880-1980. Soziale Sicherung und kollektives Arbeitsrecht (Suhrkamp, Frankfurt am Main, 1983), pp.163-7.

22. Dreissig, "Die Entwicklung der oeffentlichen Finanzwirtschaft seit dem Jahre 1950", p.738.

23. Eric Owen Smith, *West German economy*, p.105.

24. Friedhelm Hemmerich, *Die Beschaeftigungspolitik in der Bundesrepublik Deutschland 1974-78* (Duncker and Humblot, Berlin, 1982); Hans-Bodo Leibinger and Bernd Rohwer, "Die Fiskalpolitik in den Jahren 1974 bis 1979: Ineffiziente Instrumente oder unzulaengliche Anwendung?", *Konjunkturpolitik*, vol. 27 (1981), pp.261-78.

25. Hickel and Priewe, "Die Finanzpolitik seit 1974 auf dem Pruefstand", pp.5-8; Wolfgang Lerch, "Die Finanzpolitik seit 1974 und einige aktuelle Schlussfolgerungen", *WSI-Mitteilungen*, vol. 35 (1982), pp.7-15.

26. Owen Smith, *West German economy*, pp.102-6.

27. Karl Dietrich Bracher, Wolfgang Jaeger, Werner Link, *Republik im Wandel 1969-1974. Die Aera Brandt. Geschichte der Bundesrepublik Deutschland, vol. 5/I* (Deutsche Verlags-Anstalt, F.A. Brockhaus, Stuttgart, Mannheim, 1986), p.139.

28. Lampert, "The development and present situation of social policy in West Germany", p.9.

Chapter Twelve
CAPITAL AND LABOUR

Investment

During the first half of the 1950s investment subsidies and a backlog demand for goods led to investment growth rates averaging 12.8 per cent, a figure which has not been reached since and which surpassed the annual growth rate of GNP (9.4 per cent).[1] In spite of this, large increases in production were possible with relatively small investment and expansion was largely due to increased employment. After about 1954, however, expansion became possible only through heavy investment.[2] Between 1955 and 1965 annual investment growth rates slowed down to 6.9 per cent. Still, the investment rate was high enough to achieve satisfactory economic growth rates in the period 1950-65, although investment dropped markedly in the years 1953, 1958 and 1963 during the downturn of the business cycle and weakening consumer demand.

In the period 1965-70 the rate of investment sank further to only 3.2 per cent; the growth of private sector investment slowed down to below 2 per cent a year on average during the 1974-83 period.[3] The decline after 1965 affected mainly private and public construction investment, whereas producers' durable equipment rose.

The low rate of investment, one of the FRG's major economic problems of the post-1973 period, was caused mainly by structural changes as a result of the oil price explosion, declining profitability combined with changed expectations and uncertainties about the long-term effects of the *Deutsche Mark's* appreciation after the move to floating exchange rates. The risk in the future developments of exports was particularly pronounced as foreign countries' outlays for energy - except for the OPEC countries - increased. Businessmen in the Federal Republic also complained about the government's economic policies which seemed to lack medium and long term perspectives. As an example, an investment tax was levied in mid-1973, but only one and a half years later investment tax credits were granted.[4]

Figure 12.1: Investment in manufacturing 1956-1978 [a]

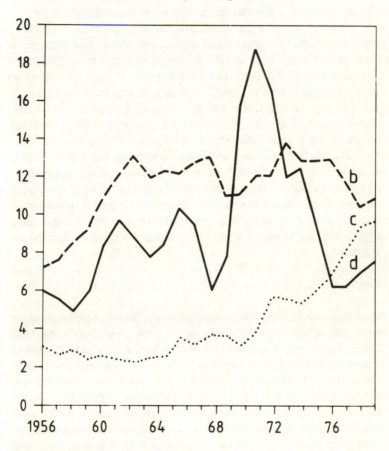

Notes: [a] in DM thousand million, 1970 prices; [b] capital deepening [c] replacement; [d] capital widening

Source: *Ifo-Schnelldienst*, vol. 31, No. 31/32 (1978), p.6

The considerable fall in the rate of return on gross capital stock through the 1970s made part of the existing capital stock unprofitable, increased the attractiveness of financial investment, reduced the propensity of outside financing and induced direct investment abroad. Capital productivity shrank and the increase in relative real labour costs up to the mid-1970s probably influenced capital deepening.[5]

Although business gross investment, measured in relation to output, declined substantially in the years immediately after the first oil price shock it has stabilised since. The share of replacement investment in gross fixed capital formation has even risen from about 32 per cent in 1972 to about 54 per cent in 1985; new investment declined continuously from 9 per cent of output in 1972 to 5.5 per cent in 1985.[6] Investment has been increasingly less efficient in terms of creating output and employment. Additional output generated by investment fell from 0.18 percentage points in the period 1960-1973 to 0.06 percentage points in 1981-85.[7] The impact of investment on employment has been comparatively small in the period after 1960 because of the large share of labour saving investment in total investment.[8] There was also a positive correlation between profits and investment which does not necessarily imply a causal relationship, but there is evidence that rising profits were - after about a year - followed by rising investment.[9]

Employment

In the period 1950 to 1985 three phases of demographic development can be distinguished: during the first phase, until the mid-1950s, there was a growing excess of births over deaths which, however, reached its maximum only during the post-war baby boom in 1964. Between 1961 and 1967 more than one million people were born in the Federal Republic every year. In the second phase, until the mid-1970s, the excess of births over deaths became smaller, mainly due to the *Pillenknick*, a downward demographic curve after the introduction of the anti-baby pill. Whereas there had been 1.065 million live births in 1964 the figure declined to 576,500 in 1978. After the mid-1970s the population in the FRG decreased owing to a surplus of deaths over births. Also, many foreign workers left the country during the recession of 1975, whilst the Act of 23 November 1973 prevented additional foreign labour from working in the Federal Republic.[10]

Demographic developments had several effects on the labour market: in contrast to the fairly constant size of the labour force in the 1960s and the decline between 1970 and 1977 there was an increased flow into the market during the late 1970s and early 1980s. At the turn of the decade probably two million more jobs will be required to accommodate this flow. Although the size of the potential labour force will no longer expand after then, the recent fall in the birth rate will bring new problems, especially for financing the social security system.[11]

Between 1949 and 1961 over three million inhabitants of the German Democratic Republic left for the FRG. Most of them were well-qualified and contributed significantly to the manpower in the Federal German economy. Labour supply was flexible and plentiful with a high degree of labour mobility.[12]

After the building of the Berlin wall in August 1961 the Federal German economy entered a phase of excess demand for labour, partly because the annual number of hours supplied by labour fell owing to such factors as a lower birth rate, delayed entry into the labour force because of an extended education, longer holidays and a shorter working week as well as a prolonged compulsory military service.[13] This brought about a demand for immigrant labour, of whom the Southern Italians, as members of the Common Market, were the first to arrive, followed by Spaniards, Greeks, Turks, Portuguese and Yugoslavs. Immigrant labour did mainly those low-paid manual jobs which German workers were, at the wages offered, no longer willing to do.[14] At an early stage of the recession of the mid-1970s, on 23 November 1973, the Federal government suspended the recruitment of foreign workers from the - then - non-EEC countries such as Greece, Spain, Portugal and also Turkey, which is not an EC member today. For this and other reasons the number of foreigners in the labour force fell from a peak of 2.5 million in 1973 to 2.0 million in 1980. Unemployment among foreigners has been relatively high because most of them have a low level of education and training.[15] The inflow of foreign workers tended to curb the upward wage trend thus raising the price competitiveness of German exports, but it has probably reduced the employment opportunities for women and older workers and also slowed down technical progress, especially labour saving investment.[16]

During the 1950s there was still a considerable pool of unemployment because of the large number of refugees and expellees and the mobility out of agriculture into industry. By the end of the decade the labour force had grown by almost 6 million to 23.6 million. However, with the economy growing, full employment was achieved at the beginning of the 1960s and a labour shortage was increasingly felt, partly caused by the reduction of working hours.[17] In 1950 the average working week for employees was 48 hours. After a reduction to 45 hours in 1956/7 the 40-hour week was introduced from 1965 onwards, although actual paid hours for manual workers (including overtime) amounted to over 41 hours in 1981. The 1979 wage round in the metal industry agreed on reducing working hours slightly below the 40-hour week. From then onwards the unions pursued the medium and long-term objective of a 35-hour week.[18]

Although unemployment rose temporarily to 460,000 during the 1967 recession it was easily eliminated in the following upswing. In nine of the years between 1960 and 1973 unemployment fell below 1 per cent and only in 1967 did it exceed 2 per cent. From 1974 to

Figure 12.2: Unemployment 1950-1985 [a]

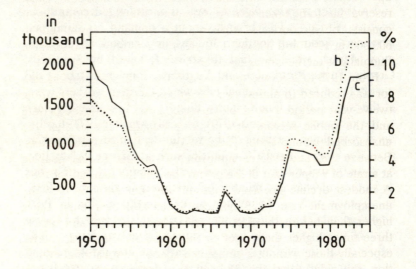

Notes: [a] until 1959 excluding Saarland and West-Berlin
           [b] actual figures; [c] unemployment rate

Source: Statistisches Bundesamt, Sachverstaendigenrat zur Begutachtung der gesamtwirtschaftlichen Entwicklung

1980 the rate amounted to about 4 per cent.[19] In the 1960s the exodus from agriculture hardly created any employment problems as the expanding public and private sectors absorbed agricultural labour to a large extent.[20]

After the period of full employment up to 1973 the situation changed in 1974: in that year, unemployment rose and vacancies fell. The upswing following the 1975 recession did not, contrary to the situation after 1967, bring about a significant decline of the unemployment rate. Each of the business cycles after 1967 started and ended with a significantly higher rate of unemployment than its predecessor.[21]

Between 1973 and 1977, when the size of the labour force shrank, the demand for labour weakened even to a greater extent and employment fell by over 1.3 million. Reflecting the relatively rapid growth of real GNP between 1976 and 1979, employment growth recovered up to 1980. Then, with real GNP weakening in the recession, employment fell again which, given the considerable growth of labour supply, drove the unemployment rate up.[22] Apart from the "official" unemployment figures, the "silent reserve" has to be taken into consideration which to a large extent consists of discouraged workers and probably amounted to 600,000 in 1980 and 800,000 in 1982.[23] There were also sizeable fluctuations on the labour market.[24]

From 1973 to 1985 the outflow of labour from the primary sector was reduced to almost two-thirds compared to the preceding twelve-year period. Net employment creation in both the private and the public sectors slowed down substantially so that the unabsorbed labour supply rose to over 2 million job seekers. Between 1982 and 1985 unemployment continued to rise, peaking at a rate of 9.8 per cent of the labour force in the first half of 1985. A modest decline occurred subsequently, but early in 1986 the unemployment rate (8.75 per cent) was still over eight times higher than before the first oil price shock in 1973 and almost three times higher than prior to the second.[25] Females, youths, especially those without a completed school or vocational education, the elderly and the disabled were particularly affected by unemployment, but also semi-skilled labour and people without work experience. Apart from the fact that the share of long-duration unemployment has increased, the regional distribution of unemployment has been rather uneven. Regions with a problematic industrial structure like coal mining, steel, shipbuilding or textiles have suffered from high unemployment, whereas areas with a more favourable industrial structure had an excess demand for skilled labour.

In analysing the causes of unemployment it is significant that, in view of the shrinking population and net emigration of foreign workers, pressures from labour supply during the period 1973 to 1979 remained weak, although there was an increasing number of school leavers after 1974.[26] The Federal German unemployment problem probably has its main roots in insufficient demand for labour and insufficient net employment creation by capital widening investment. Whereas there are some indications that the failure of real wages to adjust promptly to the decline in labour productivity played a role in the rise of unemployment in the 1970s, wage increases have most probably not been responsible for the dramatic deterioration of the employment rate since 1980.[27] From 1973 to the early 1980s output expectations were depressed and there was a further decline in profitability. Tendencies of market saturation in some manufactured goods and increasing price competition on the world market compounded the problem. Other factors have affected employment negatively such as stricter rules about hiring and lay-offs which, together with rising non-wage labour costs, have made labour input more inflexible and more costly. Increased job search time and the comparatively generous social security system, declining labour mobility because of increased home ownership and higher numbers of double-income-earning households,[28] as well as discouraged workers who have given up seeking gainful employment also played a role.

To improve the employment situation, a large number of governmental policy measures have been taken but have achieved only rather limited success.[29] The Employment Promotion Act of 1969 resulted in the Federal Labour Office assuming further responsibilities for services like placement, vocational training and counselling, job creation measures, mobility incentives and wage subsidies, a policy which was continued by the Employment Promotion Act of 1985.[30] Special objectives have been the promotion of labour market flexibility by relaxing the rules relating to fixed-term contracts in combination with extended possibilities for using temporary labour, the limitation of obligatory payments in the case of large-scale lay-offs and the improvement of the legal framework for part-time workers and job-sharing employees. The introduction of the flexible retirement age in 1973 marked an important step towards an improved employment situation as did attempts at curtailing the domestic labour supply by reducing the

potential Federal German labour force through lowering participation rates.[31]

Wages and productivity

During the 1950s and 1960s the unions put security of employment and the achievement of co-determination legislation before
wage maximisation. After the National Socialists had abolished
the principles of democratic self-government, freedom of association, free collective bargaining and employees' participation
in management, equal participation by employers and employees
was restored in 1950 in the administration of health, accident, invalidity, old age and unemployment insurance among others. The
same goes for collective bargaining and the right to strike or lock
out. In May 1951 the *Bundestag* passed the Act on the co-determination by employees on the supervisory and management
boards of the companies in the mining and steel industries. The
Act concerning industrial constitution (*Betriebsverfassungsgesetz*)
which stipulated that one-third of the supervisory board members
of all joint stock companies would have to be labour representatives, was passed by the *Bundestag* on 11 October 1952.[32]

Figure 12.3: Annual growth rates of net wages per capita 1950-1985 [a]

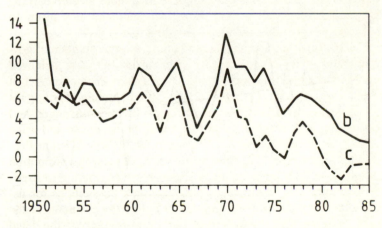

Notes: [a] until 1959 excluding the Saarland and West- Berlin
[b] current prices; [c] 1970 prices

Source: Statistisches Bundesamt, own computations

Although Federal German trade unions have generally shown few signs of militancy, labour did not lose out in the long run as is shown by the fact that wages increased substantially in the 1950s and 1960s. During the early 1970s the labour market was characterised by excess demand and wage increases were high. Between 1969 and 1970 the growth rate of the index of standard wages more than doubled and remained above the 1960s average until 1975.[33]

During the period 1970-74 the compound rate of increase in average gross monthly earnings per employee was 8.72 per cent as compared with only 4.86 per cent in the period 1975-9, mainly owing to the fact that recession had undermined trade union bargaining power. Still, during the second half of the 1970s the growth of real wages in the Federal Republic was internationally among the highest.[34] From 1980 to 1985, however, the wage-earners had to face six years of consecutive real income losses (net of taxes and social security contributions).[35]

While the number of employees and capital productivity played a decisive role in economic growth in the reconstruction period of the 1950s, the former lost that function from the middle of the

Figure 12.4: Annual growth rates of labour productivity in the manufacturing sector [a] 1952-1985 [b]

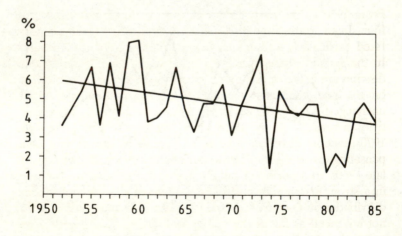

Notes: [a] including mining
        [b] 1970 = 100

Source: Statistisches Bundesamt and own computations

1950s, while the importance of the latter declined from the beginning of the 1960s. From the end of the 1950s onwards it was mainly labour productivity, especially productivity per labour hour, and the capital stock viz. capital intensity, on which economic growth was based.[36] Capital intensity grew at an average of 6 per cent per year during the period 1961-79 and most probably fostered the rise of labour productivity.[37]

In the period 1962-71 labour productivity increased 5.7 per cent, capital productivity 1.3 per cent, total productivity 3.2 percent annually in manufacturing.[38] Probably, labour productivity would not have grown as rapidly as it did had not employees moved from branches of lower productivity to those of higher productivity (structural effect).[39] Still, the annual growth rate of labour productivity has declined continuously from the early 1950s, that of capital stock and capital intensity from the beginning of the 1960s.

In the late 1960s and during the 1970s the increase in real labour costs outpaced that of labour productivity thus contributing to the decline in the demand for labour. Real wages, on the other hand, grew less rapidly than labour productivity, owing to the increasing share of public sector deductions in total compensations of employees.[40]

Income and wealth distribution

From 1950 to the early 1980s income distribution developed in four stages: during the 1950s income from profits and property fared particularly well, mainly owing to financial policy measures. In the second phase, which extended to the late 1960s, income distribution between income from entrepreneurship and property on the one hand and labour on the other remained largely unchanged. Wage policy was to a large extent related to productivity increase.[41] In the third phase, during the first half of the 1970s, income distribution favoured dependent labour thus compensating for its discrimination during the 1950s and 1960s. In the late 1960s, in a period of full employment, the trade unions were in a strong bargaining position and demanded a shift of income distribution in favour of labour, particularly as social reforms had not advanced as far as the unions had wished.[42] From 1975 onwards this development was reversed again with the exception of the years 1980 and 1981, when the net wage share rose again, reflecting the 1980/1 recession.[43] The rise in the wage share (and the corresponding fall in the profit share) during those two years was mainly due to a marked rise in import prices and - caused by this - the deterioration of the terms of trade and falling capacity utilisation.[44] Between 1981 and 1986 the labour share in national income fell, dropping to its lowest level since the late 1960s.[45]

As was common in other western nations, negotiated wage rates rose more rapidly during periods of relatively low unemployment. The recovery of wage rates during an upswing lagged behind profits, but earnings advanced more rapidly than profits during periods of low unemployment.[46] The gross wage share adjusted for increases in the number of employees was particularly high in recession periods like 1966/7, 1974/5 and 1980/1. During the 1950s and early 1960s, in a period of economic growth and rising employment, the wage share fell. This seemingly paradoxical behavi-

Figure 12.5: Wage share 1950-1985 [a]

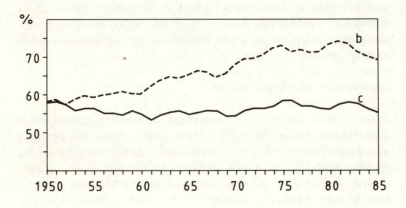

Notes: [a] Until 1959 excluding Saarland and West Berlin
          [b] unadjusted
          [c] with constant 1950 share of employees in
             gainfully employed persons

Source: Statistisches Bundesamt, own computations

our can be readily explained by the fact that the wage share and nominal (or real) income are two completely different matters. In a recession, mainly profits are negatively affected and the profit rate typically sinks, whereas the wage share, reflecting *contractual* income, typically rises.[47]

As to profits there has been a downward trend in profitability which can be traced back to the late 1950s. The profit squeeze became more pronounced in the 1970s mainly due to increased wage pressures in the first half of the decade and the appreciation of the currency in the second.[48] Wage moderation during the recession of 1980/1 led to an improvement of the profit situation from 1982 onwards. In 1983 the profit share of the non-financial sector was the highest for ten years (although it was still below the level of the 1960s) reflecting modest increases in wages and salaries and terms of trade gains. Since the early 1980s self-financing ratios have increased considerably.[49]

As far as personal income distribution, i.e. the distribution of income according to income levels, not to origin, is concerned, the share of total income, which the most affluent 10 per cent of the population received, rose from 34 to 38 per cent between 1950 and 1961, but fell after 1965 and, in 1974, sank even below the 1950 level. On the other hand, at the lower income scale, the share rose slowly from 20 per cent to 22 per cent in the period 1950-61 and has since remained at that level. Real per capita income rose, however, three and a half times reflecting a marked improvement of material welfare.[50]

The distribution of wealth is even more unequal than that of income. In 1960 a mere 1.7 per cent of all private households owned about 70 per cent of all business enterprises[51] and this percentage increased to 74 in 1966 but decreased later.[52] This reflects a growing concentration in industry, in which the share of self-employed persons in total employment fell from 16 per cent to 9 per cent during the period 1950-1980.[53]

From the late 1950s onwards there have been various political measures designed to bring about a more equal distribution of income and property after financial policy had fostered capital formation in the early 1950s. The denationalisation of the *Volkswagenwerk* and of the *Preussag* Company in 1959 and 1960 was accompanied by attempts to encourage small shareholders through *Volksaktien*, but these efforts were not very successful.[54] After housing bonuses had already been introduced in the 1950s, the policy to foster the accumulation of assets (*Vermoegensbildungsgesetze* of 1961, 1965 and 1970) achieved some success on the way to a more equal distribution of property, although these effects should not be overrated.

Notes

1. Harald Winkel, *Die Wirtschaft im geteilten Deutschland 1945-1970* (Steiner, Wiesbaden, 1974), p.90.
2. Karl W. Roskamp, *Capital formation in West Germany* (Wayne State University Press, Detroit, 1965), p.75.
3. OECD, *Economic surveys, Germany* (OECD, Paris, 1984), p.43.
4. Karl Heinrich Oppenlaender, "Einige Gedanken zu den Ursachen der aktuellen Investititionsschwaeche in der Industrie der Bundesrepublik" in Karl Erich Born (ed.), *Gegenwartsprobleme der Wirtschaft und der Wirtschaftswissenschaft* (Mohr, Tuebingen, 1978), p.186.
5. OECD, *Economic surveys, Germany* (OECD, Paris, 1983), p.153; Sachverstaendigenrat zur Begutachtung der gesamtwirtschaftlichen Entwicklung, *Vor dem Aufschwung. Jahresgutachten 1975/6* (Kohlhammer, Stuttgart, Mainz, 1975), p.136. Also Luitpold Uhlmann, "Bestimmungsgruende der Investitionsentscheidung in der Industrie", *Ifo-Studien*, vol. 1-2 (1980), pp.3-61.
6. OECD, *Economic surveys, Germany* (OECD, Paris, 1987), p.43.
7. OECD, *Economic surveys, Germany* (OECD, Paris, 1985), p.26.
8. Werner Glastetter, Ruediger Paulert, Ulrich Spoerel, *Die wirtschaftliche Entwicklung in der Bundesrepublik Deutschland 1950-1980. Befunde, Aspekte, Hintergruende* (Campus, Frankfurt am Main, New York, 1983), pp.281-5.
9. Thilo Sarrazin, "Das Laecheln der Sphinx - oder: Die Staatsverschuldung und die Krise der Globalsteuerung", *Aus Politik und Zeitgeschichte*, vol. B. 38 (1981), p.9.
10. Glastetter, Paulert, Spoerel, *Wirtschaftliche Entwicklung*, p.142.
11. Eric Owen Smith, *The West German economy* (Croom Helm, London, 1983), pp.135-65 for this and the following.
12. Klaus Hinrich Hennings, "West Germany" in Andrea Boltho (ed.), *The European economy. Growth and crisis* (Oxford University Press, Oxford, 1982), p.154; Wolfgang Koellmann, "Bevoelkerungsgeschichte 1800-1970" in Hermann Aubin and Wolfgang Zorn (eds), *Handbuch der deutschen Wirtschafts- und Sozialgeschichte* (2 vols., Klett, Stuttgart, 1976), vol. 2, pp.43-6.
13. Peter Marschalck, *Bevoelkerungsgeschichte Deutschlands im 19. und 20. Jahrhundert* (Suhrkamp, Frankfurt am Main, 1984), pp.107-11.
14. Wolfgang Franz, "Employment and the labour supply of foreign workers in the Federal Republic of Germany: a theoretical and empirical analysis", *Zeitschrift fuer die gesamte Staatswissenschaft*, vol. 137 (1981), pp.590-611.
15. Knuth Dohse, "Auslaendische Arbeiter 1974 bis 1985. Beschaeftigungsentwicklung und staatliche Regelungszusammenhaenge", *WSI-Mitteilungen*, vol. 39 (1986), pp.626-35.
16. Karl Hardach, *The political economy of Germany in the twentieth century* (University of California Press, Berkeley, Los Angeles, London, 1980), p.195.
17. Stefanie Wahl, "Langfristige Trends auf dem Arbeitsmarkt", *Aus Politik und Zeitgeschichte*, vol. B 42 (1985), pp.3-17.
18. Erwin Schudlich, "Vom Konsens zum Konflikt. Arbeitszeiten und Arbeitszeitpolitik in der Bundesrepublik Deutschland", *WSI-Mitteilungen*, vol. 39 (1986), pp.491-8; Owen Smith, *West German economy*, p.192; for the discussion on shorter working hours see, among others, Hans-Juergen Krupp, "Arbeitszeitverkuerzung: Wie unterschiedlich sind eigentlich die Positionen?", *Wirtschaftsdienst*, vol. 68 (1988), pp.183-7.
19. Owen Smith, *West German economy*, pp.46-8; Sachverstaendigenrat zur Begutachtung der gesamtwirtschaftlichen Entwicklung, *Ein Schritt voran. Jahresgutachten 1983/84* (Kohlhammer, Stuttgart, Mainz, 1983), pp.74-8.
20. OECD, *Economic surveys, Germany* (OECD, Paris, 1967), p.33.

21. Glastetter, Paulert, Spoerel, *Wirtschaftliche Entwicklung*, p.147; OECD, *Economic surveys, Germany* (OECD, Paris, 1987), p.29.

22. OECD, *Economic surveys, Germany* (OECD, Paris, 1983), p.46.

23. According to Harald Gerfin the "silent reserve" is defined as the difference of discouraged workers minus those additional employees, who have a job only as long as a family member is out of work. See Harald Gerfin, "Ursachen der Arbeitslosigkeit" in Horst Siebert (ed.), *Perspektiven der deutschen Wirtschaftspolitik* (Kohlhammer, Stuttgart, Mainz, 1983), p.42. See also Wolfgang Franz, "Challenges to the German economy 1973-1983. Supply shocks, investment slowdown, inflation variability and the under-utilisation of labour", *Zeitschrift fuer Wirtschafts- und Sozialwissenschaft*, vol. 105 (1985), pp.407-30.

24. Alfred E. Ott, "Analyse der Arbeitslosigkeit in der Bundesrepublik Deutschland" in Gottfried Bombach (ed.), *Makrooekonomie heute: Gemeinsamkeiten und Gegensaetze* (Mohr, Tuebingen, 1983), pp.16-7.

25. For this and the following see OECD, *Economic surveys, Germany* (OECD, Paris, 1987), pp.30-8.

26. Ott, "Analyse der Arbeitslosigkeit", pp.18-9; Wolfgang Franz and Heinz Koenig, "The nature and causes of unemployment in the Federal Republic of Germany since the 1970s: an empirical investigation", *Economica*, vol. 53 (1986), pp.219-44, Harald Gerfin, "Cyclical and structural elements in present unemployment: the case of West Germany" in Herbert Giersch (ed.), *Capital shortage and unemployment in the world economy* (Mohr, Tuebingen, 1978), pp.1-17.

27. Gerfin, "Ursachen der Arbeitslosigkeit", p.52. Glastetter, Paulert, Spoerel, *Wirtschaftliche Entwicklung*, pp.339, 344 maintain that there is no empirical proof for a causal link between rising real wages and falling employment and falling real wages and rising employment in the FRG. See generally E. Kowalski, "Lohnentwicklung und Beschaeftigungsgrad. Zum theoretischen Hintergrund einer wirtschaftspolitischen Evergreen-Kontroverse", *Ifo-Schnelldienst*, vol.31 (1978), pp.79-93; also Carlo Jaeger and Arnd Weber, "Lohndynamik und Arbeitslosigkeit", *Kyklos*, vol. 41 (1988), pp.479-506.

28. See, however, Joachim Wagner, "Mangelnde Faktormobilitaet - eine Ursache der Arbeitslosigkeit?", *Wirtschaftsdienst*, vol. 65 (1985), pp.297-303.

29. Fritz W. Scharpf, "Beschaeftigungspolitische Strategien in der Krise", *Leviathan. Zeitschrift fuer Sozialwissenschaft*, vol. 13 (1985), pp.1-22; Fritz W. Scharpf, "Wege aus der Arbeitslosigkeit: Die Diskussion heute", *Vierteljahreshefte fuer Wirtschaftsforschung (DIW)* (1984), pp.352-3; Peter Witterauf, "Die Wirksamkeit der Beschaeftigungspolitik in der weltweiten Depression der 70er Jahre", *Wirtschaftsdienst*, vol. 63 (1983), pp.352-6; Sachverstaendigenrat zur Begutachtung der gesamtwirtschaftlichen Entwicklung, *Unter Anpassungszwang. Jahresgutachten 1980/81* (Kohlhammer, Stuttgart, Mainz, 1980), pp.70-2.

30. Owen Smith, *West German economy*, p.166.

31. OECD, *Economic surveys, Germany* (OECD, Paris, 1987), p.38.

32. Heinz Lampert, "The development and the present situation of social policy in West Germany", *Zeitschrift fuer die gesamte Staatswissenschaft*, vol. 138 (1982), pp.352-4; Gustav Stolper, Karl Haeuser, Knut Borchardt, *The German economy 1970 to the present* (Harcourt, Brace, New York, 1967), pp.292-5.

33. Hennings, "West Germany", p.483.

34. Owen Smith, *West German economy*, pp.177, 191.

35. OECD, *Economic surveys, Germany* (OECD, Paris, 1987), p.16.

36. Glastetter, Paulert, Spoerel, *Wirtschaftliche Entwicklung*, p.108.

37. Lothar Huebl and Walter Schepers, *Strukturwandel und Strukturpolitik* (Wissenschaftliche Buchgesellschaft, Darmstadt, 1983), p.47.

38. Ernst-Juergen Horn, *Technische Neuerungen und internationale Arbeitsteilung. Die Bundesrepublik Deutschland im internationalen Vergleich* (Mohr, Tuebingen, 1976), pp.88-9. On the development of labour productivity see also Arthur Boness, Rolf Krengel and Rainer Pischner, "Langfristiges Wachstum

der gewerblichen Arbeitsproduktivitaet seit 1950 wenig veraendert", *DIW-Wochenbericht*, vol. 47 (1980), pp.504-7.

39. Sachverstaendigenrat zur Begutachtung der gesamtwirtschaftlichen Entwicklung, *Stabiles Geld - Stetiges Wachstum. Jahresgutachten 1964/65* (Kohlhammer, Stuttgart, Mainz, 1965), p.51.

40. OECD, *Economic surveys, Germany* (OECD, Paris, 1979), p.17.

41. There are of course several problems involved in this concept of income distribution between factors. Small farmers and shopkeepers, for example, belong to the entrepreneurial group whereas chief executives of large corporations belong to dependent labour. Many members of both groups receive interest payments and rents. Also, owing to the declining rate of self-employment, the share of dependent labour in total occupation rose from 77.2 per cent in 1960 to 87.5 per cent in 1981 (87.1 per cent in 1985). Peter Czada, *Wirtschaft. Aktuelle Probleme des Wachstums und der Konjunktur*, 5th edn (Leske and Budrich, Opladen, 1984), p.38.

42. Werner Abelshauser, *Wirtschaftsgeschichte der Bundesrepublik Deutschland 1945-1980* (Suhrkamp, Frankfurt am Main, 1983), pp.136-7.

43. Glastetter, Paulert, Spoerel, *Wirtschaftliche Entwicklung*, p.311; Goswin Voswinckel, "Die Entwicklung der Einkommens- und Gueterverteilung in der Bundesrepublik Deutschland von 1950 bis 1980", *Jahrbuch fuer Sozialoekonomie und Gesellschaftstheorie - Verteilungsprobleme in Industriegesellschaften* (Hamburg, Opladen, 1982), pp.64-79; Manfred Euler, "Die Einkommensverteilung und -entwicklung in der Bundesrepublik Deutschland 1962-1978 nach Ergebnissen der Einkommens- und Verbrauchsstichproben", *Konjunkturpolitik*, vol. 29 (1983), pp.199-228.

44. Rudi Welzmueller, "Einkommensverteilung im Rahmen der konjunkturellen Entwicklung in der Bundesrepublik Deutschland seit 1975", *WSI-Mitteilungen*, vol. 37 (1984), p.413.

45. OECD, *Economic surveys, Germany* (OECD, Paris, 1987), p.16.

46. Owen Smith, *West German economy*, p.186.

47. Hermann Adam, *Die Einkommensverteilung in der Bundesrepublik Deutschland* (Bund-Verlag, Cologne, 1976), p.13.

48. Hennings, "West Germany", p.495; OECD, *Economic surveys, Germany* (OECD, Paris, 1984), p.38.

49. OECD, *Economic surveys, Germany* (OECD, Paris, 1985), p.50.

50. Abelshauser, *Wirtschaftsgeschichte*, p.138. Also Klaus D. Bedau, Gerhard Goeseke and Helmut Klatt, *Verteilung und Schichtung der Einkommen der privaten Haushalte in der Bundesrepublik Deutschland 1950-1975* (Duncker and Humblot, Berlin, 1974).

51. Wilhelm Krelle, Johann Schunck, Juergen Siebke, *Ueberbetriebliche Ertragsbeteiligung der Arbeitnehmer* (Mohr, Tuebingen, 1968), p.381. This excluded, for example, private and public ownership of real estate, agricultural property, bonds and equities, cash savings and life insurance. In the same year, 1960, these 1.7 per cent had, however, a much smaller share of national wealth (about 35 per cent) which sank to 31 per cent in 1966 and showed a tendency towards more equal distribution. Meinhard Miegel, *Einkommen und Vermoegen der privaten Haushalte* (Verlag Bonn Aktuell, Stuttgart, 1983).

52. Horst Mierheim and Lutz Wicke, *Die personelle Vermoegensverteilung in der Bundesrepublik Deutschland* (Mohr, Tuebingen, 1978), p.264-5 are of the opinion that in 1969 the most affluent 1.7 per cent households owned between 55 and 60 per cent of the business enterprises, but that this share declined to 51 per cent by 1973. Owing to insufficient and partly unreliable data, investigations like these are notoriously difficult. See also Dietmar Baron, *Die personelle Vermoegensverteilung in der Bundesrepublik Deutschland und ihre Bestimmungsgruende* (Lang, Frankfurt am Main, Berne, 1988).

53. Abelshauser, *Wirtschaftsgeschichte*, pp.140-1.

54. Owen Smith, *West German economy*, p.189.

Chapter Thirteen

STRUCTURAL CHANGE

Shifts between the economic sectors

According to economic models of capitalist development there is a shift in importance from the primary sector (agriculture, forestry, fishery) to the secondary sector (the manufacturing sector, which also includes energy, mining and the construction industry) and then to the tertiary or service sector (mainly internal and foreign trade, transport, banking, insurance and the state).[1] In the first stage of development, most of the gainfully employed persons work in agriculture. In the second stage, the size of the agricultural sector declines, because mechanisation and the use of fertilizers increase agricultural productivity and raise output while making labour redundant. Redundant labour finds employment in the increasing manufacturing sector which produces an ever growing share of the gross domestic product (GDP). At the same time the tertiary sector increases, providing services for the secondary sector. During the third stage the importance of the primary sector deteriorates further, but mechanisation and rationalisation continue. This is also true of the secondary sector with the consequence that unemployment increases. People made redundant in industry are absorbed by the tertiary sector in which - at least in the early stages - rationalisation is not possible to the same degree as in the other sectors. Apart from higher productivity in the primary and secondary sectors sectoral shifts are mainly caused by the fact that with rising per capita income the demand for goods produced in the primary (and later in the secondary) sector declines relative to the secondary (and later to the tertiary) sector.[2]

At first sight the sectoral development of the Federal German economy seems to correspond well with this model.

Figure 13.1:   *Share of sectors in gross value added (left); share of gainfully employed persons in sectors (right) 1950-1985* [a]

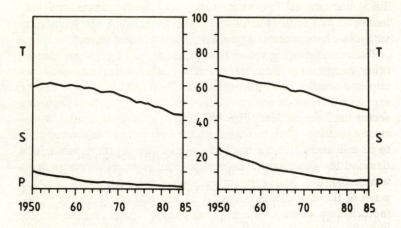

Note: [a] until 1959 excluding Saarland

Sectors: primary (P), secondary (S), tertiary (T)

Source: Statistisches Bundesamt

In the period from 1950 to 1985 the share of agriculture in GDP declined by over 80 per cent, but the monetary contribution of the primary sector to GDP increased from about DM 10 thousand million to about 38 thousand million during the same period. From the early 1950s to the middle of the 1960s there was a marked trend towards the secondary sector. After having dominated the Federal German economy from the mid-1950s to the mid-1970s in terms of gross value added the growth of the manufacturing sector was interrupted by the recession of 1974/5, in which its share in GDP fell below that of 1950. The share of the service sector in GDP rose continuously with the highest growth rates achieved after 1970.

As far as the occupational structure is concerned, in 1950 almost one in four of the working population was occupied in the primary sector. By 1985 this share had declined to just over 5 per cent. The share of labour in the manufacturing sector rose from 42 per cent in 1950 to over 49 per cent in 1965 and then declined to 41 per cent in 1985, whereas the share of people employed in the service sector rose continuously from just under 34 per cent in 1950 to almost 54 per cent in 1985. The rise of the official figures (from 6.7 million employees in 1950 to almost 13.7 million in 1985) does not tell the whole story, because the commercial and technical jobs in the manufacturing sectors, which are really "service jobs", have increased markedly during recent years.[3]

The manufacturing sector has maintained a larger share than in other comparable industrial countries and the service sector occupies a smaller share of output than is typical elsewhere. There are several reasons for the dominant role of the manufacturing sector until the middle of the 1970s and its present comparatively strong position. With the population rising from 50 million in 1950 to 62 million in 1974 (it has fallen slightly since) there was a high demand for goods which expressed itself in several consumption waves, like the "food indulgence wave" (*Fresswelle*) and clothing wave of the early 1950s followed by the household furniture and motorisation waves of the 1950s and early 1960s. Internal factors like the availability of labour and external factors like the undervaluation of the *Deutsche Mark* under the regime of fixed exchange rates contributed to this. The FRG had a strong position on the world market partly owing to the export of high quality goods which were well-suited for the world market and partly owing to the fact that she could import comparatively cheap raw materials.

Since the mid-1970s there has been a growing awareness of the social and ecological costs of industrial production, which has led to demands to pursue qualitative instead of quantitative economic growth. Of greater importance for the decline of the secondary and the rise of the tertiary sector were, however, the higher mineral oil prices and the stronger *Deutsche Mark*, the partial loss of export markets because of the huge debts of several former customers, new industrial competitors on the world market as well as government attempts to extend services like (higher) education and health care.[4]

The secondary sector is still strong, however. Export dependence has been remarkable in the 1980s (in 1982 a 27 per cent export share and a 24 per cent import share in total output). New or qualitatively improved industrial goods are constantly produced so that cases of market saturation with traditional goods are only of limited importance for the economy.[5]

The fact that the Federal German economy is a comparative laggard in structural change has led to the thesis of "overindustrialisation" which means that the service sector is underdeveloped with the negative consequence of a high dependence on exports and ecological problems. It has to be pointed out, however, that the FRG has few natural resources and is - provided the current standard of living is to be maintained - dependent on exports in order to pay for her imports and to settle her substantial deficit in the travel balance. Besides, curbing environmental pollution is also possible in a country with a large industrial sector, provided the government and the industries involved have the will to do so.[6]

The three sectors

During the period 1945-8 there were serious food shortages in the West German territories owing to manpower losses, war destruction, fuel, fertilizers and seed shortages and the loss of agricultural imports from East German territories. The deterioration of agricultural yields and reduced acreage under cultivation led to a decline in agricultural output below its pre-war level. Two other factors retarded agricultural growth: contrary to the large estates east of the Elbe the farms in West Germany were small or medium sized and often excessively fragmented. They generally did not exceed ten hectares (approximately 25 acres) and were cultivated by mixed farming. Under these circumstances efficient methods of production with rationalisation and mechanisation could only be applied to a limited degree. Improving conditions in the non-agricultural sectors induced many farmers to sell their lands and work in industry thus enabling other farmers to consolidate their holdings and make more efficient production possible.[7]

Labour productivity rose by 6.5 per cent annually in the period 1950-75 as compared to only 4.7 per cent in the economy as a whole. In 1975 7.1 per cent of all gainfully employed persons in the FRG worked in agriculture, but they contributed only 2.7 per cent to GNP.[8]

When the Korean boom was over and agricultural prices fell again it became clear that agriculture in the FRG could not face foreign competition.[9] For political and social reasons the govern-

Table 13.1: *Employment* [a] *and labour productivity* [b] *in the primary sector 1950-1985* [c]

Year	Employment	Labour productivity
1950	4819	20
1955	4158	34
1960	3581	47
1965	2876	68
1970	2262	100
1975	1773	170
1980	1437	207
1985	1360	230

Notes: [a] in thousand
         [b] 1970 = 100
         [c] until 1959 excluding Saarland

Source: Statistisches Bundesamt, own computations

ment pursued an agricultural policy which - as far as possible - aimed at conserving the rural social structure by supporting the rural *Mittelstand* as a vital pillar of the nation and by trying to secure a high degree of agricultural self-sufficiency. This policy was not cheap and did not at all agree with the concept of the social market economy: in 1950/1 agricultural marketing regulations were enacted which stipulated minimum and maximum prices and quantity controls for imports (when imports were necessary, import and warehousing agencies raised the prices of imported goods to the higher domestic levels) and guaranteed prices and sales. At the end of the 1950s the domestic price level for various agricultural goods was about 60 per cent above the world market level. This policy of agricultural protection benefited the farmers but was disadvantageous for the customers. Government subsidies for agriculture rose enormously from DM 430 million in 1956 to over one thousand million in 1960 and almost 7.5 thousand million in 1970. To this, various tax privileges and financial relief have to be added.[10]

In order to foster the consolidation of agricultural holdings the Land Consolidation Act (*Flurbereinigungsgesetz*) was enacted in 1953. By the Agricultural Act (*Landwirtschaftsgesetz*) of 1955 the government - with only partial success - aimed at improving conditions in agriculture by reducing the income gap between urban and rural areas. Annual "Green Plans" and "Green Reports" to the *Bundestag* had the purpose of outlining the aims of agricultural policy and reporting on the outcome of various policy measures. After the recession of 1966-7 the Federal and state governments, in order to reduce agricultural overproduction, inaugurated medium-term agricultural development programmes which tried to attract industry to the rural areas and encourage small farms to abandon farming.[11]

As far as agriculture was concerned the foundation of the European Economic Community in March 1957 meant an extension of Federal German agrarian protectionism to supranational Common Market protectionism, for which agricultural market regulations in the FRG provided the model. By the mid-1980s the number of statutes reached the astonishing figure of about 30,000. The Federal German politicians had some success in raising Common Market agricultural prices to the - compared with world market prices - excessive FRG level.[12] This high price level led to a markedly higher agricultural output in the EEC with surpluses in almost all fields, such as the notorious "butter mountain" or "beef mountain". If the EEC (EC after 1967) storehouses overflow, stored agricultural goods are exported or even destroyed. If they are exported the exporter is refunded the difference between the higher EC price and the generally much lower world market price. Thus the EC consumer is charged three times: first, he has to pay excessive EC prices, secondly he has to pay for the cost of storage and thirdly for the export refunds. During recent years, expenditure on agricultural policy amounted to about 60 to 70 per cent of the EC budget.[13]

Table 13.2:   *Share of selected industrial branches in gross value added of total industry 1960-1980* [a]

Industry	1960	1970	1980
chemical, mineral-oil processing, plastics	9.2	14.6	16.4
building and construction, glass	4.9	5.1	4.4
iron- and-steel producing	10.4	8.3	7.1
engineering	14.1	13.4	11.5
electrical engineering	7.4	9.4	11.5
precision engineering, optics	1.7	1.8	2.3
business machinery, computers	0.3	0.7	1.4
road vehicles	7.0	9.5	10.6
wood, paper, printing	9.2	8.6	8.0
textiles, clothing	7.7	6.0	4.5
general and luxury food industry	15.0	12.0	12.0
others	13.1	10.6	10.3

Note: [a] in 1980 prices

Source: Statistisches Bundesamt

After the rapid expansion of the consumer goods industry and housing construction in the early 1950s the capital goods industry, which gave strong incentives to the primary industries, played an increasingly larger role. Coal mining is an exception which, after the decision to rely mainly on mineral oil and partly on nuclear energy, has experienced a persistent structural crisis from 1957 onwards.

In the 1950s and 1960s the plastics processing industry had the highest annual growth rate (21.4 per cent), followed by synthetic fibres (14 per cent), the automobile industry (11.6 per cent) and the electrical engineering industry.[14] During the period 1960-80 the chemical, mineral oil and plastics industries increased their shares in total gross value added the fastest, followed by business machinery and computers, road vehicles, electrical and precision engineering. The building and construction, ceramics and glass industries, the wood, paper and printing industries and the engineering and iron-and-steel producing industries had declining shares; the relative decline of the textile and clothing industry and the general and luxury food industry was particularly pronounced.

The industries most affected by structural change have been capital-intensive branches with large plants and a highly unionised labour force. For the period 1970 to 1983 the FRG ranked third to last in international comparison as far as the magnitude of structural change was concerned, which reflected the persistent competitive strength of the traditional branches of manufacturing.[15]

As the impact of technical innovations on the economy as a whole cannot be measured precisely, productivity, especially the productivity of labour, is often regarded as an indicator of technical progress. The same is true of expenditure on research and development and of patents taken out, although these methods have severe limitations.[16]

As far as the productivity of labour is concerned it is significant that process engineering industries, like chemical engineering, had a higher labour productivity than the branches of production engineering industry, like machinery or road vehicles. In the 1950s and early 1960s labour productivity in the plastics, mineral oil processing, chemical and electrical engineering industries grew particularly fast. Labour productivity in the capital goods industries (except electrical engineering) grew below average, and the same is true of the textile and clothing industry and the general and luxury food industry. The differences in labour productivity can be mainly explained by the fact that process engineering industries lend themselves more readily to continuous working and automatic control than production engineering industries.[17]

Especially in the 1950s and 1960s the FRG imported not only labour but also technical and organisational know-how (patents, licenses, management strategies) from abroad, mainly from the USA. In technology this partly reflected the "electronic gap" which, to an extent, still exists today. Industry in the FRG tried to regain her high technological standard in non-military technology which had been partly lost during the war and the immediate post-war period.[18] These endeavours are reflected in government and business research and development expenditures which, after slow growth in the 1950s, grew at an impressive rate from the early 1960s onwards. A comparable rise did not take place in any other industrial nation.

The 1960s can be regarded as a period of catching up with the leaders in R&D, especially with the USA. R&D expenditures reached a peak in 1971 at 2.4 per cent of GNP, a figure which was only surpassed in 1979, although the share of industry in R&D outlays in GNP had been higher after 1976 and after 1977 surpassed that of the government. The general investment boom in FRG industry after the 1966/7 recession is probably reflected in these figures. The slower rise during the first half of the 1970s has to be seen in the context of generally weak industrial investment. Moreover, by that time, Federal German industry had succeeded in catching up with several of her major industrial competitors. R&D outlays were highest in the aircraft industry (strongly supported by government subsidies) and in the electrical engineering, precision engineering, optical and chemical industries, particularly in plastics processing. As far as another indicator of technical progress, patent statistics, is concerned, most patents were taken out in comparatively R&D intensive industries, especially in chemical, electrical and precision engineering, but also in the optical, machinery and motor industries.[19]

According to the economist Joseph Schumpeter and some Neo-Schumpeterians, especially Gerhard Mensch,[20] clusters of basic innovations create - as product innovations - new markets and growth industries and - as process innovations - lead to radical changes in the means and methods of production.[21] The introduction of such clusters of innovations bring about a reorganisation of the industrial structure in favour of new, dynamic growth industries.

Figure 13.2: R&D expenditures 1950-1985 ᵃ

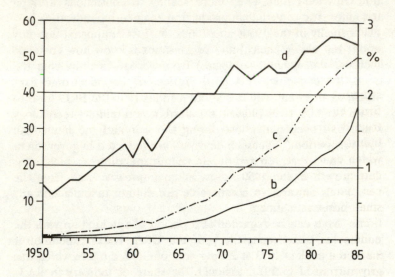

Notes: ᵃ current prices, DM thousand million
ᵇ business R&D expenditure (left scale)
ᶜ total R&D expenditure (left scale)
ᵈ total R&D expenditure in per cent of GNP (right scale)

Sources: Stifterverband fuer die deutsche Wissenschaft, *Forschung und Entwicklung in der Wirtschaft*, 1977, 1980; Bundesministerium für Forschung und Technologie, *Bundesbericht*, Bundestagsdrucksache 10/1543; Statistisches Bundesamt, *Statistisches Jahrbuch 1987*

Examining industrial innovation in German industry in the 1950s and 1960s in the light of this concept there were indeed some important innovations like plastics processing, catalytic cracking in mineral oil refining and jets, helicopters and radar in the aircraft industry which originated in the 1930s but developed their growth potential only in the 1950s and 1960s.[22] Two other industries, chemical engineering and electrical engineering, had already been important growth industries before the Second World War, whereas the motor vehicle industry, after some modest growth in the 1920s and 1930s, expanded rapidly only after the Second World War. The leading growth industries of the 1950s and 1960s were those in which "basic innovations" played a particularly large role. The slackening economic growth of the 1970s coincided with the relative stagnation of several former growth industries. Although there are indications of a fading out of some basic innovation effects, new industries or branches of already existing industries have been developed which - at least to a large extent - have made up for this slowdown. Among them are the computer and aerospace industries as well as biotechnology and new industrial materials and the application of microelectronics to various fields.

Although the Federal Republic has developed an industrial structure in which large corporations play a dominant role, small firms have by no means disappeared. Several trades have, it is true, declined or completely disappeared since the days of early industrialisation, but many have survived and perform functions which cannot be carried out by large firms, such as bricklaying, carpentry and plumbing. Trades such as radio and television and car maintenance have even increased. Although the number of small businesses - many of them subcontractors to large corporations - have declined from 886,500 in 1950 to 492,200 in 1982 the number of people employed in these firms has increased from 3.314 million to 3.973 million in the same period; turnover has grown from DM 27.0 thousand million in 1950 to 368.2 thousand million in 1982.[23]

During the 1950s and 1960s the service sector expanded only slowly. Between 1950 and 1970 its share of output even dropped by 5 percentage points. Part of the accelerated employment gains since 1970 have been due to more widespread use of part-time work, especially in trade and miscellaneous services. Of the traditional consumer services (personal and social services) and producer services (distributive services such as trade, transport, finance and business services) the most dynamic elements have been several distributive services and the social services. The relatively slow expansion of service activities during recent years can be ascribed to various political, economic and institutional factors, especially to the policy of budget consolidation, which has exercised considerable restraint on the policy of public sector employment. In education, health and welfare a considerable part of the growing service demand from households has for a long time been satisfied by the public sector at little or no direct cost to the consumer. Rising relative prices and costs for services have also led to increasing "do-it-yourself" activities aided by a shorter working life.[24]

Regional change

In the early years the Federal Republic of Germany had a varied regional structure with better infrastructure in and around urban centres than in rural areas. Government regional planning has since aimed at decentralising industry, at curbing the depopulation of rural areas and at assisting those areas in which unemployment problems were particularly pronounced. These were parts of Lower Saxony and Eastern Bavaria adjacent to the border of the GDR and Czechoslovakia (the so-called "frontier corridor"), East Friesland and, from the late 1950s onwards, the coal and iron and steel producing areas in the Ruhr and the Saar. Non-repayable investment subsidies for industry were the main instruments of assistance.[25]

For some time the gap between the economic imbalance of the FRG's southern and northern states has created problems. GNP per capita has been rising faster in the states of Hesse, Baden-Wuerttemberg and Bavaria than in the northern states of Schleswig-Holstein, Lower Saxony or North-Rhine-Westphalia and the city states of Hamburg and Bremen. Reasons for this are the catching up process of the southern states with the more industrialised states of the north, the fact that after the war many firms, which are among the most growth intensive today, settled in Hesse, Baden-Wuerttemberg and Bavaria. Also, government assistance to medium and small-scale enterprises, but also to large corporations, and the dwindling importance of many industries which had dominated the old industrial centres of the north have to be mentioned. In the case of Hamburg, the growing international competition in the shipbuilding industry and shrinking worldwide demand played a role. Of particular importance was the political division of Europe, with the missing economic hinterland in the east and, after the foundation of the EEC, the shift of the German economic gravitational centre towards the west.[26]

The Ruhr area, once the German industrial core with its wealth based on coal and steel, has been in a state of permanent economic crisis since the end of the 1950s. Ruhr coal was to a large extent replaced by mineral oil, natural gas, cheaper import coal and nuclear energy. In the FRG and worldwide the demand for steel has fallen and strong competitors have appeared in Japan, Korea and Brazil. Therefore the Rhine-Ruhr agglomeration has lost out in importance to the Rhine-Main, Rhine-Neckar and, recently, to the Munich area. The Rhine-Main area has a central location, a diversified industrial structure and houses the most important banking headquarters. The Stuttgart region's industrial structure is diversified, too, with its focus on the motor industry and on the electrical engineering and machinery industries, whereas the Munich area has its emphasis on electronics and the aerospace industry.[27]

Notes

1. See especially Colin Clark, *The conditions of economic progress*, 3rd edn (Macmillan, London, 1957); Jean Fourastié, *Le grand espoir du XXe siècle* (Gallimard, Paris, 1976).

2. Lothar Huebl and Walter Schepers, *Strukturwandel und Strukturpolitik* (Wissenschaftliche Buchgesellschaft, Darmstadt, 1983), pp.75-7; Klaus Kwasniewski, "Der Trend zur Dienstleistungsgesellschaft" in Norbert Walter (ed.), *Deutschland, Portraet einer Nation, vol. 3. Wirtschaft* (Bertelsmann, Guetersloh, 1985), p.261; Reishi Maruya, "Structural change in the German economy in the 1970s", *Kobe University Economic Review*, vol. 32 (1986), pp.69-86.

3. There are several problems with the classification criteria, because the demarcation lines between the three sectors are by no means clear cut. For example many services, like research and development, are attributed to the secondary sector. (Kwasniewski, "Der Trend zur Dienstleistungsgesellschaft", pp.262-3).

4. Werner Glastetter, Ruediger Paulert, Ulrich Spoerel, *Die wirtschaftliche Entwicklung in der Bundesrepublik Deutschland 1950-1980. Befunde, Aspekte, Hintergruende* (Campus, Frankfurt am Main, New York, 1983), pp.104-5.

5. Huebl and Schepers, *Strukturwandel*, p.77. See also Karl Georg Zinn, "Fourastié versus Neoklassik. Nochmal: Die aktuelle Strukturdiskussion im Licht der Dreisektorenthese", *Wirtschaft und Gesellschaft*, vol. 13 (1987), pp.271-80.

6. See, among others, Kwasniewski, "Der Trend zur Dienstleistungsgesellschaft", p.264.

7. Sima Lieberman, *The growth of European mixed economies 1945-1970* (Schenkman, New York, 1977), pp.61-3. On continuity and discontinuity in agriculture see Herbert Koetter, "Die Landwirtschaft", in Werner Conze and M. Rainer Lepsius (eds), *Sozialgeschichte der Bundesrepublik Deutschland. Beitraege zum Kontinuitaetsproblem* (Klett-Cotta, Stuttgart, 1983), pp.115-42.

8. Dieter Grosser, "Strukturpolitik" in Dieter Grosser (ed.), *Der Staat in der Wirtschaft der Bundesrepublik* (Leske and Budrich, Opladen, 1985), p.245.

9. Gustav Stolper, Karl Haeuser, Knut Borchardt, *The German economy 1870 to the present* (Harcourt, Brace, New York, 1967), p.264.

10. Harald Winkel, *Die Wirtschaft im geteilten Deutschland 1945-1970* (Steiner, Wiesbaden, 1974), pp.142-5.

11. Lieberman, *European mixed economies*, pp.213-5.

12. Peter Kirschke and Ulrich Koester, "Die hausgemachte Krise in der Agrarpolitik", *Wirtschaftsdienst*, vol. 65 (1985), pp.337-44.

13. Klaus Kwasniewski, "Die Ordnung und Entwicklung der wichtigsten Wirtschaftsbereiche" in Norbert Walter (ed.), *Deutschland. Portraet einer Nation, vol. 3. Wirtschaft* (Bertelsmann, Guetersloh, 1985), pp.276-7. See also Ulrich Kluge, "Vierzig Jahre Landwirtschaftspolitik der Bundesrepublik Deutschland 1945/9-1985. Moeglichkeiten und Grenzen staatlicher Agrarsubventionen", *Aus Politik und Zeitgeschichte*, vol. 33 (1986), B.42, pp.3-20; Hermann Priebe, *Die subventionierte Unvernunft* (Siedler, Berlin, 1985).

14. Wolfram Fischer, "Bergbau, Industrie und Handwerk" in Hermann Aubin and Wolfgang Zorn (eds), *Handbuch der deutschen Wirtschafts- und Sozialgeschichte*, 2 vols (Klett, Stuttgart, 1976), vol. 2, p.838.

15. OECD, *Economic surveys, Germany* (OECD, Paris, 1987), p.50.

16. Increases in labour productivity are also due to the organisation of production and managerial innovations. R&D measurements have two main shortcomings: they take input into research and development activities into consideration and not output of useful scientific and technological knowledge; secondly, a host of other activities is required before useful scientific and technological knowledge becomes marketable as useful products or production processes - that is before R&D outlays have any effect on the economy. R&D activities account for only a relatively small part of the total costs (according to some estimates between 10 and 20 per cent of commercialising a new product or production process). Patent statistics have severe limitations, too: a number of important inventions are not patentable or are not in fact patented; often the inventor does not want to disclose his technological information. Also, the value of patents varies enormously. What matters for technical progress and economic growth is not so much invention but innovation and the diffusion of innovation. (OECD, *Gaps in technology. Analytical Report* (OECD, Paris, 1970), pp.180, 205.)

17. Rationalisierungskuratorium der deutschen Wirtschaft (ed.), *Wirtschaftliche und soziale Aspekte des technischen Wandels in der Bundesrepublik Deutschland* (9 vols., Europaeische Verlagsanstalt, Frankfurt am Main, 1970), vol. 1, pp.51-95, 109.

18. Karl Hardach, *The political economy of Germany in the twentieth century* (University of California Press, Berkeley, Los Angeles, London, 1980), pp.195-6; Helge Majer, *Die "technologische Luecke" zwischen der Bundesrepublik Deutschland und den Vereinigten Staaten* (Mohr, Tuebingen, 1973).

19. Gerhard Fels and Klaus-Dieter Schmidt, *Die deutsche Wirtschaft im Strukturwandel* (Mohr, Tuebingen, 1981), pp.65-79; Rudolf-Ferdinand Danckwert, Hans-Hagen Haertel, Eberhard Thiel, *Analyse der strukturellen Entwicklung der deutschen Wirtschaft. Strukturbericht 1980* (Verlag Weltarchiv, Hamburg, 1981), pp.62-7; Kommission fuer wirtschaftlichen und sozialen Wandel, *Wirtschaftlicher und sozialer Wandel in der Bundesrepublik Deutschland (Schwartz, Goettingen, 1977), pp.244-6.*

20. Gerhard Mensch, *Stalemate in technology* (Ballinger, Cambridge, Mass., 1979). Mensch's work has met with strong criticism.

21. Although the difference between product innovations and process innovations are normally not very clear-cut. In engineering, for example, a product innovation normally implies a process innovation. See Hans-Juergen Krupp, "Innovation und Wettbewerbsfähigkeit der deutschen Volkswirtschaft" in Gottfried Bombach, Bernhard Gahlen, Alfred E. Ott (eds), *Technologischer Wandel. Analyse und Fakten* (Mohr, Tuebingen, 1986), p.216.

22. Alfred Kleinknecht, "Basisinnovation und Wachstumsschuebe: das Beispiel der westdeutschen Industrie", *Konjunkturpolitik*, vol. 25 (1979), pp.320-43.

23. Wolfram Fischer, "Bergbau, Industrie und Handwerk", pp.838-9; Kwasniewski, "Ordnung und Entwicklung", p.289.

24. OECD, *Economic surveys, Germany* (OECD, Paris, 1987), pp.48-50.

25. Eric Owen Smith, *The West German economy* (Croom Helm, London, 1983), p.143. On the role of economic policy in structural change see Frank Stiller, "Zur Rolle der Wirtschaftspolitik im Strukturwandel der Bundesrepublik Deutschland" in *"Erfolg und Misserfolg sektoraler Strukturpolitik"* (Duncker and Humblot, Berlin, 1985), pp.255-67.

26. Handelskammer Hamburg, "Herausforderung fuer den Norden. Zur Diskussion um das wirtschaftliche Sued-Nord-Gefaelle", unpublished manuscript, Hamburg, 1984.

Chapter Fourteen

FOREIGN TRADE

Commodity trade and the balance of payments

The Bretton Woods Agreement of 23 July 1944, which marked a
starting point towards the liberalisation of world trade, was followed by the General Agreement on Tariffs and Trade (GATT)
of 30 October 1947 and the beginning of European economic integration. These and other agreements resulted in a significant increase in world trade.[1]

With few material resources and dependent upon large imports
of food after the war, the Federal German government advocated
a policy of trade liberalisation. From 1950 to 1985 the FRG's
share in world imports increased from 4.5 per cent to 8.4 per cent,
her share in world exports rose even more, from 3.5 per cent to
10.3 per cent.

From the early 1950s to the mid-1960s the FRG's surplus in foreign trade grew. Mainly owing to the dramatic increase in mineral
oil prices, problems arose later, but even in 1973-4 and 1980 the
foreign trade balance was favourable. The FRG's export dependence (export share in total output) rose from 8.5 per cent in
1950 to 14.6 per cent in 1960, 18.8 per cent in 1970, 23.0 per cent
in 1980 and to 27.6 per cent in 1985. Only in the 1970s, however,
was the German pre-First World War export share - which is, of
course, not fully comparable to the post-Second World War FRG
share - regained.[2]

Three stages can be distinguished in FRG exports after the Second World War: the first, during which foreign trade expanded
rapidly, extended from 1950 to the foundation of the European

237

Figure 14.1: Export and import shares 1950-1985 [a]

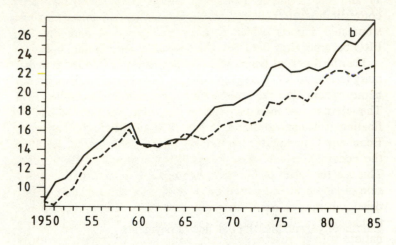

Notes: [a] 1970 prices, until 1959 excluding Saarland and West Berlin
 [b] export share
 [c] import share

Source: Sachverstaendigenrat zur Begutachtung der gesamtwirtschaftlichen Entwicklung, own computations

Economic Community in 1957/8. In that period, FRG exports rose
by 20.4 per cent a year and their share in GNP doubled.[3]

This success in exports had several causes, particularly the
strength of the world markets, the structure of Federal German
industry and the fact that the country possessed and was able to
expand exactly those industries - mechanical engineering, motor
vehicles, electrical and chemical engineering - which enjoyed constantly growing markets. Government monetary and fiscal policies, its support of export industries and the undervaluation of
the *Deutsche Mark* contributed to the success. At prevailing exchange rates export prices were comparatively low. With unemployment still persisting in the early 1950s, productivity was not
surpassed by rising wages, while, at the same time, import prices
declined. These conditions held down production costs and benefited price competitiveness in international markets.[4]

During the second period, between 1959 and 1971, world trade
grew rapidly. The removal of trade barriers within the EEC
proved vital for the expansion of FRG exports and the same goes

for the liberalisation of world trade after the Dillon Round (1960-1) and the Kennedy Round (1964-7).[5] The *Deutsche Mark*'s convertibility (after 1958) and its increasing undervaluation also stimulated exports, which rose by 10.5 per cent annually. The FRG became, after the USA, the second largest trading nation.

The third period began with the suspension of dollar convertibility in August 1971 and the collapse of the Bretton Woods monetary system after the Smithsonian agreement of December 1971. The international monetary system was rearranged on the basis of floating exchange rates and, in late 1978, the EMS, the European Economic Community's monetary system, was created. By 1983, the Federal German share in world trade shrank to 10 per cent. This was the result of significant changes in the international division of labour after the two oil price shocks, the Japanese export drive and that of some "threshold countries", the spread of new technologies and the sustained growth weakness of most industrial nations with increasing inflation, and a shift to trade protectionism and huge international debts.[6] While it was mainly the second oil price shock which had pushed the Federal German balance of current account into large deficits in 1979 and 1980, the balance of merchandise trade continued to be in surplus in these two years. This was, however, too small to compensate for the traditional deficit in the service balance reflecting mainly tourism and the deficit in the transfer balance mainly owing to Federal German contributions to international organisations.[7]

During the first three decades of the FRG's existence her current balance of payments had mostly been in a surplus position, particularly during the two recessions of 1967-8 and 1974-5 and during the recovery of the early 1980s. Deficits occurred in 1965 and in the three years following the second oil price shock, 1979-81.

Under the impact of a depreciating *Deutsche Mark* and falling domestic demand, the current external account was back in surplus again in 1982. From the mid-1970s onwards the DM exchange rate against the US dollar has been more affected by short-term speculative capital transactions[8] and the growing public deficit in the United States than by the development of the foreign trade balance.

The rapid appreciation of the dollar after 1980 and the revival in foreign demand reinforced the export orientation of the Federal German economy. In 1986 declining mineral oil prices, which improved the foreign trade balance by about 1.5 per cent of GNP, had a favourable impact on the current account balance.[9]

Figure 14.2: Components of the current account balance 1950-1985 [a]

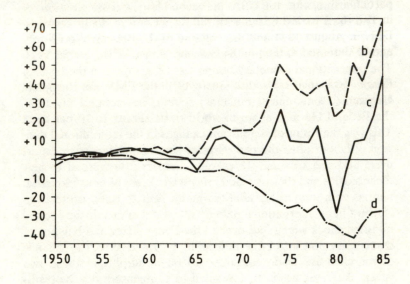

Notes: [a] in DM thousand million
          [b] foreign trade balance
          [c] current account balance
          [d] service and transfer balance

Source: Sachverstaendigenrat zur Begutachtung der gesamtwirtschaftlichen Entwicklung

Manufacturing has played the dominant role as a foreign exchange earner, easily compensating for the high deficits on transfer accounts and the net imports of services. In transfers, contributions to the European Community rose sixfold in the period 1970-80 and their share in all transfer payments rose from nearly 17 per cent in 1970 to over 36 per cent in 1980. As far as long-term and short-term capital transactions are concerned, there is no distinct trend. Reflecting the persistent current account surplus there was an adverse balance of long-term capital transactions during the 1960s and 1970s. Owing to speculation about an appreciating *Deutsche Mark* substantial amounts of short-term capital were transferred to the Federal Republic. As a consequence of the generally favourable current account balance, foreign currency reserves grew in the 1950s and 1960s under the Bretton Woods system of fixed exchange rates. Although this system broke down in 1973, growth was, mainly for political reasons, particularly strong in the 1970s (from DM 47.6 thousand million in 1970 to DM 102.8 thousand million in 1978), but declined to DM 78.9 thousand million in 1980 and fluctuated between DM 80 and 85 thousand million in the first half of the 1980s.[10]

Figure 14.3: DM/US dollar exchange rates 1953-1985, annual averages

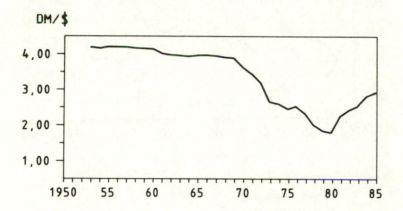

Source: Deutsche Bundesbank

Commodity structure and regional structure

Whereas during the first half of the twentieth century foodstuffs and raw materials accounted for almost three-quarters of German imports these products declined in importance continuously throughout the period 1950 to 1980. In the early 1980s they accounted for less than three-tenths of Federal German imports. During the same period the share of finished goods in FRG imports increased sixfold.[11] The development of the terms of trade influenced the behaviour of the current account balance significantly.

After the Korean boom of 1951 export prices increased con-

Figure 14.4: Average export and import prices, terms of trade, 1952-1985 [a]

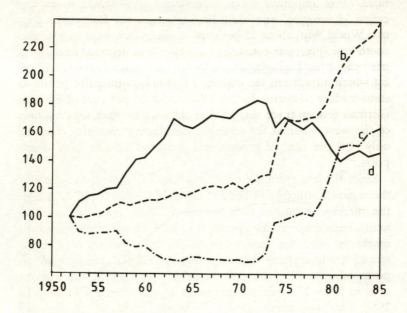

Notes: [a] 1952 = 100
 [b] average export price
 [c] average import price
 [d] terms of trade

Source: Sachverstaendigenrat zur Begutachtung der gesamtwirtschaftlichen Entwicklung, own computations

tinuously while import prices decreased and stagnated from 1962 to 1972. With increasing world inflation in the early 1970s the trend changed. As far as the terms of trade are concerned, higher import prices, particularly for mineral oil and raw materials, could no longer be compensated by high export prices. Between 1972 and 1981 import prices rose by about 80 per cent with the terms of trade deteriorating by about 15 per cent.

In exports the share of intermediate goods declined markedly; in 1980 two-thirds of all FRG exports consisted of finished goods. In the 1960s and 1970s four commodity groups provided more than half of total exports: mechanical engineering products, motor vehicles, chemicals and electrical engineering goods.

In the years immediately preceding the First World War, two-fifths of all imported goods came from areas which today are called "developing" and "state-trading" countries. Before the Second World War, about 15 per cent of all exports went to east and south-east European countries, but this figure declined to only 1-2 per cent at the beginning of the 1950s, partly due to the COCOM list which interdicted the export of technology-intensive goods to state-trading countries. In the 1960s about 85 per cent of Federal German foreign trade was carried out with the industrial nations of the west, whereas the so-called developing countries received only 12.8 per cent of exports and provided 8.4 per cent of imports.[12]

Since the late 1950s the creation of the EEC has led to shifts in the regional structure of Federal German foreign trade. Although the member countries had, because of their proximity to Germany, been major trading partners before, foreign trade increased markedly after the foundation of the EEC. There have been strong "trade creating" effects within the EEC - the share of exports going to EEC countries in total FRG exports was 50.8 per cent in 1985, 15.5 percentage points higher than it had been in 1958. This was mainly due to the larger "domestic" market and large-scale production,[13] but there were also many hindrances, setbacks and "trade diversion" effects,[14] partly because of the agricultural sector's isolation from the world market. Japan has gained an increasing share of the domestic market, although in relatively few products. Trade with non oil-exporting "developing countries" grew less rapidly than total foreign trade, partly because those countries exported mainly agricultural products for which Federal German demand was low, due to agricultural protection. Some "threshold countries" have been quite successful in selling industrial products to the FRG while Federal German exporters have only to a small extent made use of the growing markets in east and south-east Asia.

During the 1970s the OPEC countries raised their share in the value of FRG imports because of higher oil prices. Federal German exporters availed themselves of the increasing purchasing power in those countries so that exports to OPEC countries more than doubled during the 1970s. From the early 1980s, however, exports to OPEC members declined because of lower income through deteriorating mineral oil prices and the competition of threshold countries.[15]

Trade with the state-trading countries also increased during the 1970s, consisting mainly of imported fuels and exported capital goods. With a share of about 6 per cent in total Federal German foreign commodity trade the Federal Republic was the most important western market for goods from state-trading countries. In FRG exports, however, these countries in total did not exceed the importance of a country like Switzerland or Austria.[16]

For the trade between the two parts of Germany - "interzonal trade", later "inner-German trade" - the political dimension has always been dominant for the Federal German government which regarded inner-German trade as a binding link between the two German states, whereas the GDR government's motives for trade were purely economic ones. The FRG has never considered the GDR as a foreign country so that no "foreign trade" in the strict sense could exist between the two parts of Germany and, indeed, there have never been any customs duties. As a result of the currency reform, a new accounting unit (*Verrechnungseinheit, VE*) was created with a value corresponding to that of the Federal German *Deutsche Mark*, as well as a clearing account held at the *Bundesbank* and the State Bank of the GDR, and "the swing", an interest-free overdraft, of which, so far, only the GDR has availed herself.[17]

With the "Grand Coalition" (Christian Democrats and Social Democrats) after 1967 and the Social-Liberal Coalition after 1969 inner-German trade expanded and, after the "basic treaty" of December 1972, developed relatively steadily. The cumulative trade volume rose from *VE* 22 thousand million in the period 1951-65 to 95 thousand million during 1966-80. The FRG exported mainly basic goods, production goods and capital goods, especially non-electrical machinery and chemicals, whereas the emphasis of GDR exports was on lignite, petroleum and textiles.[18]

In 1955 the share of inner-German trade in Federal German GNP was 2.2 per cent, but subsequently it declined to 1.7 per cent in 1985;[19] for the GDR inner-German trade has been of far greater importance.[20] With about 28 per cent of total inner-German trade in 1980 West-Berlin's share of trade with the GDR was disproportionally large. The GDR has benefited from the special status of inner-German trade within the EEC in that goods exported from the German Democratic Republic have never been subject to EEC tariffs and can be moved freely within the community. This has led to frequent criticism by other EEC members who complained about the FRG's "open border" with the GDR.[21]

Multinational corporations and international competitiveness

Multinational corporations had already existed in Germany before the First World War, especially in the chemical, electrical and metal industries.[22] After confiscations in two world wars Federal direct investment abroad was interdicted by the Allies until 1952.[23] Between 1952 and 1980 FRG firms invested DM 74 thousand million abroad, mainly in the chemical, electrical, machine tool and motor vehicle industries.[24]

Figure 14.5:   Federal German foreign direct investment 1956-1985 and foreign direct investment in the FRG 1962-1985 [a]

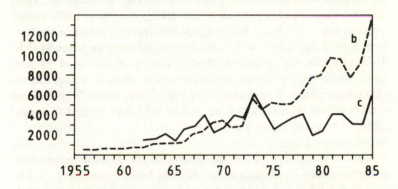

Notes: [a] in DM million
          [b] FRG foreign direct investment
          [c] foreign direct investment in the FRG

Sources: Henry Kraegenau, *Internationale Direktinvestitionen 1950-1973* (Verlag Weltarchiv, Hamburg, 1977); Joerg Beifuss, *Direktinvestitionen im Ausland, Exportkonkurrenz oder Marktsicherung?* (Deutscher Instituts-Verlag, Cologne, 1987).

From 1952 until the mid-1960s direct investment abroad did not rise significantly. From 1965 until the early 1970s, however, there was an upward trend with no significant fluctuations. From the early 1970s onwards marked fluctuations developed around an upward trend, but from about 1977 the trend continued similar to that of the second half of the 1960s. In the late 1960s about half of the Federal German foreign assets were in Europe, about one-fifth in Latin America and one-tenth in the United States.[25]

Until the mid-1960s Federal German investors were reluctant to invest abroad, partly because of unpleasant experiences with expropriations after two world wars.[26] Secondly, and more importantly, domestic investment opportunities in the 1950s abounded, often assisted by government subsidies. Also, the ample labour supply until the early 1960s led to a comparatively low domestic wage level and the undervaluation of the *Deutsche Mark* made buying plants and equipment abroad expensive.

From the late 1950s onwards the picture changed and direct investment abroad picked up: the large EEC market favoured direct investment in other EEC countries and the growing dependence on exports and rising foreign trade surpluses induced investors to support exports by direct investment abroad. Also, growing profits could often not be absorbed by the domestic market and the DM revaluations of the 1960s and early 1970s made exports more difficult, fostering direct foreign investment. Between 1972 and 1980, with a floating exchange rate from March 1973 onwards, the *Deutsche Mark* appreciated by about 50 per cent, which made foreign investment attractive. It is significant that a year after the revaluations of 1961, 1969 and 1973 there was a marked rise in direct investment abroad.[27] Also, fears of foreign counter-measures against the large Federal German foreign trade surplus played a role.

As far as foreign direct investment in the FRG is concerned there has been no distinct trend. In 1970 half of the foreign holdings in the FRG belonged to North Americans and the other half to Europeans. After the end of the Second World War foreigners, especially Americans, often continued production in plants which they had owned before the war and the high economic growth rates during the early years of the Federal Republic made direct investment attractive.[28] These increased after the foundation of the EEC: between 1957 and 1967 American direct investment in the FRG grew fourfold.[29]

One of the reasons why Americans invested in the Federal Republic after the creation of the Common Market was to remain competitive in an increased market. Owing to the unprecise notion of "international competitiveness" different - indirect - indicators have to be used for evaluation. A distinction has to be made between price competitiveness and technological competitiveness, although there are some links between the two. As far as technological competitiveness is concerned, R&D expenditures or "technology intensity" (R&D expenditures and human capital intensity) as well as patent applications, especially patents taken out abroad, can be used as indicators, although the link between international competitiveness on the one hand and R&D expenditures and patent applications on the other is rather loose.[30]

The FRG is well endowed with physical capital, technological know-how, a well-trained labour force and a good infrastructure, vital prerequisites for technological competitiveness.[31] In patents taken out abroad she held second place in the period 1972-81 with 20 per cent of the total, behind the USA (31 per cent) and ahead of Japan (10 per cent); in R&D expenditure the FRG was second to the USA, too. She is particularly strong in those exports in which price competitiveness does not play a major role and in which the exact fulfilment of orders, delivery on time, reliability and continuous technical development are predominant.[32] At present, she has an excellent competitive position in automatic control technology, equipment for the distribution of electricity, optical instruments, nuclear reactors, pharmaceutical goods and products of organic chemistry, while there are competitive gaps in computer technology, in which she holds third place in exports behind Japan and the United States and in communications technology.[33] Regulations and some lack of efficient R&D management may be the reasons why the switch to some new technological fields has not been managed as rapidly as in Japan or the United States.[34] While the FRG has, comparatively speaking, lagged behind in designing and making microcircuits, her industry has, however, been usually quick in putting microcircuits to work in its products.[35] It is possible that the discussion about a supposedly widening "high technology gap" is looking the wrong way at that wrong goal and that it would be better to ignore recent high technology trends and, instead of copying the world's latest "high tech", concentrate rather on new, untapped areas.[36]

Price competitiveness as opposed to technological competitiveness is mainly determined by the development of unit labour costs, the exchange rate, capital costs, taxes and business cycles.[37] Unit labour costs in the FRG rose by 7 per cent during the period 1975-9, but fell again by 4 per cent from 1980-3, while the exchange rate (the real average rate on the basis of consumer prices) rose against the dollar during 1975-9, but fell during 1980-3. The FRG's share in manufacturing in world exports rose in the period 1966-74. There was, however, a slight downward trend in the late 1970s and early 1980s mainly due to a lower demand from her industrial trading partners after the two oil price shocks and the fact that the FRG was not prepared well enough for the rapid expansion of third world markets.[38] The alleged loss of international competitiveness[39] was mainly due to the strong *Deutsche Mark*. In the early 1980s, with the DM falling against the dollar, the situation improved and in 1986 and 1987, even in spite of the FRG's strong currency, she was the world's largest exporter.[40]

Examining total factor productivity in an international perspective, the FRG's level in manufacturing compared to the United States was just 0.5 in 1952, but improved to almost 0.75 in 1960 and to over 0.9 in 1980 (United States = 1).[41] A FRG-US comparison also shows that in the 1960s the FRG was behind the US in factor productivity in all manufacturing industries. By the end of the 1960s industries like plastics, fabricated metal and leather caught up, while mining, primary metal, precision engineering and the construction sector succeeded in catching up in the 1970s. While the gap in the chemical, machinery, motor vehicle and communication industries has narrowed continuously, branches like electrical machinery, printing and textiles have not shown any tendency to catch up with the US level of total productivity.

As far as Japan is concerned most Japanese industries were well behind their Federal German counterparts in total factor productivity in the early 1960s. However, during that decade, chemicals, machinery and precision instruments lost their productivity advantage; in the seventies, the same is true of primary metals, electrical machinery and textiles. No closing of the productivity gap can be found in industries like plastics or fabricated metal.[42]

Foreign trade policy

Shortly after the Second World War American foreign policy aimed at integrating West Germany into a liberal, multilateral world trade system. The Paris agreement on European economic cooperation of 16 April 1948 envisaged, as part of the Marshall Plan, general preferences, the reduction of tariffs and of trade discriminations and subsidies.[43] Shortly after her foundation, the Federal Republic became a member of the OEEC (Organization for European Economic Cooperation), and, from 1951 onwards, reduced tariffs on imported industrial goods. In 1951 the FRG joined GATT (General Agreement on Tariffs and Trade), and, a year later, the International Monetary Fund (IMF) and the Bretton Woods Agreement. Owing to the Korean boom and the liberalisation of foreign trade the FRG's gold and foreign exchange reserves increased continuously from 1952 onwards.[44]

Several members of the Federal German government, especially Ludwig Erhard, Minister of Economic Affairs, advocated a programme for establishing free world trade and included it in the general concept of a social market economy. The attempts to liberalise commodity trade were complemented by the liberalisation of international payments. On 1 July 1950 the European Payments Union (EPU) was founded, which organised a European clearing system by establishing current accounts through which the EPU member nations (the FRG among others) could balance their mutual claims. The existence of the EPU led to the hardening of European currencies and, in 1958, to the resumption of general convertibility, although the *Deutsche Mark* had, in fact, been freely convertible for some years.[45]

As negotiations in GATT turned out to be rather protracted the FRG lowered her tariffs (with the exception of agricultural tariffs) between 1955 and 1957 partly to counteract foreign criticism of the Federal German export drive. Still, the FRG's foreign trade policy was anything but an epitome of a liberal market policy. There were export subsidies of many sorts: the 1951 act to foster exports, which remained in force until 1955, stipulated tax rebates for exports and granted lower interest rates which, in turn, exporters could offer to foreign customers.[46] From 1949 exports could be insured against the risk of insolvent foreign customers (*Hermes Kreditversicherung*), which nowadays mainly covers risks connected with exports to "developing countries". Also, subsidies for special industries played a role, especially for coal mining, the iron and steel industry and shipbuilding, but also for the chemical, electrical and air and space industries. These subsidies improved export conditions, although the official reason for granting them was often connected with regional policy. The Federal government also improved exports by financing research and development, particularly in the chemical, electrical, engineering and air and space industries.[47] Another means of stimulating exports was the undervaluation of the *Deutsche Mark*, especially in the 1960s.

From the mid-1950s to the early 1970s the *Deutsche Mark* was probably below the level compatible with external stability. Continuing balance of payments surpluses led to several speculative capital inflows which forced the revaluations of 1961 and 1969 (5 per cent and 9.3 per cent) among others which, however, proved to be too small and too late. The fact that the price level in the FRG rose more slowly than that of other major trading partners fuelled international speculation and contributed to domestic inflation. The undervalued currency and the accumulation of reserves led to inflationary pressures not only via an increased domestic money supply, but also via the additional demand for Federal German goods.[48]

There were other reasons why the undervaluation of the *Deutsche Mark* created problems for the Federal German economy: while it promoted exports, it led to a domestic misallocation of production factors that were tied to industrial branches which, if exchange rates conducive to international monetary stability had prevailed, would not have been internationally competitive. Goods and resources were given away too cheaply; home supply and therefore domestic material welfare was reduced in favour of high export rates and the consequent accumulation of foreign currency, assets of rather dubious merit because of their frequent devaluations by the *Deutsche Mark*'s appreciation.[49] Foreign trade surpluses also provoked trading partners to take protective countermeasures and enhanced the Federal Republic's dependence on the vagaries of the world market. On the other hand, economic development after the early 1950s has proved foreign trade to be an engine of growth which led the Federal German economy out of recession in many business cycles, compensating for weak domestic demand. A large export share also fostered economies of scale. Moreover, to compensate for her traditionally adverse service and transfer balances and to meet international obligations like contributions to international organisations (EEC, UNO, IMF among others) and development aid, the FRG required a sizeable surplus in commodity trade.[50]

This is also true of the settlement of pre-war debts and for restitution payments. In the London debt negotiations the Federal government acknowledged the principal of all old debts and was ready to pay back interest at a reduced rate. According to the London Agreement of February 1953 the total debt amounted to about DM 14 thousand million. Foreign obligations existed in addition to those dealt with in London, such as the payments to the state of Israel agreed to in 1952 as a partial material compensation for the National Socialist crimes committed against Jews. The FRG incurred obligations to pay DM 102.6 thousand million as restitution,[51] of which DM 78.7 thousand million have so far been paid.

In the early 1950s institutions like the European Coal and Steel Community (*Montan-Union*) were founded, which led to the Treaty of Rome of 25 March 1957 and the foundation of the European Economic Community. The main motives of Federal German politicians in taking part in the creation of the EEC were political ones with economic objectives playing only a secondary role. Industrialists voiced differing opinions on Common Market membership. Although they generally welcomed the prospect of exporting goods to France, Italy and the Benelux countries free of tariffs, they would have preferred the foundation of a large free-trading community including the United Kingdom, the Scandinavian countries, Austria and Switzerland. Ludwig Erhard advocated this "greater free trading area" fervently and did not think much of the idea of achieving political integration via economic integration, mainly because he doubted French readiness to give up her national sovereignty. The FRG strongly supported the reduction of tariffs on industrial goods vis-à-vis non-member countries.[52] In 1970, average nominal tariffs amounted to 8.8 per cent. In spite of these achievements much remains to be done on the way to a complete economic - let alone political - integration.

Notes

1. Rainer Vollmer, "The structure of West German foreign trade", *Zeitschrift fuer die gesamte Staatswissenschaft*, vol. 13 (1981), pp.575-87 for this and the following.

2. Walter G. Hoffmann, Franz Grumbach, Helmut Hesse, *Das Wachstum der deutschen Wirtschaft seit der Mitte des 19. Jahrhunderts* (Springer, Berlin, Heidelberg, New York, 1965), pp.520-5.

3. Juergen B. Donges, "Die Exportorientierung der deutschen Wirtschaft: Erfahrungen, Probleme, Perspektiven" in Erwin Dichtl and Otmar Issing (eds), *Exporte als Herausforderung fuer die deutsche Wirtschaft* (Deutscher Instituts-Verlag, Cologne, 1984), p.16.

4. Gustav Stolper, Karl Haeuser and Knut Borchardt, *The German economy 1870 to the present* (Harcourt, Brace, New York, 1967), pp.248-9.

5. Wolfgang Ernst, "The free movement of goods and services within the European Economic Community within the context of the world economy", *Zeitschrift fuer die gesamte Staatswissenschaft*, vol. 137 (1981), p.563.

6. Donges, "Die Exportorientierung der deutschen Wirtschaft", p.17.

7. Vollmer, "The structure of West German foreign trade", p.577.

8. Dieter Grosser, "Internationale Wirtschafts- und Waehrungspolitik" in Dieter Grosser (ed.), *Der Staat in der Wirtschaft der Bundesrepublik* (Leske and Budrich, Opladen, 1985), p.461.

9. OECD, *Economic surveys, Germany* (OECD, Paris, 1987), p.38.

10. Werner Glastetter, Ruediger Paulert, Ulrich Spoerel, *Die wirtschaftliche Entwicklung in der Bundesrepublik Deutschland. Befunde, Aspekte, Hintergruende* (Campus, Frankfurt am Main, New York, 1983), pp.492, 540-51.

11. Vollmer, "The structure of West German foreign trade", pp.578-84 for this and the following.

12. Werner Abelshauser, *Wirtschaftsgeschichte der Bundesrepublik Deutschland 1945-1980* (Suhrkamp, Frankfurt am Main, 1983), p.160.

13. Gerold Ambrosius, "Europaeische Integration und wirtschaftliche Entwicklung der Bundesrepublik Deutschland in den fuenfziger Jahren" in Helmut Berding (ed.), *Wirtschaftliche und politische Integration in Europa im 19. und 20. Jahrhundert, Geschichte und Gesellschaft*, Sonderheft 10 (Vandenhoeck and Ruprecht, Goettingen, 1984), p.274.

14. Hanns Juergen Kuesters, *Die Gruendung der europaeischen Wirtschaftsgemeinschaft* (Nomos, Baden-Baden, 1982).

15. Donges, "Die Exportorientierung der deutschen Industrie", p.19.

16. Vollmer, "The structure of West German foreign trade", p.580.

17. Franz Roesch and Fritz Homann, "Thirty years of the Berlin agreement - thirty years of inner-German trade: economic and political dimensions", *Zeitschrift fuer die gesamte Staatswissenschaft*, vol. 137 (1981), p.529.

18. Stolper, Haeuser, Borchardt, *German economy*, p.298.

19. Reinhold Biskup, "Einfluesse auf die Entwicklung des Aussenhandels in beiden Teilen Deutschlands seit dem Zweiten Weltkrieg", *WiSt, Wirtschaftswissenschaftliches Studium*, vol. 15 (1986), p.331.

20. Stolper, Haeuser, Borchardt, *German economy*, p.298. See also Horst Lambrecht, "Innerdeutscher Handel - Entwicklung, Warenstruktur, wirtschaftliche Bedeutung", in Claus-Dieter Ehlermann, Siegfried Kupper, Horst Lambrecht, Gerhard Ollig (eds), *Handelspartner DDR - Innerdeutsche Wirtschaftsbeziehungen* (Nomos, Baden-Baden, 1985), pp.77-144.

21. See Reinhold Biskup, *Deutschlands offene Handelsgrenze (Ullstein, Berlin, 1976)*; Roesch and Homann, "Thirty years of the Berlin agreement", p.548.

22. Thomas R. Kabisch, *Deutsches Kapital in den USA. Von der Reichsgruendung bis zur Sequestierung (1917) und Freigabe* (Klett-Cotta, Stuttgart, 1982); Lawrence G. Franko, *The European multinationals. A renewed challenge to American and British big business* (Harper and Row, London, 1976); Walther Kirchner, *Die deutsche Industrie und die Industrialisierung Russlands 1815-1914* (Scripta Mercaturae, St. Katharinen, 1986); Hans-Joachim Braun, "The National Association of German-American Technologists and technology transfer between Germany and the United States, 1884-1930", *History of Technology*, vol. 8 (1983), pp.15-35.

23. Manfred Holthus, Rolf Jungnickel and others (eds), *Die deutschen multinationalen Unternehmen* (Athenaeum, Frankfurt am Main, 1974), p.8.

24. Erich Owen Smith, *The West German economy* (Croom Helm, London, 1983), p.67.

25. Karl Hardach, *The political economy of Germany in the twentieth century* (University of California Press, Berkeley, Los Angeles, London, 1980), p.194.

26 Holthus and Jungnickel (eds), *Die deutschen multinationalen Unternehmen*, p.10.

27. Ursula Schulz, *Deutsche Direktinvestitionen im Ausland. Struktur, Bestimmungsgruende und Wirkungen auf die Wirtschaft der Bundesrepublik Deutschland* (Hochschule Bremen, Bremen, 1978), pp.12-8.

28. Friedrich-Wilhelm Froehlich, *Multinationale Unternehmen. Entstehung, Organisation und Management* (Nomos, Baden-Baden, 1974), p.27-8; Henry Kraegenau, *Internationale Direktinvestitionen 1950-1973* (Verlag Weltarchiv, Hamburg, 1975).

29. See Mira Wilkins, *The maturing of multinational enterprise. American business abroad from 1914 to 1970* (Harvard University Press, Cambridge, Mass., London, 1974).

30. See also my remarks on technical change in the chapter on structural change. Also Hans-Juergen Krupp, "Innovation und Wettbewerbsfaehigkeit der

deutschen Volkswirtschaft" in Gottfried Bombach, Bernhard Gahlen and Alfred E. Ott (eds), *Technologischer Wandel - Analyse und Fakten* (Mohr, Tuebingen, 1986), p.216.

31. Bernhard Gahlen, Fritz Rahmeyer, Manfred Stadtler, "Zur internationalen Wettbewerbsfaehigkeit der deutschen Wirtschaft", *Konjunkturpolitik*, vol. 32 (1986), p.136. See also Reinhard Neebe, "Technologietransfer und Aussenhandel in den Anfangsjahren der Bundesrepublik Deutschland", *Vierteljahrschrift fuer Sozial- und Wirtschaftsgeschichte*, vol. 76 (1989), pp.49-75.

32. H. Schmalholz, L. Scholz, H. Maier, "Innovationsdynamik der deutschen Industrie in den achtziger Jahren", *Ifo-Schnelldienst*, vol. 40 (1-2/1987), pp.20-8; W. Gerstenberger, "Wettbewerbsfaehige Strukturen gestatten Expansionspolitik. Zusammenfassung der Ergebnisse der Strukturberichterstattung 1987", *Ifo-Schnelldienst*, vol. 41 (1/1988), pp.5-22; Ole Boernsen, Hans H. Glismann, Ernst-Juergen Horn, *Der Technologietransfer zwischen den USA und der Bundesrepublik* (Mohr, Tuebingen, 1985); Ernst-Juergen Horn, "Die Entwicklung der internationalen Wettbewerbsfaehigkeit der Bundesrepublik Deutschland", *WiSt, Wirtschaftswissenschaftliches Studium*, vol. 14 (1985), pp.337-40.

33. Bundesministerium fuer Forschung und Technologie (ed.), "Zur technologischen Wettbewerbsfaehigkeit der deutschen Industrie", Allgemeine Informationen aus Forschung und Technik, December 1986, unpublished manuscript.

34. W. Gerstenberger, "Wettbewerbsfaehige Strukturen", p.10.

35. "The right to smile. A survey of West Germany", *Economist*, 6-12 Dec. 1986.

36. *Financial Times*, 28 Oct. 1987, interview with Prof. Erich Staudt, University of Bochum. According to the product cycle hypothesis (Robert Vernon, "The product-cycle hypothesis in a new international environment", *Oxford Bulletin of economics and statistics*, vol. 41 (1979), pp.255-67) the FRG has to produce new and qualitatively high products continuously in order to maintain her real income level. In view of the competition by Japan, the USA and several threshold countries she has to keep running in order to stay in the same place. (See Gahlen, Rahmeyer and Stadtler, "Zur internationalen Wettbewerbsfaehigkeit der deutschen Industrie", p.142).

37. Krupp, "Innovation und Wettbewerbsfaehigkeit der deutschen Volkswirtschaft", pp.199-215; Gahlen, Rahmeyer and Stadtler, "Zur internationalen Wettbewerbsfaehigkeit der deutschen Industrie", p.136.

38. Sachverstaendigenrat zur Begutachtung der gesamtwirtschaftlichen Entwicklung, *Investieren fuer mehr Beschaeftigung. Jahresgutachten 1981/2* (Kohlhammer, Stuttgart, Mainz, 1981), pp.185-90.

39. Hans-Hagen Haertel and Eberhard Thiel, *Analyse der strukturellen Entwicklung der deutschen Wirtschaft*, Strukturbericht 1983 (Verlag Weltarchiv, Hamburg, 1984).

40. Gerstenberger, "Wettbewerbsfaehige Strukturen".

41. Laurits R. Christensen, Dianne Cummings and Dale W. Jorgenson, "Relative productivity levels 1947-1973: an international comparison", *European economic review*, vol. 16 (1981), pp.61-94.

42. Klaus Conrad and Dale W. Jorgenson, "Sectoral productivity gaps between the United States, Japan and Germany, 1960-1979" in Herbert Giersch (ed.), *Probleme und Perspektiven der weltwirtschaftlichen Entwicklung. Schriften des Vereins fuer Socialpolitik*, New Series, vol. 148 (Duncker and Humblot, Berlin, 1987), pp.335-47; Klaus Conrad, "Sektorale Produktivitaetsluecken zwischen den USA, Japan und Deutschland 1960-1979" in Gottfried Bombach, Bernhard Gahlen and Alfred Ott (eds), *Technologischer Wandel - Analyse und Fakten* (Mohr, Tuebingen, 1986), pp.221-41. See also OECD, *Economic surveys, Germany* (OECD, Paris, 1988), pp.45-50.

43. Abelshauser, *Wirtschaftsgeschichte*, pp.147, 153.

44. See on this among others Hartmut Berg, *Internationale Wirt-*

schaftspolitik (Vandenhoeck and Ruprecht, Goettingen, 1976).

45. Stolper, Haeuser, Borchardt, *German economy*, p.239.

46. Grosser, "Internationale Wirtschafts- und Waehrungspolitik", p.466; Henry C. Wallich, *Mainsprings of the German revival* (Yale University Press, New Haven, 1955), pp.244-52.

47. Klaus-Dieter Schmidt and others, *Im Anpassungsprozess zurueckgeworfen - Die deutsche Wirtschaft vor neuen Herausforderungen* (Mohr, Tuebingen, 1984); Donges, "Die Exportorientierung der deutschen Industrie", pp.33-4.

48. Hennings, "West Germany", p.487.

49. Peter Czada, *Wirtschaft. Aktuelle Probleme des Wachstums und der Konjunktur*, 5th edn (Leske and Budrich, Opladen, 1984), p.284; Donges, "Die Exportorientierung der deutschen Industrie", p.35.

50. Abelshauser, *Wirtschaftsgeschichte*, p.162; Glastetter, Paulert, Spoerel, *Wirtschaftliche Entwicklung*, p.469.

51. Stolper, Haeuser, Borchardt, *German economy*, pp.252-3.

52. Grosser, "Internationale Wirtschafts- und Waehrungspolitik", p.469.

SELECT BIBLIOGRAPHY

Twentieth Century, economic surveys

Abelshauser, W. and D. Petzina, "Krise und Rekonstruktion. Zur Interpretation der gesamtwirtschaftlichen Entwicklung Deutschlands im 20. Jahrhundert", in W.H. Schroeder and R. Spree (eds), *Historische Konjunkturforschung* (Klett-Cotta, Stuttgart, 1981), pp.75-114.

Ambrosius, G., *Der Staat als Unternehmer. Oeffentliche Wirtschaft und Kapitalismus seit dem 19. Jahrhundert* (Vandenhoeck and Ruprecht, Goettingen, 1984).

Aubin, H. and W. Zorn (eds), *Handbuch der deutschen Wirtschafts- und Sozialgeschichte* (vol.2, Klett, Stuttgart, 1976).

Berghahn, V.R., *Modern Germany. Society, economy and politics in the twentieth century* (Cambridge University Press, Cambridge, 1982).

Borchardt, K., *Wachstum, Krisen, Handlungsspielraeume der Wirtschaftspolitik. Studien zur Wirtschaftsgeschichte des 19. und 20. Jahrhunderts* (Vandenhoeck and Ruprecht, Goettingen, 1982).

Deutsche Bundesbank (ed.), *Waehrung und Wirtschaft in Deutschland 1876-1975* (Knapp, Frankfurt am Main, 1976).

Hallgarten, G.W.F. and J. Radkau, *Deutsche Industrie und Politik von Bismarck bis in die Gegenwart* (Rowohlt, Reinbek near Hamburg, 1981).

Hardach, G., *Deutschland in der Weltwirtschaft 1870-1970. Eine Einfuehrung in die Sozial- und Wirtschaftsgeschichte* (Campus, Frankfurt am Main, New York, 1977).

Hardach, K., *The political economy of Germany in the twentieth century* (University of California Press, Berkeley, Los Angeles and London, 1976).

Henning, F.-W., *Das industrialisierte Deutschland 1914 bis 1972* (Schoeningh, Paderborn, 1974, 6th edn, 1988).

Henning, F.-W., "Deutschland von 1914 bis zur Gegenwart" in Wolfram Fischer and others (eds), *Handbuch der europaeischen Wirtschafts- und Sozialgeschichte* (vol.6, Klett-Cotta, 1987), pp.416-81.

Henning, F.-W., *Landwirtschaft und laendliche Gesellschaft in Deutschland* (vol. 2, Schoeningh, Paderborn, 1978).

Hoffmann, W.G., F. Grumbach and H. Hesse, *Das Wachstum der deutschen Wirtschaft seit der Mitte des 19. Jahrhunderts* (Springer, Berlin, Heidelberg, New York, 1965).

Kellenbenz, H., *Deutsche Wirtschaftsgeschichte* (vol. 2, Beck, Munich, 1981).

Kitchen, M., *The political economy of Germany* (Croom Helm, London, 1978).

Sommariva, A. and G. Tullio, *German macroeconomic history, 1880-1979. A study on the effects of economic policy on inflation, currency depreciation and growth* (St. Martin's Press, New York, 1987).

Stolper, G., K. Haeuser and K. Borchardt, *The German economy 1870 to the present* (Harcourt, Brace, New York, 1967).

Walter, N. (ed.), *Deutschland. Portraet einer Nation*, vol.3, *Wirtschaft* (Bertelsmann, Guetersloh, 1985).

1870-1933

Aldcroft, D.H., *From Versailles to Wall Street* (Allen Lane, London, 1977).

Baudis, D. and H. Nussbaum, *Wirtschaft und Staat in Deutschland vom Ende des 19. Jahrhunderts bis 1918/19* (Topos, Vaduz/Liechtenstein, 1978).

Blaich, F., *Der Schwarze Freitag. Inflation und Weltwirtschaftskrise* (Deutscher Taschenbuch Verlag, Munich, 1985).

Brady, R.A., *The rationalisation movement in German industry* (University of California Press, Berkeley, 1933).

Feldman, G.D., *Army, industry and labour in Germany, 1914-1918* (Princeton University Press, Princeton, 1966).

Feldman, G.D., C.-L. Holtfrerich, G.A. Ritter and P.-C. Witt (eds), *Die deutsche Inflation. Eine Zwischenbilanz* (de Gruyter, Berlin, New York, 1982).

Feldman, G.D. and E. Mueller-Luckner (eds), *Die Nachwirkungen der Inflation auf die deutsche Geschichte 1924-1933* (Oldenbourg, Munich, 1985).

Fischer, W., *Deutsche Wirtschaftspolitik 1918-1945,* 3rd edn (Leske, Opladen, 1968).

Fischer, W. (ed.), *Sachzwaenge und Handlungsspielraeume in der Wirtschafts- und Sozialpolitik der Zwischenkriegszeit* (Scripta Mercaturae, St. Katharinen, 1985).

Hardach, G., *The First World War, 1914-1918* (Allen Lane, London, 1977).

Hardach, G., "Zur politischen Oekonomie der Weimarer Republik" in R. Kuehnl and G. Hardach (eds), *Die Zerstoerung der Weimarer Republik*, 2nd edn (Pahl-Rugenstein, Cologne, 1979), pp.14-37.

Hentschel, V., *Wirtschaft und Wirtschaftspolitik im wilhelminischen Deutschland. Organisierter Kapitalismus und Interventionsstaat* (Klett-Cotta, Stuttgart, 1978).

Holtfrerich, C.-L., *The German inflation, 1914-1923* (de Gruyter, Berlin, New York, 1986).

James, H., *The German slump. Politics and economics 1924-1936* (Clarendon Press, Oxford, 1986).

Kocka, J., *Facing total war. German society 1914-1918* (Harvard University Press, Cambridge, Mass., 1984).

Kindleberger, C.P., *The world in depression 1929-1939* (Allen Lane, London, 1973).

Kolb, E., *Die Weimarer Republik* (Oldenbourg, Munich, 1984).

Mommsen, H., D. Petzina and B. Weisbrod (eds), *Industrielles System und politische Entwicklung in der Weimarer Republik* (2 vols., Athenaeum, Droste, Kronberg/Ts., Duesseldorf, 1977).

Nussbaum, M., *Wirtschaft und Staat in Deutschland waehrend der Weimarer Republik* (Topos, Vaduz/Liechtenstein, 1978).

Petzina, D., *Die deutsche Wirtschaft in der Zwischenkriegszeit* (Steiner, Stuttgart, 1977).

Winkel, H. (ed.), *Waehrungs- und Finanzpolitik der Zwischenkriegszeit* (Duncker and Humblot, Berlin, 1973).

1933-1945

Blaich, F., *Wirtschaft und Ruestung im "Dritten Reich"* (Schwann, Duesseldorf, 1987).

Boelcke, W.A., *Deutschlands Ruestung im Zweiten Weltkrieg. Hitlers Konferenzen mit Speer 1942-1945* (Akademischer Verlag Athenaion, Frankfurt am Main, 1969).

Boelcke, W.A., *Die deutsche Wirtschaft 1930-1945. Interna des Reichswirtschaftsministeriums* (Droste, Duesseldorf, 1983).

Carroll, B.H., *Design for total war. Arms and economics in the Third Reich* (Mouton, The Hague, Paris, 1968).

Dlugoborski, W. (ed.), *Zweiter Weltkrieg und sozialer Wandel* (Vandenhoeck and Ruprecht, Goettingen, 1981).

Eichholtz, D., *Geschichte der deutschen Kriegswirtschaft 1939-1945* (2 vols., Akademie-Verlag, Berlin (GDR), 1969, 1985).

Erbe, R., *Die nationalsozialistische Wirtschaftspolitik 1933-1939 im Lichte der modernen Theorie* (Polygraphischer Verlag, Zurich, 1958).

Farquharson, J.E., *The plough and the swastica: The NSDAP and agriculture in Germany 1928-45* (SAGE, London, 1976).

Fischer, W., *Deutsche Wirtschaftspolitik 1918-1945*, (Leske, Opladen, 3rd edn, 1968).

Forstmeier, F. and H.-E. Volkmann (eds), *Kriegswirtschaft und Ruestung 1939-1945* (Droste, Duesseldorf, 1977).

Forstmeier, F. and H.-E. Volkmann (eds), *Wirtschaft und Ruestung am Vorabend des Zweiten Weltkrieges* (Droste, Duesseldorf, 1975).

Gillingham, J.R., *Industry and politics in the Third Reich* (Franz Steiner Verlag Wiesbaden, Stuttgart, 1985).

Hayes, P., *Industry and ideology. IG Farben in the Nazi era* (Cambridge University Press, Cambridge, 1987).

Henning, F.-W. (ed.), *Probleme der nationalsozialistischen Wirtschaftspolitik* (Duncker and Humblot, Berlin, 1976).

Herbert, U., *Fremdarbeiter, Politik und Praxis des "Auslaender-Einsatzes" in der Kriegswirtschaft des Dritten Reiches* (Dietz, Berlin, Bonn, 1985).

Herbst, L., *Der totale Krieg und die Ordnung der Wirtschaft. Die Kriegswirtschaft im Spannungsfeld von Politik und Propaganda 1939-1945* (Deutsche Verlags-Anstalt, Stuttgart, 1982).

Homze, E.L., *Foreign Labour in Nazi Germany* (Princeton University Press, Princeton, N.J., 1967).

Janssen, G., *Das Ministerium Speer. Deutschlands Ruestung im Krieg* (Ullstein, Berlin, 1968).

Klein, B.H., *Germany's economic preparations for war* (Harvard University Press, Cambridge, Mass., 1959).

Kindleberger, C.P., *The world in depression, 1929-1939* (Allen Lane, London, 1973).

Ludwig, K.-H., *Technik und Ingenieure im Dritten Reich* (Droste, Duesseldorf, 1974).

Mason, T.W., *Sozialpolitik im Dritten Reich. Arbeiterklasse und Volksgemeinschaft*, (Westdeutscher Verlag, Opladen, 2nd edn, 1977).

Militaergeschichtliches Forschungsamt (ed.), *Ursachen und Voraussetzungen der deutschen Kriegspolitik. Das deutsche Reich und der Zweite Weltkrieg*, vol.1 (Deutsche Verlags-Anstalt,

Stuttgart, 1979).

Milward, A.S., *The German economy at war* (Athlone Press, London, 1965).

Milward, A.S., *War, economy and society 1939-1945* (University of California Press, Berkeley, Los Angeles, 1979).

Overy, R.J., *Goering, The "Iron Man"* (Routledge and Kegan Paul, London, 1984).

Overy, R.J., "Hitler's war and the German economy. A reinterpretation", *Economic History Review, Second Series*, vol.35 (1987), pp.272-91.

Overy, R.J., *The Nazi economic recovery 1932-1938* (Macmillan, London, 1982).

Petzina, D., *Autarkiepolitik im Dritten Reich. Der nationalsozialistische Vierjahresplan* (Deutsche Verlags-Anstalt, Stuttgart, 1968).

Petzina, D., *Die deutsche Wirtschaft in der Zwischenkriegszeit* (Steiner, Wiesbaden, 1977).

Recker, M.-L., *Nationalsozialistische Sozialpolitik im Zweiten Weltkrieg* (Oldenbourg, Munich, 1985).

Schweitzer, A., *Big Business in the Third Reich* (Eyre and Spottiswoode, London, 1964).

Teichert, E., *Autarkie und Grossraumwirtschaft in Deutschland 1930-1939. Aussenwirtschaftliche Konzeptionen zwischen Wirtschaftskrise und Zweitem Weltkrieg* (Oldenbourg, Munich, 1984).

Thomas, G., *Geschichte der deutschen Wehr- und Ruestungswirtschaft (1918-1943/45)*, ed. by Wolfgang Birkenfeld (Boldt, Boppard, 1966).

Turner, H.A. jr., *German big business and the rise of Hitler* (Oxford University Press, Oxford, New York, 1985).

Wagenfuehr, R., *Die deutsche Industrie im Kriege 1939-1945*, 2nd edn (Duncker and Humblot, Berlin, 1963).

Werner, F.W., *"Bleib übrig". Deutsche Arbeiter in der nationalsozialistischen Kriegswirtschaft* (Schwann, Duesseldorf, 1983).

Winkler, D., *Frauenarbeit im "Dritten Reich"* (Hoffmann and Campe, Hamburg, 1977).

Zilbert, E.R., *Albert Speer and the Nazi Ministry of Arms. Economic institutions and industrial production in the German war economy* (Fairleigh Dickinson University Press, Rutherford, London, 1981).

Zumpe, L., *Wirtschaft und Staat in Deutschland 1933 bis 1945* (Topos, Vaduz/Liechtenstein, 1980).

1945-1985

Abelshauser, W., "West German economic recovery 1945-1951: a reassessment", *Three Banks Review*, No. 135 (1982), pp.34-53.

Abelshauser, W., *Wirtschaft in Westdeutschland 1945-1948. Rekonstruktion und Wachstumsbedingungen in der amerikanischen und britischen Zone* (Deutsche Verlags-Anstalt, Stuttgart, 1975).

Abelshauser, W., *Wirtschaftsgeschichte der Bundesrepublik Deutschland 1945-1980* (Suhrkamp, Frankfurt am Main, 1983).

Adam, H., *Die Einkommensverteilung in der Bundesrepublik Deutschland* (Bund-Verlag, Cologne, 1976).

Altvater, E., J. Hoffmann and W. Semmler, *Vom Wirtschaftswunder zur Wirtschaftskrise. Oekonomie und Politik in der Bundesrepublik* (Olle and Wolter, Berlin, 1980).

Ambrosius, G., *Die Durchsetzung der Sozialen Marktwirtschaft in Westdeutschland 1945-1949* (Deutsche Verlags-Anstalt, Stuttgart, 1977).

Backer, J.H., *Priming the German economy. American occupation policies 1945-1948* (Duke University Press, Durham, N.C., 1971).

Berghahn, V.R., *The Americanisation of West German industry 1945-1975* (Berg, Leamington Spa, 1986).

Blum, R., *Soziale Marktwirtschaft. Wirtschaftspolitik zwischen Neoliberalismus und Ordoliberalismus* (Mohr, Tuebingen, 1969).

Borchardt, K., "Die Bundesrepublik in den saekularen Trends der wirtschaftlichen Entwicklung", in W. Conze and M.R. Lepsius (eds), *Sozialgeschichte der Bundesrepublik Deutschland* (Klett Cotta, Stuttgart, 1983), pp.20-45.

Danckwert, R.-F., H.-H. Haertel and E. Thiel, *Analyse der strukturellen Entwicklung der deutschen Wirtschaft. Strukturbericht 1980* (Verlag Weltarchiv, Hamburg, 1981).

Donges, J.B., "Die Exportorientierung der deutschen Wirtschaft: Erfahrungen, Probleme, Perspektiven" in Erwin Dichtl and Otmar Issing (eds), *Exporte als Herausforderung für die deutsche Wirtschaft* (Deutscher Instituts-Verlag, Cologne, 1984), pp.11-41.

Fels, G. and K.-D. Schmidt, *Die deutsche Wirtschaft im Strukturwandel* (Mohr, Tuebingen, 1981).

Franz, W. and H. Koenig, "The nature and causes of unemployment in the Federal Republic of Germany since the 1970s: an empirical investigation", *Economica*, vol.53 (1986), pp.219-44.

Gahlen, B., F. Rahmeyer and M. Stadler, "Zur internationalen Wettbewerbsfaehigkeit der deutschen Wirtschaft", *Konjunkturpolitik*, vol.32 (1986), pp.130-50.

Glastetter, W., R. Paulert and U. Spoerel, *Die wirtschaftliche Entwicklung in der Bundesrepublik Deutschland 1950-1980. Befunde, Aspekte, Hintergruende* (Campus, Frankfurt am Main, New York, 1983).

Grosser, D. (ed.), *Der Staat in der Wirtschaft der Bundesrepublik* (Leske and Budrich, Opladen, 1985).

Grosser, D., Th. Lange, A. Mueller-Armack and B. Neuss (eds), *Soziale Marktwirtschaft. Geschichte - Konzept - Leistung* (Kohlhammer, Stuttgart, Berlin, 1988).

Haertel, H.-H. and E. Thiel, *Analyse der strukturellen Entwicklung der deutschen Wirtschaft, Strukturbericht 1983* (Verlag Weltarchiv, Hamburg, 1984).

Hamel, H. (ed.), *Bundesrepublik Deutschland - DDR. Die Wirtschaftssysteme. Soziale Marktwirtschaft und sozialistische Planwirtschaft im Systemvergleich*, (Beck, Munich, 4th edn, 1983).

Hardach, G., "The Marshall Plan in Germany", *Journal of European economic history*, vol.16 (1987), pp.433-85.

Hennings, K.H., "West Germany", in Andrea Botho (ed.), *The European economy. Growth and crisis* (Oxford University Press, Oxford, 1982), pp.472-501.

Hogan, M.J., *The Marshall Plan. America, Britain and the reconstruction of Western Europe, 1947-1952* (Cambridge University Press, New York, 1987).

Holthus, M., R. Jungnickel and others (eds), *Die deutschen multinationalen Unternehmen* (Athenaeum, Frankfurt am Main, 1974).

Horn, E.-J., *Technische Neuerungen und internationale Arbeitsteilung. Die Bundesrepublik Deutschland im internationalen Vergleich* (Mohr, Tuebingen, 1976).

Huebl, L. and W. Schepers, *Strukturwandel und Strukturpolitik* (Wissenschaftliche Buchgesellschaft, Darmstadt, 1983).

Jerchow, Friedrich, *Deutschland in der Weltwirtschaft 1944-1947. Alliierte Deutschland- und Reparationspolitik und die Anfaenge der westdeutschen Aussenwirtschaft* (Droste, Duesseldorf, 1978).

Kirchgaessner, G., "Size and development of the West German shadow economy", *Zeitschrift fuer die gesamte Staatswis-*

senschaft, vol.139 (1983), pp.197-215.

Klein, Ph.A., "Postwar growth cycles in the German economy" in W.H. Schroeder and R. Spree (eds), *Historische Konjunkturforschung* (Klett, Stuttgart, 1980), pp.115-40.

Kleinknecht, A., "Basisinnovation und Wachstumsschuebe: Das Beispiel der westdeutschen Industrie", *Konjunkturpolitik*, vol.25 (1979), pp.320-43.

Kloten, N. and K.H. Ketterer, "Fiscal policy in West Germany: anticyclical versus expenditure reducing policies" in Stephen F. Frowen (ed.), *Controlling industrial economies. Essays in honour of Christopher Thomas Saunders* (Macmillan, London, 1983), pp.291-307.

Klump, R., *Wirtschaftsgeschichte der Bundesrepublik Deutschland. Zur Kritik neuerer wirtschaftshistorischer Interpretationen aus ordnungspolitischer Sicht* (Steiner Verlag Wiesbaden, Stuttgart, 1985).

Knapp, M. (ed.), *Von der Bizonengruendung zur oekonomischpolitischen Westintegration. Studien zum Verhaeltnis zwischen Aussenpolitik und Aussenwirtschaft in der Entstehungsphase der Bundesrepublik Deutschland (1947-1952)* (Haagen and Herchen, Frankfurt am Main, 1984).

Koerner, H., P. Meyer-Dohm, E. Tuchtfeld and C. Uhlig (eds), *Wirtschaftspolitik - Wissenschaft und politische Aufgabe. Festschrift zum 65. Geburtstag von Karl Schiller* (Haupt, Berne, Stuttgart, 1976).

Kommission fuer wirtschaftlichen und sozialen Wandel, *Wirtschaftlicher und sozialer Wandel in der Bundesrepublik Deutschland* (Schwartz, Goettingen, 1977).

Lampert, H., "The development and the present situation of social policy in West Germany", *Zeitschrift für die gesamte Staatswissenschaft*, vol.138 (1982), pp.351-66.

Lieberman, S., *The growth of European mixed economies 1945-1970* (Schenkman, Cambridge, Mass., 1977).

Milward, A.S., *The reconstruction of Western Europe 1945-1951* (Methuen, London, 1984).

OECD, *Economic surveys, Germany* (OECD, Paris, 1953-88).

Roesch, F. and F. Homann, "Thirty years of the Berlin-agreement - thirty years of inner-German trade: economic and political dimensions", *Zeitschrift fuer die gesamte Staatswissenschaft*, vol.137 (1981), pp.525-55.

Roskamp, K.W., *Capital formation in West Germany* (Wayne State University Press, Detroit, 1965).

Sachverstaendigenrat zur Begutachtung der gesamtwirtschaftlichen Entwicklung, *Jahresgutachten* (Kohlhammer, Stuttgart, Mainz, 1965-88).

Sarrazin, Th., "Die Finanzpolitik des Bundes 1970 bis 1982. Eine kritische Wuerdigung", *Finanzarchiv*, vol.41 (1983), pp.373-87.

Scharf, C. and H.-J. Schroeder (eds), *Politische und oekonomische Stabilisierung Westdeutschlands 1945-1949. Fuenf Beitraege zur Deutschlandpolitik der westlichen Alliierten* (Steiner, Wiesbaden, 1977).

Scherf, H., *Enttaeuschte Hoffnungen - vergebene Chancen. Die Wirtschaftspolitik der Sozial-Liberalen Koaliton 1969-1982* (Vandenhoeck and Ruprecht, Goettingen, 1986).

Schmidt, K.-D. and others, *Im Anpassungsprozess zurueckgeworfen - Die deutsche Wirtschaft vor neuen Herausforderungen* (Mohr, Tuebingen, 1984).

Shonfield, A., *Modern capitalism. The changing balance of public and private power* (Oxford University Press, London, 1965).

Siebert, H., *Perspektiven der deutschen Wirtschaftspolitik* (Kohlhammer, Stuttgart and Mainz, 1983).

Smith, E.O., *The West German economy* (Croom Helm, London, 1983).

Vollmer, R., "The structure of West German foreign trade", *Zeitschrift für die gesamte Staatswissenschaft*, vol.35 (1981), pp.575-89.

Wallich, H.C., *Mainsprings of German revival* (Yale University Press, New Haven, 1955).

Watrin, C., "The principles of the Social Market Economy - its origins and history", *Zeitschrift fuer die gesamte Staatswissenschaft*, vol.135 (1979), pp.405-25.

Welteke, M., *Theorie und Praxis der sozialen Marktwirtschaft. Einfuehrung in die politische Oekonomie der BRD* (Campus, Frankfurt am Main, New York, 1976).

Winkel, H., *Die Wirtschaft im geteilten Deutschland 1945-1970* (Steiner, Wiesbaden, 1974).

Winkler, H.A. (ed.), *Politische Weichenstellungen im Nachkriegsdeutschland 1945-1953* (Vandenhoeck and Ruprecht, 1979).

INDEX

Adenauer, Konrad 182
aerospace industry 190,
  233, 235, 249
agricultural
  land 44, 146, 226
  machinery 20, 29, 99, 126
  policy 56, 87, 97-101, 180,
  227-8
    *Flurbereinigungs-
    gesetz* 228
  production, *see* production
agriculture 1, 19, 26, 54-6,
  65-6, 71, 73, 82, 85, 97-101,
  125-7, 148, 180, 198, 203,
  211, 224, 227, 234
  see also primary sector
air attacks 123, 131, 133
aircraft 129, 135, 137, 149,
  190
  gasoline 118, 133, 152
  industry 111, 125, 135, 231,
  232
  production 96, 111, 124,
  131-2, 136-8, 149
air force 128, 131, 133
*Allgemeine Elektricitaets-
Gesellschaft (AEG)* 50
Allied economic institutions
  Allied Bizonal Control Office 178
  Allied Control Council
  148, 196
  Allied High Commission
  178
  Allied Military Govern-

ment 151, 153-4
  Allied Reparation
  Commission 34
  Bipartite Economic
  Control Croup (BICO)
  150
  Cooperative for American
  Remittances to Europe
  (CARE) 152
  Government and relief in
  occupied areas
  (GARIOA) 152, 156
  Joint Export-Import
  Agency (JEIA) 156-7
  *Office du Commerce
  Exterieur (OFICOMEX)*
  156
  United States
  Reconstruction and
  Rehabilitation
  Administration (UNRRA)
  152
  US War Department 152
Alsace-Lorraine 33, 113, 144
American zone of
  occupation 146, 148-51,
  156
armament 28, 30, 73, 80, 85,
  96, 98, 109, 111, 130-1
  in depth 110, 135
  in width 110
  materials 34, 85
  production 93, 110-11,
  123-4, 126-32, 134-8, 149,
  178

see also rearmament *and* war production
Austria 102, 144, 244, 251
autarky 9, 85-6, 97, 99, 101-2, 125
automobile industry 52, 65, 83, 92, 180, 229-32, 235, 238, 242, 245

balance of payments 34, 39, 60, 86, 157, 168-9, 237, 239, 249
bank(ing)
  crisis 9, 67-9
  notes 31, 39
Bank Deutscher Laender 153, 179, 181
banks 20-1, 39, 64, 68-9, 91, 114, 155, 188, 223, 235
  Commerzbank 151
  Danat Bank 68-9
  Deutsche Bank 151
  Dresdner Bank 68, 151
  Oesterreichische Creditanstalt 68
Badische Anilin- und Sodafabrik (BASF) 39, 151
Bayer 151
Belgium 34, 36, 49, 116-17, 121, 157, 251
Berlin 10, 30, 64, 118-19, 153, 176, 244
Berlin Wall 168, 211
Bichelonne, Jean 121
bilateralism 101-2
birth rate 19, 210-11
Bizone 147-51, 156-7, 177
black market 26, 155, 176
Blitzkrieg 3, 110-11, 121
blockade 25-6, 48, 102, 176
BMW (Bayerische Motoren Werke AG) 136
Boehm, Franz 176
bonds 44, 186
  public treasury 91, 114-15
boom 7, 12, 47, 49, 64, 172, 181, 184-5, 231
  baby 210
  Korean 172, 227, 241, 249
Braunkohle Benzin AG (BRABAG) 81
Brauns, Heinrich 71
Brest Litowsk 30
Bretton Woods Agreement 237, 239, 241, 249
Britain 14, 20, 30, 34, 37, 52, 55, 58, 69, 85, 99, 110, 114, 133, 138, 148-9, 153, 251
British zone of occupation 146, 148-52, 156
Bruening, Heinrich 3, 68-72, 91
Buchner, Hans 79
budget 179, 182-3, 189, 196, 233
  balanced 69
  deficit 37, 39, 70, 89, 90, 187-8, 190, 201, 203-4, 239
buna (synthetic rubber) 26, 86, 88
Bundesbank 173, 182-6, 188, 244
bureaucracy 19, 72, 98, 156, 178, 190
business
  big 80-2
  cycles 2, 9, 10, 12, 21, 47-50, 64, 166-8, 170-4, 177, 181-2, 185-6, 188-9, 204, 208, 212, 247, 250
Byrnes, James F. 150

capacity
  excess 47, 50, 52, 65, 148,
  172-3, 187, 190, 218
  production 10, 48, 82, 134,
  145-6, 149, 178, 187
capital
  account 47, 239-40
  exports 22, 46
  foreign 37, 45, 47, 65, 69,
  70
  goods 47, 49, 50, 66, 125,
  230, 244
  imports 46, 60, 64
  market 68, 89, 91
  productivity 167, 171, 181,
  210, 217
  stock 14, 89, 145-7, 149,
  151, 166, 169, 171, 208,
  210, 217, 247
  see also investment
cartel(s) 50, 70, 98, 151
  law 180
cartelisation 21, 47, 49, 50,
  52
central bank 35, 116
  council 181
  money stock (CBM) 188
  see also *Bundesbank,*
  Reichsbank, Rentenbank,
  or GDR (state bank of)
cereal(s) 56-7, 67, 98, 100,
  125-6, 152, 156
  yields 55, 85, 99, 226
chemical industry 20, 28-9,
  51, 57-8, 80-1, 87, 97, 125,
  148, 151, 180, 229-32, 242,
  245, 248-9
Christian Democratic Party
  (CDU) 176, 182-3, 189,
  190, 202, 244
  Ahlen Programme 176
civil

servants 41, 67, 71, 128
  service 53
clearing 116
  account 119, 244
  system 118-19, 249
coal 27, 45, 57, 80, 113, 117,
  119, 125, 135, 148-50, 172,
  176, 234, 249
Colm, Gerhard 154
Colm-Dodge-Goldsmith
  Plan 154
colonies 20, 33, 102
Common Market 197, 211,
  228, 246, 251
communism 79
competition 21, 35, 58, 80,
  151, 177, 180, 184, 214,
  227, 234
competitiveness 14-15, 70,
  149, 170, 211, 225,
  230-1, 234, 238, 246-8,
  250
concentration 21, 47, 49, 50,
  129, 132, 177, 180, 184, 219
  see also industrial
  concentration *and*
  cartelisation
concentration camp 124
concerted action
  (*Konzertierte Aktion*)
  183
constitution, *see also*
  Grundgesetz 54, 177
construction industry 28, 65,
  72-3, 82-4, 92, 96, 125,
  172, 204, 223, 229-30,
  248
  see also housing
consumer goods industry 20,
  29, 47, 49-50, 58, 64-6,
  80-1, 92-3, 125, 136,
  179, 230

consumption 29, 39, 45, 64,
114, 119, 169, 173-4, 184,
203, 225
see also demand
convertibility 239
Coordinating Committee for
East-West-Trade-Policy
(COCOM) 243
corporation(s) 39, 78, 93, 96,
151, 177, 181, 187, 233-4
multinational 121, 245-6
cost of living 21, 53, 116
Council of Economic
Experts
(*Sachverstaendigenrat zur
Begutachtung der
gesamtwirtschaftlichen
Entwicklung*) 182-3, 187
credit 40, 64-5, 69, 91, 114,
153, 180
demand 44, 202-3
expansion 47, 72
foreign 68
investment 209
crowding out 47, 202-3
currency 9, 39, 45, 118-19,
153, 219, 249
foreign 35, 44-5, 47, 60, 86,
181, 250
reform 3, 44, 46, 148,
154-6, 171, 244
reserves 68-9
stabilisation 9, 36, 70
see also foreign exchange
current account 65, 103, 168,
173, 188, 190, 239,
240-1, 249, 250
customs 197, 244
see also tariffs

Darré, Walther 98
Dawes, Charles 45

Dawes Plan 36, 45-6, 60
debts 4, 36, 39, 56, 67, 71,
154-5, 225, 239
foreign 68-9
inter-allied 34
public 31, 40, 90, 114-15,
154-5, 173, 188-9, 200-4
service 200, 204
short-term 30, 65, 114
deflation 21, 65, 69, 101
deindustrialisation 148
demand 25, 66, 93, 99, 154-5,
169, 170, 172-3, 179,
182, 185, 187, 223, 239,
243, 250
consumer 169, 183, 187,
225
foreign 169-70, 172-3, 182,
186, 188, 239, 247
management 11-12, 184,
see also stabilisation policy
democracy 1, 11, 13, 22, 30,
81, 150-1
demographic development
3, 4, 198, 210-11
see also population
Denmark 126
deposits ratio 64, 180
depreciation 35, 70, 173,
183, 185, 239
depression 3, 9, 64, 66-7, 70,
103, 184
see also Great Depression
Deutsche Mark (DM) 154,
169-86 *passim*, 208,
225, 239-50 *passim*
*Deutsch-Nationale
Volkspartei (DNVP)* 97
Deutsche Werke 91
devaluation 36, 66, 70, 170,
184
developing countries 243

Dillon Round 239
discount rate 68, 181-2, 185
dismantlement 145-6, 148-9
Dodge, Joseph 154
Dornier 137
Dresden 133
"dynamic pension" 203

ecology 4, 153, 204, 225-6
economic system 8, 21, 64,
  68, 79, 150
  capitalist 4, 11, 13, 26, 151,
  166
  liberal 70, 152, 154, 176
  socialist 4, 11, 13
  see also social market
  economy
economic
  growth 1, 3, 7, 10-14, 22,
  46-7, 49, 52, 83, 85, 92, 130,
  146, 148, 154-6, 165-71,
  173, 177-80, 183-4, 188,
  190, 198, 203, 208, 216-18,
  225, 232, 234, 241, 246, 250
  structure 15, 33, 124, 165-
  6, 198, 223
economies of scale 243, 250
education 14, 20, 168, 198-9,
  211, 214, 225, 233
  *Bundesausbildungs-
  foerderungsgesetz* 204
election(s) 65, 81, 180, 182
electrical industry 20, 29, 50,
  65, 97, 148, 180, 229-32,
  235, 238, 242, 247-9
emigration 20
employment 4, 19, 20, 52,
  55, 72, 84, 96, 124, 173,
  185-6, 189, 208, 210-15,
  218-19, 224, 227, 233
  full 10-11, 14, 37, 168, 183-
  4, 190, 203, 212-13, 217

over 94
policy 10, 37, 187
programmes 34, 37, 71-3,
  82-4, 90-2, 172, 178, 188,
  204
see also labour
energy 12, 51, 87, 117, 144,
  154, 172, 179, 209, 223
  nuclear 168, 230, 234, 247
engineering industry 20, 28,
  58, 65, 81, 148, 229-32,
  235, 238, 242
entrepreneurs 20, 72, 80, 88,
  121, 217
Erhard, Ludwig 155, 177-8,
  182, 249, 251
Ersatz (substitutes) 25-6, 39,
  135
ERP-Sondervermoegen
  (European Recovery
  Programme Special Fund)
  153
Erzberger, Mathias 36-7
estate system 79, 80
  see also Staende
Eucken, Walter 176, 184
European
  Coal and Steel Community
  251
  Community (EC) 211, 228,
  239-40
  Economic Community
  (EEC) 211, 228, 234, 238,
  243-4, 246, 250-1
  Monetary System (EMS)
  239
  Payments Union (EPU)
  249
  Recovery Programme
  (ERP) 148, 152-4
  see also Marshall Plan *and*
  Common Market

exchange rate 37, 39, 47, 59, 116, 119, 182, 186, 208, 225, 239, 241, 246-7, 250
expellees 144, 203, 211
export(s) 1, 21-2, 29, 33, 35, 45, 47, 57-60, 65-6, 81, 86, 101-3, 119-20, 153, 156-8, 168-86 *passim*, 208, 211, 225-51 *passim*
industry 238
prices 58, 118, 156, 238, 241-2
quota(s) 35
subsidies 70, 101, 179, 249
see also foreign trade

fascism 177
see also National Socialists
Feder, Gottfried 78-9
fertilizers 20, 26, 29, 34, 56, 98-9, 126, 152, 156, 223, 226
fiscal policy 14, 33, 36-7, 69, 170-90 *passim*, 196, 201, 203-4, 217, 219, 238
flow production 29, 50
food 32, 51, 54, 57-8, 98, 100, 109, 119, 125, 146-56 *passim*, 225-6, 230, 237
rationing of 26, 30, 123, 126, 148
supply 26, 29-30, 41, 126
foreign
claims 9, 70
deposits 65, 69
exchange 40, 98-100, 102, 109, 169, 185, 240, 249-50
-exchange controls 69, 184
-exchange reserves 65, 101,

103, 241
policy 22, 83, 112
trade 4, 22, 47-8, 57-60, 66, 70, 101-3, 117-21, 150, 156-8, 169, 172, 189, 223, 237-44, 246, 249-50
-trade balance 66, 70, 101, 237, *see also* current account
-trade policy 20, 101-2, 248-51
Hermes Kredit-versicherung 249
Four Year Plan 80-1, 85-8, 98, 121, 127-8, 130-1
France 19, 21-2, 30, 36, 49, 52, 68, 83, 117, 119, 121-2, 126, 144, 150, 251
Free Democratic Party (FDP) 182, 186, 189-90, 202
"Freiburg School" 176
French zone of occupation 146-7, 150, 156-7
Fuehrer 71, 89, *see also* Hitler, Adolf
fuels 51, 85, 226, 244
synthetic 81, 85-6, 133, 135

General Agreement on Tariffs and Trade (GATT) 158, 237, 248-9
Gereke, Guenther 73
German Democratic Republic (GDR) 2, 10, 146, 153, 211, 234, 244
state bank of the 244
Gilbert, Parker 45
Goebbels, Josef 90

Goering, Hermann 86, 113,
128, 133
gold
reserves 44, 65-6, 103, 249
standard 8-9, 21, 44
"golden twenties" 44, 46
Goldmark 35-6
Goldsmith, Raymond W.
154
government
borrowing 200, *see also*
debts
consumption 173, 200
expenditures 9, 85, 89-91,
112, 114, 166, 180, 195-200,
228, 231
revenue 89, 90-1, 114, 189,
195-8
"grand coalition" 183, 244
Great Depression 3, 7, 21-2,
64-73, 86-7, 91-2, 101,
149, 166, 177
Great Inflation 37-9
gross
domestic product (GDP)
223-4
national product (GNP) 7,
85, 92, 167, 170-1, 184-239
passim
value added 224, 229-30
growth
see economic growth
cycles 166, 171, *see also*
business cycles
Grundgesetz (basic law)
196, 198
Gruenderkrise (foundation
of the Reich crisis) 21

heavy industry 20, 29, 52, 81
see also
coal/metal/iron and

steel industry, mining
Helfferich, Karl 40
Henschel 137-8
high-precision industry 20,
231
see also engineering
industry
Hindenburg, Paul von 67, 71
Hindenburg Programme
26-7
Hitler, Adolf 3, 73, 78-83,
85, 89-90, 93,
101-37 *passim*
Hoechst 151
Hoover, Herbert 68
Hoover moratorium 46, 68
housing 51, 64-5, 71, 144,
172, 179-80, 198-9, 203,
208, 219
see also construction
industry
Hugenberg, Alfred 97-8
Hungary 102, 116-17
hyperinflation, *see* inflation

IG Farben(industrie) 50,
87, 102, 118, 121, 151
Ilgner, Max 102
immigration 20, 94, 168, 211
see also refugees
import(s) 20-1, 25-6, 29, 33,
35, 37, 39, 48, 54, 57-60, 66,
85, 98, 100-3, 119-20, 126,
153, 156-8, 170, 174, 188,
225-6, 234, 237-51 *passim*
prices 39, 59, 86, 156, 170,
218, 227, 238, 241-2
quota(s) 67, 97, 227
income 13, 40-1, 79, 114,
187, 198-9, 204, 216, 219,
223, 227
agricultural 66, 98, 100

distribution 40, 177, 217-19
redistribution 178
  Kindergeldgesetz 203
industrial
  concentration 2, 20
  goods 35, 58, 154, 156, 158,
    226, 248, 251
  output 80
industrialisation 2, 9, 19-21,
  47, 66, 102, 233
industrialists 4, 26, 40, 79,
  80, 111, 113, 121, 123, 129,
  186-7, 251
  Ruhrlade 81
  see also entrepreneurs
industry 20, 22, 29, 33, 36,
  45, 51-2, 54, 67, 70, 80-2,
  88, 91, 110-14, 124, 146,
  150, 202-3, 211, 219, 231-4
  see also under branches
inflation 1, 10, 12-14, 31,
  35-41, 44, 47, 50, 69-70, 86,
  89-91, 109, 117, 154-5, 168-
  9, 172, 181-2, 184-8, 190,
  200, 239, 242, 250
  "imported" 182
  hyper- 46, 56
"inner-German" trade 244
innovations *see* technical
  innovations
insurance companies 40, 68,
  91, 114, 180, 223
interest rates 47, 56, 64, 97,
  116, 170, 185, 187-90,
  202-3, 249-50
International Monetary
  Fund (IMF) 248, 250
investment 21, 46-7, 52, 54,
  64-5, 72-3, 79-80, 88, 111,
  113, 116, 145-6, 149, 153-5,
  170-3, 179, 182-3, 185-9,
  196, 202-3, 208-11, 214, 231

control 86, 148
direct 22, 245-6
foreign 34, 149, 245-6
military 85, 87
public 200, 208
ratio 46-7
subsidies 179, 234, 246
iron 21, 25, 33, 82, 85-6, 117
  and steel industry 51,
  80-2, 92, 113, 117, 133,
  148, 151, 153, 176, 179,
  190, 215, 229-30, 234,
  249
  ore 113, 117, 134
  see also mining
Israel 250
Italy 14, 30, 34, 36, 52, 79,
  117, 126, 169, 211, 251

Japan 46, 118, 234, 239, 243,
  247-8
Jews, Jewish 79, 99, 250
Juliusturm (Julius Tower)
  179-80
Junker 67, 71

Kaiser 30
Kaiserreich 19
Karstadt 68
Kennedy Round 239
Keynes, John Maynard 12,
  34-5, 183, 201
Kiesinger, Kurt Georg 183
Klasen, Karl 186
Koerner, Paul 131
Korean War 172, 178
Krupp 91

labour 33, 48, 50, 52, 54, 72,
  79, 87, 93-7, 113, 121-5,
  133-4, 136-8, 146, 166, 168-
  9, 181, 210-17, 223, 225,

246
agricultural 19, 55-6, 97,
99, 126, 213, 223, 226
Betriebsverfassungsgesetz
215
conscription 95
control 95, 123
costs 40, 198, 210, 214, 217,
247
female 27, 29, 41, 94, 96,
122, 124, 211, 213
foreign 34, 122-5, 210-11,
214
Gastarbeiter 169
imports 27, 231
industrial 19, 22, 124, 226
juvenile 124, 213
market 20, 34, 94-7, 131,
190, 204, 211, 213-14, 216
mobilisation of 27, 94, 121-
4, 136
mobility 27, 87, 169, 204,
211, 214
organised 27
productivity 29, 47, 53, 125,
134, 169, 214, 216-17, 226-7
retirement age 168, 214,
233
unskilled 29, 41, 169
Laender see also states 71,
155, 183, 196, 198, 204
Lausanne Conference 46, 72
licenses 149, 231, *see also*
patents
living standard 10, 93, 95,
196, 226
loan(s) 21, 40, 44, 65, 115-16
foreign 47
long-term 56, 91
marriage 96-7
war 30
lock out 215

London Agreement 250
Luftbruecke 176
luxury goods 31, 229-30

machinery 22, 50, 57, 73,
80-1, 102, 118, 136-7,
149, 230-1, 235, 248
machine tools 29, 135, 138,
245
manufacturing sector 230,
240
see also secondary
sector
market
black, *see* black market
regulation 21, 180, 227-8
saturation 58, 169, 214,
226
Marshall, George 152
Marshall Plan 3, 148, 152-4,
156-8, 248
mass production 52, 93, 125,
129, 132-3, 136
mechanisation 50, 99, 223,
226
Mefo (= *Metallurgische
Forschungs GmbH*,
Metal Research Ltd.)
91
- bills 73, 91, 115
Messerschmitt 124, 136
metal(s) 117, 128, 135-6, 248
industry 51, 57, 87, 98,
125, 212
Milch, Erhard 131
militarisation 26, 95
military 26, 110-11, 127-8
service 94, 98, 126, 211
mineral oil 85, 87-8, 102,
117-18, 129, 135, 170, 186,
225, 229-30, 232, 234, 237,
239, 242-3

mining 21, 28, 49, 51, 81-2, 92, 113, 125, 148-9, 172, 179-80, 190, 213, 215, 223, 230, 248-9
modernisation 55, 149
monetary
  policy 8, 12-3, 47, 64, 89, 172-3, 177, 181, 184-90, 203, 238
  stability 180-1, 250
  target 188
money supply 31, 37-9, 44, 72, 90, 116, 154, 169, 186, 250
monopolies 113, 176, 180, 196
Montanunion, *see* European Coal and Steel Community
Morgenthau, Henry 148
Morgenthau Plan 148
mortality rate 19, 210
mortgage 44, 98, 155, 203
  debtors 40
motorisation 83-4
Mueller-Armack, Alfred 177-8
municipalities 40, 73, 155, 182-3, 196, 198
Mussolini, Benito 79

national
  income 7, 21, 52, 89, 92, 95, 112, 121, 218
  product 37
  see also gross domestic product
National Socialist economy:
  economic ideology 78-80
  laws and institutions
    Anleihestockgesetz 89
    Deutsche Arbeitsfront
    (DAF) 94
    Organisation Todt
    (OT) 128, 131, 136
    Reichsarbeitsdienst
    (RAD) 94, 96
    Reichsnaehrstand 98
    Reichswerke Hermann
    Goering 82, 111, 113
    see also Four Year
    Plan, *Mefo, Neuer*
    Plan
National Socialists 1, 3, 65, 71, 73, 78-103 *passim*, 109-38 *passim*, 215, 250
Nationalsozialistische
  Deutsche Arbeiterpartei
  (NSDAP) 79, *see also*
  National Socialists
nationalisation 78-9, 176
navy 111, 128, 131
neo-liberalism 165, 176-8
Netherlands 25, 27, 101, 117, 121, 157, 251
Neuer Plan (New Plan) 101-2
nitrogen 29, 99
Nordstern insurance company 68
Nordwolle 68
Norway 25, 117, 121, 126
nutrition 30, 41, *see also* food

occupation 2, 49, 117, 119, 156
  costs 34, 114, 116, 119, 149
occupied territories 34, 116, 118-19, 121, 152
Oder and Neisse 144
oil price shock 169-70, 173, 188, 198, 201, 208, 210, 213, 239, 248

optical industry 20, 58, 65, 231, 247
Organisation for European Economic Cooperation (OEEC) 153, 248
Organisation of the Petroleum Exporting Countries (OPEC) 169, 209, 243
"organised capitalism" 21
Osthilfe 56

Papen, Franz von 72-3, 81-2, 97
paper and printing industry 28, 51, 92, 229-30, 243
Paris Agreement 248
patents 34, 230-1, 247
pharmaceutical industry 58
Pleiger, Paul 82, 113
Poland 3, 14, 27, 109-11, 117, 123, 126, 144
policy
  anti-cartel 151
  anticyclical *see* stabilisation
  competition 182
  de(re-)flationary 45, 47, 69-70, 173, 184
  economic 3, 168, 178-90
  Mittelstandspolitik 180
  Ordnungspolitik 181
  social 3, 180, 203-5, 227
  Strukturpolitik 153, 182
  supply-side 179, 187, 189
  see also agricultural, employment, fiscal, foreign, monetary, stabilisation (policy)
population 19, 30, 33, 97, 99, 114, 124, 126-7, 133, 156, 168-9, 199, 200, 210, 214, 219, 234
Potsdam Conference 148, 150-1
powder and explosives industry 25, 29
Preussag company 219
price(s) 8, 9, 11, 25, 30-1, 35, 39, 40, 50, 58, 70-1, 86, 96, 114-16, 149, 172, 184, 186, 211, 227-8, 233, 246, 250
  agricultural 20, 56, 66, 98, 228
  controls 37, 117, 154, 156
  freeze decree 87
  regulated 21, 227
  stability 11, 179, 183-4, 190
  wholesale 21, 38
  see also export/import prices
primary sector 19, 58, 100, 125, 213, 223-5, 227, 230, 243
prisoners of war 34, 122-3, 126, 144
privatisation 181, 190, 219
production
  agricultural 20, 25-6, 29, 30, 34, 54-5, 66, 98-102, 117, 125-6
  armament 26, 29, 86, 100
  artisan 53, 125, 136
  costs 136
  industrial 19, 21-2, 27, 29, 33, 37, 46-53, 66-7, 88, 91-3, 118, 121, 147-56, 172, 178, *see also* mass production
  quota 98
  targets 26
productivity
  agricultural 20, 55-6, 99, 126, 223, 226

growth 21
of capital *see* capital
of labour *see* labour
profit(s) 31, 40, 52, 78, 81,
179, 186, 203, 208, 210,
217, 219, 246
protectionism 20, 22, 35, 45,
65-7, 97, 228, 239, 243, 246,
250
Prussia 26, 33, 56, 144, 179
public
borrowing 190
expenditure 13, 36, 47, 84,
169, 172, 185-9, 200-1,
203-4
finance 36-7, 44, 65, 89-91,
114-17, 187-8, 195-205
passim
granaries 67
see also government, state

R&D 20, 110-11, 113, 135,
230-2, 246-7, 249
racism 123
railway(s) 34, 83, 119, 134,
179, 183
rolling stock 34, 48
Rathenau, Walther 130
rationalisation 49-52, 55, 93,
125, 128-30, 135-6, 223, 226
raw materials 25-6, 33, 48,
50, 57, 59, 85-7, 93, 101-2,
109, 117, 119, 134-6, 156,
158, 170, 190, 225, 241-2
control of 25, 86, 131
rearmament 10, 73, 80-1,
84-6, 101
programmes 79, 92
see also armament
recession 12, 22, 37, 39, 47-9,
53, 65, 67, 172-4, 183-9,
200-5, 211-18, 224, 228,

231, 239, 250
reconstruction 7, 10-11, 14,
133, 150-1, 166-8, 176, 178,
216
refugees 144, 146, 150-1,
196, 203, 211
Reichsbank 30, 44-5, 47, 65,
68-9, 91, 114, 116
Reichsmark (RM) 30, 59,
119, 154-5
Reinhardt, Fritz 83
Rentenbank 44
Rentenmark 36, 44
rents 70, 78, 154
reparations 21, 34-7, 39-40,
58-9, 68-70, 72, 101, 149-50
research and development
see R&D
resistance 29
passive 49
resources
agricultural 102
industrial 102
revaluation 172, 184, 208,
219, 246, 249
revolutionary disturbances
48
Rheinmetall 91
Roumania 116-18
Ruhr (industrial region) 20,
30, 33, 49, 81, 113, 148-9,
234
Ruhrkampf 36

SA (Sturmabteilung) 71
Saar region 39, 144, 234
Sauckel, Fritz 123, 131
savings 3, 41, 155, 179, 196,
203
Schacht, Hjalmar 73, 86,
101-2, 127
Schaeffer, Fritz 179-80

Schiller, Karl 183-6, 204
Schleicher, Kurt von 71, 73, 82
Schieber, Walther 130
Schmidt, Helmut 186
science-based industries 20
secondary sector 2, 19, 86, 216, 223-6
  see also manufacturing sector
securities 65, 114
shadow economy 198
shipbuilding 22, 92, 130, 149, 179-80, 190, 213, 234, 249
Siemens 50, 91
Smithsonian Agreement 239
social
  question 20, 177
  reform 203, 217
  security 4, 10, 123, 177, 198-9, 203-5, 211, 214-16
    benefits 182, 187, 190, 198, 200
    contributions 54, 189, 198
Social Democratic Party (SPD) 176, 183, 186, 188, 244
social-liberal coalition 186, 189, 204
social market economy 3, 154-5, 165, 176-8, 179-80, 184, 227, 249
socialism 1, 177
Soviet Union 9, 14, 30, 66, 117-19, 123, 126, 129, 144, 149-50, 176
Soviet zone of occupation 146, 149-50
speculation 65
  international 181, 239, 249
Speer, Albert 121, 129-31, 134, 136
SS (Schutz-Staffel) 71, 124, 130, 133
  Deutsche Erd- und Steinwerke (DEST) 124
stabilisation policy 9, 73, 168, 172, 177, 179, 181-90, 201, 204
  Globalsteuerung 183-5, 204
  Investitionshilfegesetz 179
  Stabilitaetsgesetz 183, 190
  Zukunftsinvestitionsprogramm (ZIP) 204
Staende 80,
  see also estates
stagflation 12, 185
stagnation 47, 52, 57, 102-3, 146
standardisation 29, 50, 93
state(s) 73, 177, 183
  finance 26, 36-7, 40
  see also public finance *and Laender*
state-trading countries 243- 4
steel 19, 21, 54, 65, 87-8, 129, 136, 151, 213
  see also iron and steel industry
Stinnes 47
stock(s) 64, 67
  exchange 40, 79
  market crash 4
Strasser, Gregor 79
strike(s) 30, 48, 93, 124, 215
subsidies 83, 93, 179, 183, 190, 199-200, 203, 208, 214, 231, 248-9
  agricultural 56, 67, 70, 228
substitutes 128, 135
  see also Ersatz
Sweden 9, 25, 134

tariffs 244, 248-9, 251
  agricultural 56, 67, 97
  see also customs
tax(es)
  corporate 36, 185, 196-7
  credit 72, 91, 209
  direct 36, 196-8
  excise 31, 114, 196
  income 36, 54, 71, 114, 185, 196-7
  indirect 23, 36, 189, 196, 198
  mineral oil 196-7
  occupation 196
  property 36, 196
  reform 172, 196
  revenue 31, 89, 114, 180, 182, 196-8
  tobacco 114, 196-7
  turnover 31, 36, 196
  value-added (VAT) 196-7
  war profits 31
taylorism 50
technical innovations 50-2, 135, 168, 190, 230, 232-3, 247
Technische Hochschulen 20
technology 135-8, 153, 231, 243, 247
terms of trade 58-9, 66, 85, 170, 218-9, 241-2
  see also export/import prices
tertiary sector 223-6, 233
textile industry 26, 28, 51-2, 57-8, 92-3, 113, 135, 154, 229-30, 248
Third Reich 82, 200
Thomas, Georg 110
Todt, Fritz 129-30
trade
  agreements 118, 157

barter 39, 154
foreign, *see* foreign trade, *also* "inner-German" trade
trade unions 40, 71, 183, 188, 216-17
transfer
  account 240, 250
  payments 240, *see also* reparations
transport(ation) 3, 27, 30, 50, 84-5, 119, 121, 144, 146, 148, 199, 204, 223, 233
treasury bill(s) 30-1, 114
Treaty of Rome 251
Trizone 152, 156

Udet, Ernst 131
Ukraine 126
unemployment 35, 37, 52, 66-9, 71-3, 82-3, 91-4, 168-73, 178, 187, 201, 211-15, 218, 223, 234, 238
  benefits 67, 71, 91, 204, 215
  insurance 71
  statistics 67, 91, 94, 213
  see also employment
unions 212
  see also trade unions
United Nations
  Organisation (UNO) 250
United States 20, 30, 34-9, 45-6, 51-2, 55, 60-9, 85, 93, 99, 110, 133, 149-54, 158, 172, 178, 231, 239, 245-8
Upper Silesia 30, 33

Vereinigte Stahlwerke 50, 151
Versailles peace treaty 34, 135
victuals 127, 152

see also nutrition
Volkswagenwerk 181, 219

wage(s) 3, 39, 41, 47, 52, 55,
  67-8, 70, 94-6, 98, 100, 117,
  123-5, 148, 154, 172-3, 183,
  186, 189, 198, 204-5, 211,
  214-17, 219, 238
  costs 172, 186-7
  freeze 87, 96
  nominal 30, 53-4, 95, 218
  real 29, 53, 67, 96, 125, 214,
  216-17
  share 52, 95-6, 217-19
wage drift 54, 96
war
  bonds 30-1
  debts 9, 65, 68, 250
  expenditure 26, 31
  finance 30-1, 114-17
  contribution 114
  industries 28, 138, 148
  losses 33-4, 144-6
  material 26, 118-19
  preparations 81, 85, 91, 97,
  109-11, 127
  production 27, 121, 124,
  129, 131, 134-8
  profiteers 31
war economy
  First World War:
    Gesetz ueber den
    Vaterlaendischen
    Hilfsdienst 27
    Kriegsrohstoffabteilung
    (KRA) 25
    Waffen- und
    Munitionsbeschaffungs-
    amt (WUMBA) 27
  Second World War:
    Grossraumwirtschaft
    102-13, 126

Reichskuratorium fuer
Wirtschaftlichkeit 130
Reichsministerium fuer
Bewaffnung und Muniton
(Ministry of Armament
and Munition) 121, 127-
8, 136
Reichsministerium fuer
Ruestung und
Kriegsproduktion
(Ministry of Armament
and War Production)
131
Wehrwirtschafts- und
Ruestungsamt (War
Economy and Armament
Office) 127-8, 130-1
Zentrale Planung 131
wealth 155, 203
  distribution 204-19
    Vermoegensbildungs-
    gesetz 219
    Volksaktien 219
Wehrmacht 109, 119, 129
Weimar Republic 1, 3, 50,
  52-8, 67, 71, 79, 81, 155
Wirtschaftswunder
  ("economic miracle")
  165-6, 179, 203
"wonder weapons" 133, 135,
  138
wood 25
  -working industries 28, 51,
  229-30
work(ers) *see* labour
workers committees 27, 54,
  130
workers' councils
  (*Betriebsraete*) 27, 54, 94
working time 30, 41, 48, 54,
  67, 73, 94, 125, 131, 134,
  211-12, 233

world depression 46, 55
world market 20-2, 55, 58,
   86, 148-9, 156, 166-7, 214,
   225-48 *passim*
World War
   First 8, 19, 25-31, 37, 39,
   48, 52-7, 114, 126, 130, 135,
   166, 237, 243, 245
   Second 2, 7, 109-38
   passim, 144, 166-8, 198,

232, 237, 246, 248

Young Plan 46, 60, 69-70
Yugoslavia 102, 117, 169

zones of occupation
   see American, British,
   French *or* Soviet zone of
   occupation